Netta

This edition published 2025
by Living Book Press

Originally published by Routledge Kegan Paul, published by arrangement with Routledge, an imprint of the Taylor & Francis Group, an Informa business.

© Monk Gibbon 1960

ISBN: 978-1-76153-830-8 (hardcover)
        978-1-76153-836-0 (softcover)

All rights reserved. No part of this publication may be reproduced, stored in a retrieval system, or transmitted in any other form or means–electronic, mechanical, photocopying, recording or otherwise, without the prior permission of the copyright owner and the publisher or as provided by Australian law.

 A catalogue record for this book is available from the National Library of Australia

NETTA

A Biography of Henrietta Franklin

BY

MONK GIBBON

INTRODUCTION

The Honourable Henrietta Franklin was a rich woman, born into aristocratic British society in the late 19th century. She could have spent her life within her social circle, attending social gatherings and focusing on a refined home environment. Her father, Samuel Montagu, 1st Baron Swaythling, was a wealthy banker given a peerage because of his social service and work as a political figure in the House of Commons. Franklin married early and married a banker, Ernest Louis Franklin, who in his own right was quite wealthy. She could easily have "rested on her laurels" as a very wealthy woman, but she did not.

As you read this biography, you will notice that as a young mother concerned about the education of her children, Franklin worked tirelessly for many causes. She became of great importance to the Charlotte Mason community after they were introduced in 1894. The Parents' National Education Union (PNEU) then became one of her causes. In the summer of 1894 she became the PNEU Organising Secretary, and for seventy years until her death in 1964, she worked tirelessly to promote the educational theories and practices of Charlotte Mason.

In fact, Mrs. Franklin's commitment to Mason's work was so strong that Mason dedicated her third volume, *Home and School Education*, to Franklin by writing: "Henrietta Franklin: This volume is affectionately inscribed, in very grateful recognition, not only of her generous life's labour given to the spread of certain educational ideas, but also of her singular apprehension of those ideas." Of course, it was never enough for Mason for anyone to have just mechanical acknowledgement of an idea; one must have deeper and stronger beliefs as to why one is investing time and energy into a set of principles. Without a change from within, one's practice does not change. Thus, Mason acknowledged that not only did Henrietta Franklin work tirelessly to promote Mason's philosophy and practices, she (Franklin) absorbed them into herself.

Franklin believed them so strongly that in 1896 she opened the first PNEU school in London in Linden Gardens, attended by approximately 16 students taught by two teachers trained at the House of Education (later called the Charlotte Mason College). But Franklin was also involved with other schools, such as the English public school for girls called Overstone and the boys preparatory school called Desmoor. She was involved in the opening of schools that used Mason's programmes of study designed for the Parents' Union School (PUS), ran the PNEU office in London, and worked on a host of other projects such as the annual PNEU conference. In addition, she was a member of the National Union for Women Suffrage Societies serving as President from 1916-1917. You will learn more about her many social and cultural efforts as you read this biography.

It is important to note that through all her work, Henrietta Franklin had a medical condition that would have interfered with leading a routine life for many people. In 1909 she was diagnosed with cancer in one of her legs, and the leg had to be amputated. She insisted that a female doctor perform the amputation. Not long after she was up and about with a prosthesis. Although such a traumatic experience would have caused many to sit down and quit, it never seemed to daunt her. She continued her very busy life.

So what you will find between these pages is the life story of a person who gave her all for various causes, women's issues, the war effort, charity efforts, and the list goes on. No, she did not "rest on her laurels" until she was laid to rest on 7 January 1964 in London at the age of 97.

Why the republication of this book? Henrietta Franklin is a primary source of information about Charlotte Mason. As a young mother, Mason was Franklin's mentor and example. As a more experienced adult, Franklin was very much a leader in her own right. For those of us in the Mason community, seeing her through the eyes of author Monk Gibbon, provides a historical record of aspects of Mason's work, of the PNEU, and of various schools using Mason's PUS programmes. Monk Gibbon has written about a person directly involved with Mason and all aspects of her work.

The republication of this historical record is important for us to have a deeper understanding of not only Henrietta Franklin, but also Charlotte Mason and the work of the PNEU.

                                              J. Carroll Smith, EdD
                                              Founder, Charlotte Mason Institute
                                              Roanoke, VA
                                              January 2025

Contents

Chapter 1	1
Chapter 2	5
Chapter 3	16
Chapter 4	23
Chapter 5	28
Chapter 6	37
Chapter 7	43
Chapter 8	51
Chapter 9	58
Chapter 10	67
Chapter 11	76
Chapter 12	83
Chapter 13	89
Chapter 14	96
Chapter 15	103
Chapter 16	112
Chapter 17	120
Chapter 18	128
Chapter 19	139
Chapter 20	144
Chapter 21	152
Chapter 22	158
Chapter 23	169
Chapter 24	180
Chapter 25	189
Chapter 24	199
Chapter 27	206
Chapter 28	210
Chapter 29	216
Chapter 30	222
Chapter 31	229
Chapter 32	239
Chapter 33	242

AUTHOR'S FOREWORD

BIOGRAPHERS WHO ATTEMPT a living subject tempt providence. Just as painters must often feel embarrassed when the sitter gets up and slowly approaches the easel—still more when a candid friend is brought to the studio and declares that the nose is a little too long, the chin a shade receding, the eyes and hair the wrong color, but everything else a triumph of masterly accuracy—so the biographer of the living knows that he has to reckon not only with his victim but with his victim's friends. He will be accused of being too flattering, too malicious, too outspoken, too reticent; and it will be delicately hinted that the whole thing is on a completely wrong note, but that otherwise it would have been a magnificent success.

I have known Netta—more explicitly the Hon. Mrs. Franklin, C.B.E.—for thirty-six years. I was urged to write her life by two other long-standing friends, Winifred Raphael and Dr. Annis Gillie, neither of whom could ever fall under suspicion of wishing to do her an ill turn. But it is significant that I have not yet dared to show them my work. If what they hoped for was a vigorous depiction of the public-spirited propagandist, member of forty-two committees, it was a vain hope. It seemed to be more practicable, and perhaps more interesting for the reader, to create a Conversation Piece against an intimate background. Netta's life has been full of action and service; but her dynamic personality is best revealed in relation to persons. She is a figure of central significance for a whole clan; moreover, she has the gift of making her friends feel that they have to some extent been absorbed into the family circle. This role of extended matriarchy reveals her more fully than any.

I have tried, then, to trace the career of this courageous altruist, drawing on my own memories and those of certain members of the Franklin family with whom I have long been friends and who have endured repeated cross-examination without complaint. I am most grateful to them. I would like also to express my sincere gratitude to Mrs. Wilkins, who in typing my manuscript had to display a patience even more exemplary.

MONK GIBBON

June 7th, 1960

1

NETTA WILL BE ARRIVING at six. Ordinarily, she is here before any of us, but a conference has kept her in London. I have been her guest on countless occasions, first as a shy and frightened newcomer, plunged into a household which I found combined considerable unobtrusive organization with great personal liberty; then as a confident habitué; and now as a sort of super-guest, making a family arrival to the tune of six or seven persons, to take possession of a three-storeyed octagonal tower in the grounds.

It is wonderful to be back, yet Glenalla is not completely itself without its presiding goddess. She creates its whole spirit and atmosphere. She has made this haven of periodic bliss for herself, for her family, for her friends. She thinks of everything. On my first visit, years ago, all the speculative qualms of youth, as to what might be a suitable leaving tip for the domestic staff, were allayed by a small white card at one side of my bedroom door, informing me that no tips were expected or would be accepted, compensation having already been made for this deprival in the appropriate quarter. There were two distinct modes of life at Glenalla, then as now: the formal one and the bohemian one. The formal one assumed that you would appear on the glass-roofed terrace for breakfast punctually at nine o'clock. This was for the benefit of the very young, the middle-aged, and the elderly. Fortified by boiled eggs or trout, toast and honey, and as many red currants or small amber gooseberries as they chose to consume, the young were expected to join Netta in podding an immense garden basket of peas or beans, wheeled by the gardener onto the terrace alongside her chair. The breakfast things were cleared away, and the young podded happily around the table, frequently joined by a suppliant adult who found this restful occupation had definite psychotherapeutic virtues. At lunch, the grey-haired host, Ernest, helping himself to peas for the second time, would remark with grave courtesy to his seven-year-old neighbor, "How well these peas are podded," a conversational gambit which invariably brought a delighted smile to the flushed face of the individual so addressed. As the peas were being shelled, plans would be made for the afternoon.

Meanwhile, the bohemian portion of the household continued to sleep, had their breakfast later—perhaps a little cold—in the dining room, or, if privileged, taken up to them on a tray. They would descend to find Netta at work at her desk in the drawing room, while the young scattered joyously to various corners of the wooded demesne.

When she comes this afternoon, there will be no fuss, only one small act of time-honored ritual. Winding its way towards Glenalla, past the gate lodge, over the yellow surface of the long avenue embedded with countless minute fragments of sea shells, under the oaks, under the beeches, past the rhododendrons, and the first open glade which discloses a field of ripening oats, the vehicle will come at last to a second break in the trees. At this point, the arriving car invariably gives a series of long blasts on its horn, and all those who may have been listening for this signal hurry to the front of the house to welcome the newcomer. This avenue is a one-way street. The only time it is used in the opposite direction is when a member of the family, or a guest, is departing at the end of their holiday. Then the whole household, including the servants, assemble by the huge garage in the yard, follow the car out to the front gravel, watch it as it goes past the small painted NO EXIT board stuck in the grass edging, and, when it comes to the three brief open sections of the avenue, there is a last, Rolandesque tooting on the horn, and a tremendous waving of handkerchiefs on both sides.

Generally, Netta comes before her guests. Only Kay Daly, who lives in Glenalla all the year, is here to welcome her. The order of her coming, Kay says, is nearly always the same. She descends from the car a little slowly. If it is at Easter, she looks up instantly at the creeper-covered house and says, "I've been longing to see my *Spooneri Clematis*, it has done well." Later in the year, her conversation may be different. "How is Nelly Moser doing? Has she got over that bad setback last year?" This is not an inquiry for the offspring of one of the cottagers up on Peat Hill. All the clematis are referred to by their proper names, and, when it comes to pronouns, their sex is strictly observed. She does not enter the house. Certain pet roses have to be inspected first, which grow below the wooden pillars of the glass-roofed terrace. She walks past the porch with its stout, wood, rose-twined single pillar, past the projecting end of the drawing-room, up which creeps a clematis whose stem must be thicker than that of many a full-size birch, and up the three steps onto the terrace. There she stands, near the lemon-scented verbena, and a little in front of the swing door, which forms a part of the drawing-room bow window, and allows her gaze to travel in a complete semicircle from the flowering shrubs on the extreme left, backed by the huge monkey-puzzle and the rising woods of intensely green trees, on round by the waterfall and the stream, to the bog-garden, with the cornfield beyond; then past the two immense lime trees behind the tennis court until it comes to the water-garden and the pink limestone wall of the back avenue on the extreme right, before resting finally on the herbaceous border immediately at her feet. She is silent for a minute or two. Then she says slowly, "How lovely it all is," and makes her way into the house. Her guests will be following the next day. But already, full directions have been dispatched to Miss Daly from London: the number of the room into which each guest is to go, even the books which are to be put in that room. "In fact, I get a fairly accurate idea of their character before ever they arrive," Kay declares, "from the books chosen for them."

Today it was different. We were already here, and she arrived punctually at six. She had left London at one, reaching the airport near Belfast an hour and forty minutes later. There she got into the car and was driven off, only stopping for a picnic tea in Dungivvan Pass at the exact spot at which she has stopped for years, then continuing on her way to Londonderry, Letterkenny, and Ramelton until she reached the bridge at Ray beside Lough Swilly and turned up towards the well-loved green woods at Glenalla.

Almost as soon as she had arrived, she was in her chair by the open drawing-room door, through which came a drift of sweet-scented verbena, chatting away about books, world events, people—people the most absorbing subject of all to her, except for one even more absorbing—children.

Her life radiates out in a hundred different directions. Her friends are in every walk of life, of every political and social colour and complexion, and part of her own great vitality springs from this merging of herself into the lives of other people. There we sit, talking away, while the light on the Glenalla woods takes on a deeper emerald radiance as the sun sinks lower in the sky. She does not appear to be tired, and she would never admit it if she were. And yet, she has every excuse to be tired—an aeroplane flight, followed by a hundred-mile drive in a motor car, and now, in a few minutes, dinner and a number of guests. After all, Netta is not young, even if her animation is still the animation of youth, and her clear, incisive voice giving some patient direction to a child out on the terrace is essentially a youthful voice. When it comes to reading Shakespeare aloud in the evenings, her Malvolio is definitely better than anyone else's, full of a rich, pompous, impenetrable self-complacency, which justifies all Maria's plots and plannings to tumble it in the dust. No one hearing her reading the part would ever guess the truth of the situation. For Netta, "according to Fates and Destinies and such odd sayings, the Sisters Three and such branches of learning," is indeed ninety-three years of age and will, before very long, be celebrating her ninety-fourth birthday.

2

NETTA'S ARRIVAL into this world was awaited in a mood of considerable despondency, for her mother had already lost a stillborn child, followed by four miscarriages. Actually, she was the first of eleven living children and was to have three younger sisters and a brother before she herself was five and a half years old.

"I caught measles at birth from my mother. She had visited a family whose children were ill with it but whose doctor was of the opinion that no pregnant woman ever catches an infectious disease. There was consternation when my mother developed it, and I, at a few days old, was dispatched to a childless aunt in the hope that I would escape. I didn't. The rash appeared shortly afterwards, and as I have nursed all my own children through the complaint without getting it, there can be no doubt at all that what I had was measles."

Netta learnt to talk early, and it is not surprising that her memories can go back to when she was only two and a half. She was sitting in a hip-bath in lodgings at Brighton when her mother came into the room, saying that she was getting a German under-nurse. "I was transfixed with horror, why I cannot imagine, for Rosie proved the best and kindest of friends, and remained with the family for fifty years. Her name was on the lips of my brother Edwin, the Secretary of State for India, when he died." At five, she was already a fluent reader. She would sit on the floor beside the tall nursery fender at the top of the house, her eyes riveted in morbid fascination on the pages of *Grimms' Fairy Tales*. She admits she hated the book. It gave her frightful nightmares, despite the consolation of a well-sucked thumb. "But I could not take my eyes away from it—I read on and on, and suffered accordingly."

A shiny-surfaced Carte De Visite photograph, taken in Bayswater nearly a century ago, shows a diminutive one-year-old Netta set down on a hideous, velvet-bottomed Victorian chair. In the high forehead, the black curly hair, the steady, rather challenging look in the eye—I can trace likenesses to child, grandchild, and even great-grandchild. A certain Signor

Lombardi of Brighton—whoever he may have been—has recorded the Netta of a few years later. This time, she sits up very straight on the edge of a heavy mahogany table with ornately carved bulbous legs. Her sashed white dress is spread out gracefully around her; she is wearing white socks and buttoned kid boots, and has crossed her ankles, with her feet resting on a leather-seated music stool. With her hands in her lap and her head erect, she appears confident and assured, if a little sad; and, wonder of wonders, her thick hair is tied in a ponytail, anticipating modern fashion by more than eighty years.

Netta grew up in a home where there was love, devotion, and courtesy. She remembers how, when she was only ten, her great, bearded, grave-looking father insisted on carrying quite a small burden for her on the grounds that women must be taken care of. But, though she was surrounded with affection, she was in some degree a victim of the prevailing mood of the time. A hundred years ago, children's responsibilities were mountainous and were constantly being dinned into their ears. The more advantageous their worldly circumstance, the more the doctrine of moral obligation was preached to them day and night. If they had the misfortune to be royal, the treatment, so far from being milder, was ten times more severe.

Fate seemed weighted against the young. Netta told me once of an incident that took place when she cannot have been more than ten or eleven. She was to go shopping with her mother, her four small sisters, and the German governess. In a spirit of lighthearted forgetfulness, she ran down the steps and climbed into the waiting carriage, whereat her Teutonic companion immediately took great affront. "I haf been insulted by Netta!" So serious was the offence that the lady refused to accompany them and retreated indignantly up the steps, pursued by Netta's distressed and pleading mother, who did not relish the idea of going shopping with five little girls unaided.

In a scene like this, we get the whole schoolroom atmosphere of the time. If you loved your governess, you were made desperately unhappy by her moods or by the faintest suggestion of a tiff between her and your parents. If you detested her, you soon found that you were helpless against her machinations.

Punctuality was regarded by Netta's mother as a cardinal virtue. "If we were late for a meal, there was no reproof, only dead silence, which was worse than any reproof[1]. The whole meal was spoilt for everyone. A dark shadow hung over it until we got up from the table. My brother Edwin, as a schoolboy, once remarked, 'If we committed a murder, Mother would sit sympathetically at the foot of the gallows, but if we were late for tea she would never forgive us.'"

Harshness was unknown in their home. The atmosphere was loving, but it was also desperately earnest where religious observance was concerned. As the firstborn, Netta soon acquired a keen sense of responsibility. In general company, she was not self-assertive. Rather, by all accounts, she was extremely shy. But she had a deeply ingrained sense of duty and an almost heroic resolution to be of service to others.

Netta's verdict on herself at this time is: "I was distinctly priggish." She certainly had cultural aspirations well in advance of her time. She wanted to learn Latin like her brothers; she wanted to learn algebra, and her headmistress sagely suggested that she should hem a shirt exquisitely for her father in order to convince him that algebra would not in any way detract from her womanly qualities. She had a great admiration for her headmistress's partner, who taught her Latin. "In fact, my *schwärmerei*, or 'pash', was such that nowadays it would not be encouraged. I would stand long at the window, regardless of rules, in the hope of seeing her pass on the way to church. She was a High Anglican, and, later on, after I was married, when this *grande passion*, if it were a *grande passion*, had come to be more on her side than mine, she told me one year that it was her custom to give up something that she cared for greatly in Lent and that therefore she would give up coming to tea each week with me! Shortly afterwards, she appeared at tea, and I learnt to my amusement that she had decided to give up sugar instead!"

In her own eyes, Netta was a prig, but in her pre-school days, she seems to have had her attractions for the opposite sex.

"I came across the other day letters from several of my boy cousins aged about seven or eight, each signing himself 'your loving husband'. One of them announces that his heart 'has gone pit-a-pat' at the mere news that I had a cold."

As a little girl, too, she was once 'capped' daily by the Kaiser. She and

---

1   Olive, her daughter, tells me the same story. 'If we were staying with my grandfather and came back from a walk late for a meal the whole room turned round to stare at us. We preferred to starve.'

her sisters were staying in a rented house in Shanklin in the Isle of Wight. It was summer, and in the adjoining house, the future ruler of Germany was residing with his younger brother in charge of a tutor. Every morning, when the two boys came out to go for a walk, the tutor would see that they doffed their caps politely to the four small girls in white piqué dresses on the balcony of the house next door. "Years later, I saw him again when he was travelling in Norway on a holiday. Ernest shook hands with him, but I remained in the background and did not tell him that I had once been a part of his education in good manners."

Other holidays spent at Brighton do not gleam so radiantly in memory. They were heavily interlarded with lessons, and as a relaxation from these, Netta would walk up and down the promenade in button boots and stiffly starched London clothes with the German governess of the moment, who was a terrible tyrant.

Later, on their annual summer holiday, the whole vast family often travelled in a specially reserved saloon carriage. On one occasion, on their way to North Berwick, there was some kind of railway accident. Her mother was thrown from her seat, and strange objects like perambulators, cots, a tin bath with a lid, and numerous leather hat-boxes cascaded from the roof. On these journeys, Emma, their nurse, would cook Welsh rarebit for them on a spirit lamp, despite the fact that she herself and several of the children suffered acutely from train sickness. Emma was a pleasant memory. There were others less pleasant. Netta's younger sister Ethel, for example, suffered grave pangs of conscience because she had told a lie and had informed their father that the bruises on her temple had been caused by a fall, whereas really they were the handiwork of the German governess. Netta rose to the occasion, went to her father, and the governess was sent packing to become, shortly afterwards, the spouse of an English widower and stepmother to several children, scarcely the role that Netta or Ethel would have chosen for her.

Netta was twelve and staying on holiday at Folkestone when she had an adventure which might have cut short her career. She was taking riding lessons and was given a mount that had kicked to pieces a victoria only the day before. They had no sooner set off with the riding master than her horse bolted.

Folkestone sea front is not the ideal setting *for une course hippique*. There was the danger that the horse might at any moment come off the road proper onto the asphalt promenade, which ran parallel with it on a slightly lower level; in which case, it would almost certainly have slipped and fallen. "I remember saying the Shema[2], and not being in the least frightened. After about three miles, the horse gradually slackened pace. It was beginning to get tired. Its rein was grabbed by a bystander, and it came to a halt in front of a house. A gentleman, getting into a victoria with his wife, offered to drive me home. I had been brought up never to talk to strangers, so I refused, saying that I would wait for the riding master. He went back to his wife, and she came over to me and insisted. I was driven home in the victoria, and Rosie, our dear old German nurse, opening the door, threw up her hands in horror when she saw who it was and called up the stairs with Teutonic fervour to my mother, 'Here is the child come home killed!', a rather Irish way of indicating that there had been some kind of an accident."

At school, she had very speedily justified herself. It was not only her fine memory and great receptive powers that endeared her to her teachers, but her attitude to them, which was one of gratitude rather than resentment. One of them wrote later, "I had so much pleasure in teaching you, both on account of your aptitude and generous consideration towards those who gave you your lessons." Thanks to her German nurse and a succession of German governesses, she had learned enough German by thirteen to abandon lessons and to begin specializing in French. Later in life, she continued to study languages, learning Greek, Latin, Russian, Italian, Spanish, and Norwegian.

At one time, both the boys and the girls of the family attended Doreck College. On wet days, relays of Montagus descended from a series of hackney cabs to the amusement of the onlookers.

The Montagu girls were regarded as highbrows by their relatives and friends. There is the recorded remark of Lady Magnus, mother of the charming Mrs. Freddie Franklin, Netta's sister-in-law, and one of her dearest friends: "It's no use the Montagus going to a dance. They only talk Greek to their mother." This lady was noted for her acid outspokenness. On one occasion, she greeted a young person: "Good afternoon, Betty," only to be told coldly, "My name is Miss Jones." "Yes, and likely to remain so!" came the stinging reply. However, time takes its revenge upon all. In old

---

[2]   The declaration of faith in the unity of God.

age, Lady Magnus became extremely deaf. She had a hearing aid in the shape of a fan, which she held between her teeth. It was not very effective. She would sit in her armchair with the fan projecting from her mouth, while her granddaughter, Dulcie, played for her the most outrageously cacophonous ragtime of the 1920s. Then the old lady would nod gratefully, while Dulcie explained to her that she had been listening to Beethoven's Moonlight Sonata!

Whether or not Netta talked Greek with her mother, she did certainly coach a future philosopher. He was her cousin, Herbert Samuel. He had lost his own father, and Samuel Montagu was his guardian. Bribed by a promise of a present from his mother if she succeeded, she helped him to secure a first prize at his school. When, later, as an undergraduate at Balliol, he was asked by his mother to discuss his attitude to Jewish orthodoxy with Netta's father, he replied—"I shall be pleased to discuss the question of religion with Uncle Montagu as my guardian, though there is no likelihood of such a discussion having the least effect upon me. My opinion of Uncle Montagu's theology and his philosophical qualities is not such as to lead me to bow to his wishes in the matter." Nevertheless, in earlier days, he had listened tractably to Rabbi Singer's occasional sermons to children in synagogue, as had Netta, who was expected to narrate the chief points back to the rabbi on the following Sunday at their weekly lesson. "Writing on the Sabbath was a sin, but we had a box of alphabet letters for games, and I used to spell out the headings of the sermon with these, laying them in a drawer, which later had to be very delicately opened lest it should throw the words into confusion. And in this way, I was able to satisfy the inspired and beloved teacher the following week."

A home of Jewish orthodoxy had its embarrassments. Her sister Lily sometimes found it a little difficult to explain to her hostess when she went out to a meal that all sorts of restrictions were necessary. She must not eat any kind of meat, not even chicken, unless prepared according to Mosaic rites, nor cakes or cream for at least one and a half hours after meat. "I saw what trouble my father took even on his travels to deny himself any forbidden food. At a grand hotel table d'hôte, he would contentedly sit and eat bread and cheese if the manner of cooking vegetables made him suspicious."[3]

---

3   *The Faith of a Jewish Woman* by Lily H. Montagu.

Netta tells much the same story: "We were allowed to play tennis on the Sabbath but not allowed to play croquet! My father said that we chipped the mallets when we played croquet, and according to the strictest rabbinical interpretation of the Mosaic law, breaking or damaging things is a form of work. There was an even subtler distinction to be observed when we went to Brighton. There we could hire a bath-chair on the Sabbath, pushed by a man, but we might not drive in an open victoria. The man was a rational being and could observe his day of rest the next day if he chose. But the horse was a member of the 'brute' creation and would be given no choice in the matter. We could not take the risk of making it work on our Sabbath since it might be forced to take someone else out for a sea drive along the promenade the following day as well, and then we would have broken the injunction in the fourth commandment, which conceded the ox and the ass their weekly respite as well as man."

To Netta in afterlife, her home seemed not so much a religious home as a home of strict religious observance. To the young Bethel Solomons, the future Master of the Rotunda, their father always seemed a figure of stern and terrifying orthodoxy. Nevertheless, the big, bearded Mosaic-looking man who, traveling on small cargo steamers to France as a young bank courier in charge of bullion, used to deny himself even a cup of soup lest he should thereby be breaking the law, could be wonderfully gentle in his dealings with his children. Lily has told how he might be called in to soothe their night terrors. Very gently, he would repeat the words: "The Lord is with me, I shall not fear. Stand in awe and sin not. Commune with your own heart upon your bed and be still.—Selah." Or the mother would soothe the frightened child off to sleep with the words: "You know, Papa is such a good man, God would never make him unhappy by letting his little daughter die."

It is Lily, too, who writes: "He never imposed his religious opinions on his children and was satisfied so long as they conformed with the observances which he practiced. He did not insist on weekly synagogue attendance, and partly, perhaps, because no compulsion was used, nearly all the children grew up to appreciate regular public worship. He liked family gatherings, especially in connection with religious observances, such as the feast of Purim and the Passover nights, and punctiliously attended any family celebrations."

She goes on to say, "He was always particularly fond of any educational successes achieved by his children, for he liked to see the tangible results of strenuous effort. He esteemed intelligence above many other attributes and was indeed always rather intolerant of 'stupidity.'" Many of these traits reappeared in his eldest daughter—the moral earnestness, the intense family feeling, the respect for the things of the mind, and the impatience with all trifling and ineptitude.

Netta left school at fifteen, owing to a curvature of the spine for which, in those days, lying on a specially constructed couch was considered the only cure. It was her first encounter with physical disability, and she rose superior to it, just as she was to triumph so decisively in later life. Stretched on her invalid couch, she had private lessons from a Mr. Vigniols. Later she was able to pass both the Senior Cambridge and the College of Preceptors examinations, and, having recovered from her spinal trouble, she went on to attend classes at King's College for Ladies under the famous Miss Faithful. She was already a seriously minded individual. A poem written in April 1881 makes this abundantly clear. It has twelve solemn and fairly carefully scanned verses, beginning with the portentous reflection—

> I stand now on the very line
> 'Twixt childhood and maturity.
> It is so narrow and so fine
> That it dwells in the mind only.

From there, it continues on its earnest and rather gloomy way to a wholly characteristic encounter with a vague, heavenly figure who announces—

> I am the goddess of duty,
> And for those there is perpetual light
> Who never cease to follow me,
> Whilst others dwell in endless night.

The heavenly figure does at least vouchsafe that those who take its advice "will truly happy be."

If one were looking for the whole text and tenor of Henrietta Franklin's life, one could find it in these ink-faded and prophetic stanzas, which predict both the line she was to take and the reward she would earn as a result of taking it. Another visiting-card photograph, taken in May 1883 at the age of seventeen, depicts her as already the youthful devotee of the stern goddess of duty. She is wearing a heavy bead necklace and a high-collared blouse with a tucked fringe that just touches the curve of her neck and her chin, and her large black eyes look out on life already with the steadfastness of the dedicated soul. The forehead is higher than ever, and the black hair, divided in the center, is drawn down smoothly on either side of the head. If she were a Roman Catholic and not a daughter of the synagogue, one would say that she was definitely destined for the convent.

Her commonplace book, dated 1882, full of ponderous and earnest moral pronouncements, contains nothing more obliquely frivolous than this observation from Paine: "On croit trop volontiers en France que si une femme cesse d'être poupée elle cesse d'être femme." Netta was to be in the forefront of a generation whose set determination was that woman should cesser d'être poupée. She grouped the quotations under vast and comprehensive headings, such as Duty, Friendship, and Education. A resolute idealist, she notes Charles Kingsley's impassioned plea for "a well-educated moral sense, a well-regulated character." She garnered Carlyle's "A man thinks as a slave, a coward, till he have got Fear under his feet," and Emerson's "Always do what you're afraid to do." She reminded herself, "Better be a nettle in the side of your friend than his echo."

Lily bears witness to the forceful young woman who was her senior by seven years: "Although she married when she was so young, she left an impression on the home life which convinced us that her opinion was worthwhile. She was strong-willed, and her intelligence was so alive and her interests so diverse that she loved to be told details of every passing incident in the lives of her brothers and sisters. She was always consulted by our mother before any decision was made, and our father enjoyed hearing her opinion about passing events. Very much the eldest of the family, our lives were very much dominated by her."

She might be her mother's consultant on most topics, but Victorian reticence prevailed in the Montagu house, as elsewhere, in one particular respect. Although she already possessed five sisters and three brothers, Netta was banished from 96 Lancaster Gate at the age of seventeen, before the arrival of her youngest brother Lionel. "I was sent away because I was supposed to know nothing about babies and their advent. Of course, I did. If my mother had breakfast in bed, we knew the reason for it. I have never known either of my Spartan parents have a fire in their bedroom. Only when a baby arrived were any modifications made in the severity of the régime which both parents imposed on themselves. My father hated the sight of sickness or anything to do with illness. From the age of four, he could not remember a single day's illness until he reached the age of seventy-six."

In her dealings with her younger brothers and sisters, she was the good friend but also, it is plain, the firm dictator. But in her contacts with the outer world, her self-confidence was liable to melt away. The prelude to her coming-out dance, despite all the monitions of Carlyle and Emerson, was a fit of abandoned weeping upon her bed, followed presently by a reading of Schiller's *Wallenstein* as a means of reassurance!

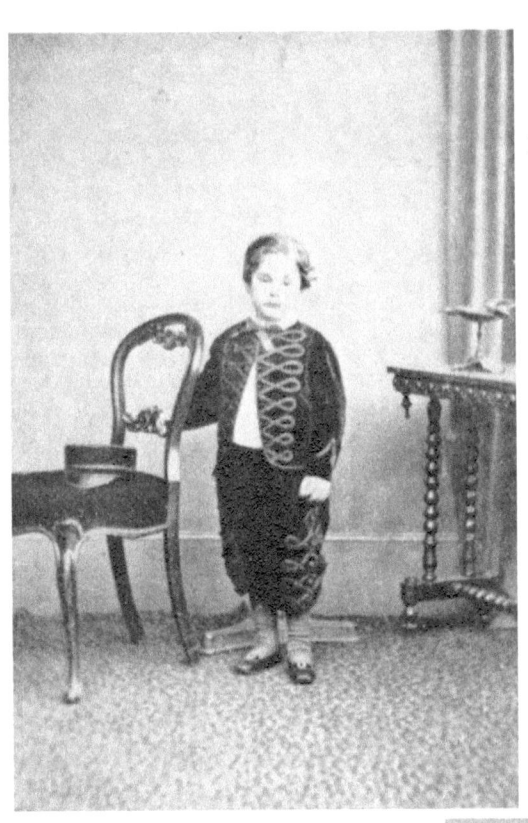

ERNEST AGED 4 IN 1863

NETTA AGED 3 IN 1869

3

IN 1885, NETTA MARRIED her cousin, Ernest Louis Franklin. He was seven years older than she, and his earliest recorded appearance is in a *carte de visite* photograph dated 1 October 1863—a slightly wistful Dickensian figure that might be David Copperfield at some early stage of his career, standing with one white-gloved hand fallen to his side and the other resting on the back rung of a cloth-seated chair drawn alongside. One would think that this was sufficient support for a healthy four-year-old, but two of the three legs of a much-contracted photographic headrest splay out on either side of the tiny feet of the subject of the photograph. No doubt this infernal machine, firmly clamped to the back of his head, may account for some of the wistfulness in his expression. A small ornamental table supports what looks like a brazier for burning incense, but it may be a fruit stand. On the side of the chair rests a very smart peaked cap like the cap of a French *cuirassier*, and an amazing velvet jacket decorated with elaborate coils of braiding down the front and down the sides of the rather baggy trousers—exactly like the Chocolate Soldier—adds to this slightly continental air.

It is difficult to envisage a person in their youth whom one has only known mellowed by seventy years of living. Even then, Ernest did not suggest age, nor did he seem to grow any older with the years. He played golf, climbed Peat Hill, could tell an excellent story, and was obviously beloved by his sons and daughters, his son-in-law and daughters-in-law. To a new acquaintance, he seemed to possess something of the courteous charm of an elderly Frenchman. His humor and his quiet self-sufficiency—liking his own routine but never giving trouble, always ready to arrange his own orderly days—were a sort of foil to Netta's dynamic energy and her gift for extroversion.

He had retained vivid memories of the 'sixties and wrote some of them down for his grandchildren. Apart from the fact that there was then hardly any income tax, no death duties, and relatively small national expenditure, he was without nostalgic regret for that epoch. Furniture, he maintained, was heavy and hideous; men and women ate far too much, mixed the wines they drank at dinner ignorantly and indiscriminately, and took little or no exercise, so that "old age crept on very quickly, and a man or woman of sixty was physically older than one of eighty at the present time." He remembered the jugs of tea-water and toast-water in the nursery for children when they were thirsty, the Lipscombe water-filter, and the cotton nightcaps—a survival from the days when men wore wigs and required protection for their cropped heads during sleep. His toys had been Dutch dolls, the Wheel of Life—a forerunner of the cinematograph—and the ever-popular Noah's Ark. There was one golf course in all of England; pajamas were unknown; their introduction by some returned Anglo-Indian sent a comic story going the rounds—Binks: "Do you like bananas?", Jinks: "No, I prefer the old-fashioned nightgown." Most vividly of all, he remembered the bathing machine of those days and the ritual of a woman's bathe: the door at the back, with its huge calico canopy furnishing even greater privacy against prying eyes; the fisherman mounted on his great horse to draw the box into water waist-high; the mob-capped bathing woman to "dip" or "duck" the screaming children; and the heavy cloth bathing overall from neck to feet, tied at the waist and concealing equally heavy undergarments of the same material. When he saw his grandchildren running naked upon some Donegal beach, it may or may not have occurred to him that it was his wife and her friends who had helped to change all this. During his lifetime, there was a revolution in manners and customs, and it had come partly because women insisted that it should come.

Ernest had married someone who, even if she had tried deliberately to subdue her own personality, would have found it impossible to make herself a well-intentioned cipher in any home. Netta was born to direct and to explore, if not to dominate. And it says a good deal for Ernest's strength of character that, even after sixty-five years of married life to this tornado of energy and high endeavor, he remained firmly and implacably himself in all that really mattered, while at the same time admirably patient and cooperative in lesser trifles. There were a few who thought he had too little say in things. But actually, he had all the say he either wanted or needed. Netta was as solicitous about his golf or his game of bridge at the club as the most self-effacing wife could ever be. She encouraged his interest in pictures, freely acknowledging that in this respect his knowledge far outran hers, and, if she snapped his head off sometimes, he nevertheless appeared to survive it very well. They had sailed the seven turbulent seas of matrimony with fair success and had brought the ship into quiet waters at last, refusing to abandon it when storms ran highest. Now, in old age, they presented a modified version of Baucis and Philemon, based less on sentiment than on a certain basic underlying respect.

Two years before Netta's marriage to her cousin, her parents had moved in 1883 to No. 12 Kensington Palace Gardens, whose wide avenue, wrought-iron gates, and liveried attendant at either end to prevent its being used as a thoroughfare gave it a slightly ducal air. Her father, who finished his schooling at the High School of the Mechanics' Institute in Liverpool at the age of sixteen and came to London to seek his fortune, had begun life as Montagu Samuel, but at an early age, his parents had reversed the order of these two names. It was only the first of a series of changes of nomenclature. At the age of sixty-two, he would become Sir Montagu Samuel Montagu, Bart., and on the morning of the 18th of July 1907, he would wake up to find himself 1st Baron Swaythling of Swaythling in the county of Southampton. Netta, whose grandparents could hardly have anticipated it and whose father's early life had been one of ceaseless industry, was born to the purple. She grew up in a setting of footmen and chambermaids. And, though she would shock some of her contemporaries by insisting rebelliously on her right to push her own perambulator in the park, she was forced to some extent to pass on the same setting to her own children. Her daughter Olive remembers her lady's maid exclaiming reproachfully, when as a teenager she had hung her own clothes up in the wardrobe, "What have I done to offend you? You don't want me anymore!"

In overstaffed households, excessive domestic assistance can defeat its own end. When there are three or four flunkeys to tidy the poker and tongs, one can forget about the poker and tongs; but one is only at the beginning of one's worries in regard to the flunkeys. From this excess of domestic help, however, Netta learnt the importance of organization. In her nineties, she still directs the Glenalla household when she comes to Ireland. There may be a house party of twenty, and though the domestic staff has dwindled to one versatile male and three seasoned and accomplished females, all of local origin, a daily morning consultation in the drawing room with Kay Daly ensures that everything runs smoothly, thanks to a wise simplification of the various issues involved.

The relationship between the Franklin and the Samuel families reads like an early Victorian parable of The Two Good Apprentices. Netta's great-grandfather, Menachem Samuel, had come to England about the year 1774 and had married there. He was the grandson of another Menachem Samuel who, with his son Asher, had been driven from Breslau by Frederick the Great's Jewish policy in Silesia, and had settled in the town of Kemper in the Polish province of Posen. The later Menachem married Hannah Israel, and his sons, Louis and Moses, married two sisters, Henrietta and Harriet, daughters of Israel Israel, and, in all likelihood, cousins. The portraits of Louis and his wife suggest two kindly, benevolent, Pickwickian characters, in contrast to the extremely forceful countenance of the other brother, Moses. Louis's son became Netta's father, while his daughter married Ellis Abraham Franklin, Ernest's father, whose gentle, slightly plaintive, rabbinical countenance can be found also in one of the many photographs in *The Samuel Family of Liverpool and London*.

The Franklin family name was originally Franckel, and the family were distinguished members of the Jewish community in Breslau and had produced a succession of rabbis down the centuries. A Benjamin Wolf Franckel went to London about 1763 and anglicized his name to Franklin. He was appointed rabbi of the Talmad-Torah Heura, a school for religious instruction. Benjamin and his wife died during an epidemic in 1785, and their son Abraham was brought up by a childless London couple called Marks. He was given a money box and encouraged to fill it. At the age of eight, he was taken to the Jewish burial ground in Mile End, and, noticing that his parents' graves had no headstones, he insisted on going to a stonemason, offering him all his savings, which amounted to eight pounds, and commissioning two headstones from him. After half a century, he replaced these headstones with new ones, burying the old.

This Abraham was a volunteer during the Napoleonic scare in 1803. Thirty years later, returning from his daughter's marriage in Holland, he travelled back with the Prince Consort, who was coming to England on courtship bent. The Prince liked him so well that he wanted to present Abraham with a souvenir set of Saxe-Coburg coins, but he could only be persuaded to accept one. He died in Holland. Ellis Abraham, Ernest's father, the eleventh of his twelve children, was born in 1822 and lived to see George V ascend the throne. He was an intelligent boy and a pupil at Manchester Grammar School, where he stood during school prayers out of respect to those who were kneeling but refused to kneel himself. He studied drawing and painting before beginning first a business and then a banking career. His work as an independent bullion broker brought him the acquaintance of Samuel Montagu, Netta's father, who was his junior by ten years. They used to meet at an eating house in the evening and discuss their different transactions. When, in 1852, the younger man, with his father's assistance, launched forth as an independent banker in London, Ellis Franklin joined him in the venture and was presently made a full partner[4]. For a time, they lived together. Ellis married his partner's sister, Adelaide, in 1858. Her picture, in later life, shows a sensitive, refined face, with steadfast fine eyes. If we are to judge from her epitaph in the Jewish cemetery at Willesden, she had a good deal in common with her niece, Netta. Translated from the Hebrew, it reads: "Sacred to the Cherished Memory of Adelaide, for six and forty years the devoted wife of Ellis A. Franklin. Her simple, noble life was passed in unswerving allegiance to the divine precepts of her inherited faith, in the zealous and cheerful discharge of her responsibilities as wife and mother, in loving solicitude for the well-being of all her kindred, and in unceasing kind and generous service to hosts of friends and acquaintances, who never turned to her in vain for sympathy, wise counsel, or material help."

Samuel Montagu continued to live with his sister and brother-in-law until he married Ellen Cohen in 1862. Now, a generation later, a further link was forged between these two men by the marriage of their children. Netta was nineteen at the time. Her Jewish wedding ought, by the social usage of her time, to have taken place in her parents' drawing room, but she considered this a snobbish differentiation between the classes, as well as a lessening of the religious significance of the occasion. So she insisted on its being celebrated in the New West End Synagogue, which her father had helped to found in St. Petersburg Place, Bayswater. A faded news cutting in a bottom drawer of the escritoire in the drawing room at Glenalla records the decorations in the synagogue for the occasion: "palms, dracaenas, and other sub-tropical plants, with charming greenhouse flowers, almost concealing the sacred ark from view."

As well as her own sisters, Netta had as bridesmaid her much-beloved school friend, Rose Leney, whose beauty, even now, seventy-three years later, is a family legend. She was, by all accounts, a living Undine, her long fair hair reaching almost to her ankles. Another person at the wedding was to

---

4   In the firm of Samuel Montagu and Co., bankers.

figure in one of the most famous political scandals of modern times. He was Captain William O'Shea, the plaintiff in the Parnell divorce case. Samuel Montagu was an ardent Gladstonian, and O'Shea was a Nationalist M.P. and amongst Gladstone's supporters. At the reception after the wedding, it was Willie O'Shea who proposed the bridesmaids' health.

He continued to be a family friend, but on one occasion, a visit from him caused Netta no small perturbation. "We were living at 9 Pembridge Gardens, our first house. It was afterwards turned into a nursing home, and suffragettes used to be taken there when they were released temporarily under the 'Cat and Mouse' Act. Sydney was born there in August 1886, and I was still semi-convalescent and resting on the sofa one afternoon when the parlourmaid announced 'Captain O'Shea.' I was very shy and quite unaccustomed to the society of gentlemen other than my own relations. I am afraid he was a little the worse for drink. He rushed into the room and gave me a kiss, which shocked me considerably. He then presented me with a charming shagreen skin *étui*, which I still possess."

FIRST BORN—SYDNEY

LAST BORN—MICHAEL

4

ERNEST HAD TRAVELLED through Germany the year before he married and had enjoyed it greatly. Anxious that his bride should share his pleasure, he suggested that they should spend their honeymoon making a similar tour. On her first trip abroad at the age of twelve, the crossing had been so rough that Netta assured her father he would never again be put to travelling expenses on her account. But she had changed her mind later. Now, travelling without a lady's maid, she found herself faced with a new problem. "I was unused to tackling my own long and very thick hair. Ernest had to do the best he could. It was not very good. He was always knocking out the hairpins, which flew to the ground. As for our packing, it was beyond description. How the modern girl with her two suitcases would have laughed at our immense trunk, which held my many garments, some of them embodying half-hoops that would not lie down."

Doing her hair was not the only difficulty Netta encountered. The two young people passed eagerly from town to town, sightseeing avidly. At Nuremberg, Netta felt so unwell that she was obliged to inquire for a doctor. Hitherto, she had always had her mother's support on such occasions. Without her, she felt painfully shy—not so much, strange to say, at consulting him on her ailment, but in relation to the payment of his fee. "It seemed to me that I would sink through the floor with shame if I had to rifle my bag in order to produce the right amount. And so Ernest and I did up a number of coins in small packages in preparation for this contingency. We began at two guineas and worked our way down by easy stages to ten shillings. Alas, when the moment came and the question was asked, the wretched man demanded only five shillings, and instead of the neat little package which I had hoped to slip into his hand, I had to fumble in my bag and hand him two coins as though he were a railway porter."

After the honeymoon, Netta and Ernest returned to London to start their married life in 9 Pembridge Gardens. While she was on her wedding tour, her mother had chosen her maids—a little German housemaid, recommended by the German governess, a parlourmaid, and a cook. On

Christmas Eve, Ernest declared the cutlets to be uneatable. Too shy to tell the cook this outright, Netta went to the top of the basement stairs and handed her a Christmas present of pocket handkerchiefs, at the same time remarking that the cutlets were overdone. The cook began to weep and said that it was the anniversary of her son's death. Always quick to sympathize, the inexperienced bride returned to the dinner table and said to the parlourmaid, "Mrs. Jones is very upset. It's the anniversary of her son's death." The parlourmaid's reply caused great consternation. "Upset, ma'am? She's as drunk as a lord." That brought the curtain down. "We were so terrified at the idea of having a drunken cook in the house that when she went out after dinner, we locked her out for the night. The tradespeople told us the next day that she was a well-known drunk in the district."

In the England of that day, it was not difficult to replace domestics. Maids were so plentiful that after an advertisement there would be a long queue of applicants in the hall. It was easy enough to engage them. Getting rid of them was a different matter. Netta dreaded having to do so. "On one occasion Ernest said that I really must give notice to the parlourmaid. I was terrified of doing so, and I gambled on the baseness of human nature, and when he was away for a night or two, I wrote a postcard to him on which I said, 'I really think I must let Emma go.' I left it on the hall table, calculating that Emma would be sure to read it. She did, and came promptly, as I had hoped she would, to give *me* notice first." It was not only with servants that Netta felt shy. "You may not believe it, but I was too timid and ingenuous for words. Even as a young married woman, I was terrified of walking alone in the street in case anyone should speak to me. Once I stopped to buy daffodils from a woman with a basketful. I gave her a gold sovereign to go and get change. Needless to say, I never saw her, or the daffodils, or the sovereign again."

Maids might terrorize a youthful employer, but in the general run of things, they did not have much of a time. A little German maid who had been ill-treated in her former post was found by Netta hiding under the bed because she had broken a gas globe. The bullying that went on in many posts may be partly responsible for the dislike of the younger generation for domestic service today. But the very persons who were supposed to simplify life often helped only to complicate it. These early trials engraved themselves on Netta's memory. What she learned from them bore fruit in later years when she won the name of an outstandingly considerate employer and was rewarded by years of faithful service from her employees.

At the time of her first confinement, which lasted eighteen difficult hours, she was not so fortunate. The next day, the parlourmaid, whom she looked upon as a real friend, asked to be allowed to see the baby. She no sooner had entered the room of this exhausted young mother than she promptly gave notice. "This reduced me almost to a state of hysteria. I had counted upon her to care for me and the new baby." The story, however, had a happier ending. A few days later, the parlourmaid came upstairs again and said that she would stay even though she did not like babies. Netta, greatly touched, thought that her better feelings had prevailed. Some weeks later, however, she discovered that her kindly father-in-law, who had been in the house at the time, had stopped the maid on the stairs, given her a pound, and told her that her behaviour was uncharitable and unkind and that she must not worry her mistress at such a time.

When Netta was well, she and Ernest went for a holiday to Italy, leaving the baby, nurse, and wet nurse at Kensington Palace Gardens with Netta's mother. The nurse, who had been recommended by a lady who sang her praises loudly, was taken suddenly ill and removed to St. George's Hospital. "When I returned, I went to visit her. I had never been in a hospital before and I felt nervous and frightened. When I got there and asked to see the patient, I was told that she had died the night before. This was a shock, and it was a still greater shock to learn that she had been suffering from an advanced stage of heart trouble and might have dropped dead at any time when carrying my baby. The ward sister told me that the patient's last wish had been that she should be buried in her native Gloucestershire and that she hoped we would defray the expense. She had been only a few weeks with us, and twelve years with her former mistress. But when I wrote to the latter, who had expressed so much interest in and affection for her, suggesting that she might care to help also, my letter remained unanswered."

Life was not all domesticity and the worries attendant thereon. Social activities occupied a large part of it. When Netta gave her first dinner-party, her father arrived late because, as a member now for Tower Hamlets, he had waited in the House of Commons to hear Gladstone introduce his first Home Rule Bill. Later, when the Grand Old Man dined at Kensington Palace Gardens, Ernest and Netta met him at coffee. There was much entertaining, at her parents' and in her own home. Ernest did not quite conform to Montagu standards of punctuality. "I remember, soon after we were married, we were dining with the Countess d'Avigdor. It was winter, there was a very hard frost, and straw had been laid in the streets. Ernest had not hurried unduly, and when we got into the four-wheeler, we found that we must go at a snail's pace, and that the horse could scarcely keep its feet. I realized that we were going to be terribly late. We arrived. It was a dinner party for twenty-four, and we found twenty-two people already seated around the dinner table. There was a vacant place either side, as though not only Banquo but Banquo's wife were expected. I hurried towards my hostess, desperately shy, and barely able to murmur my apologies. She remarked in a very cold voice, 'I suppose you couldn't help it.' And then in a deathly silence, which fully indicated society's disapproval of such behaviour, Ernest made his way to one side of the table and I to the other."

On 22 February 1887, Netta's parents gave a fancy dress ball at 12 Kensington Palace Gardens, duly commemorated in a whole series of photographs taken on the occasion. The costumes are magnificent, and were probably hired. The most frivolous-looking member of the family, garbed as an Italian maiden and with a tambourine, is, paradoxically, Lily, the future earnest social worker and lay minister in the Liberal Jewish Movement. Netta is a decidedly serious-looking young Roman matron, in flowing white robe, with a kind of black cope over one shoulder. Her dark hair is wound close to her head and bound with a fillet, and she carries a bunch of lilies. She is seen turning towards a heavily-embossed Victorian plush chair, with her hand resting on an equally anachronistic Japanese fire-screen. In the background waves a forest of tenuous palms. In fact, the only Roman thing in the picture is the stern and earnest expression of the extremely handsome young matron. Ernest was a dashing Italian of the Renaissance, and might have walked straight out of the pages of one of Shakespeare's plays. His jet-black eyebrows, his dark eyes, and his light growth of moustache are clearly his own; but his dark curling locks may have been borrowed for the occasion. Seated at her desk, seventy-one years later, Netta holds this portrait up, gazes at it, and then says reflectively, "It may seem strange to you to hear it, but Ernest was an extremely good waltzer."

NETTA CIRCA 1888

5

IN THE SUMMER of 1888, Ernest and Netta took a house for the holidays in Caterham. The Oakfield Visitors' List and a number of limericks written by the guests and host on that occasion still exist. Rose Leney and Rosie Stiebel, with whom Netta used to read Horace and Virgil, both figure in them. Netta's virtues are celebrated in more than one limerick.

> The name of our hostess is Netta,
> 'Twould be hard to discover a better,
> She's so kind to each guest
> That I really am blest
> If she doesn't make each one her debtor.

Of all the limerick composers, Rosie Stiebel was the gayest—

> There was a young party named Sigismund[5]
> Who rode a most beautiful gee-gee,
> This remarkable steed
> Was of wonderful breed
> For it came from the island of Fiji.

She was also a frequent source of inspiration to her rival poets: they celebrated her not only in English, but in French and Latin as well, which throws a sidelight on the erudition of the frivolous young in 1888:

> Il y avait une demoiselle Rose,
> Écoute, je t'en dirai quelqu' chose,
> Elle s'appelle aussi Stiebel,
> C'est un nom bien horrible,
> Mais ce n'est pas sa faute, je suppose!

And this, by Harry Cohen, a talented member of a talented family who, later, was killed in the Alps—

---

[5] Sir David (Sigismund) Waley, later Secretary to the Treasury and U.K. Delegate Tripartite Commission on German Debts.

AD ROSAM

Te, Rose, voce peto tremula, dulcissima florum
Namque 'vale' tandem dicere Fata jubent
Quid nimium versus vario sermone jocosos
Ludimus insulsi? Sed! mihi parce precor.
Vulnera non numquam risus dedit inter amicos
Inque loco, dicunt, desipiisse juvat.

Jaques Franklin produced a charming anagram which might have been taken out of one of Portia's caskets at Belmont:

R ippling laughter only shows
O utward signs of mirth; and woes
S ilently may in their throes
E ven merry hearts enclose –
S o at least the saying goes
T is not proven, still who knows?
I ll too oft a sadness sows
E 'en where joy and gladness grows
B ut a flow'r there is that blows
E xcepted aye—who'd suppose
L atent evil 'neath the Rose?

When she left, after one of her visits, Rosie would continue versifying in the rain up to London and would presently dispatch a rhymed 'Collins' to her hostess. Later in life, she would become the official translator into English of Puccini's *Madame Butterfly*.

Family contacts, and friendships like this with the animated Rose Stiebel, meant everything to Netta. She had known Rosie since childhood. The latter, at the age of ten, had been told one day by her mother, "Mrs. Montagu has asked you to tea. Her little girl is just the right age for you two to be companions to one another." It was not the most promising beginning, but young Miss Stiebel had gone, or been dispatched. When she returned home later, she made one very clear observation on the situation, which she remembered long afterwards. "Do you know, Mama, people don't tell Netta what to do—*she tells them!*"

Rosie had reason to be grateful later for this trait. One of her own limericks at Caterham was about a fellow-guest.

> There was a young fellow called Elkin
> The cheekiest man 'neath the welkin,
> His name it was Willy
> And both clever and silly
> Could be this young party called Elkin.

Cheek must have triumphed; or perhaps cleverness; for presently Netta was pleading the cause of Willy Elkin with Rosie's mother, who strongly opposed the match for financial reasons. Many years later, Mrs. Elkin would say to a friend, "I owe my happy married life to Netta, so happy that I cannot bear to speak of it." Netta gave an engagement party for the young couple. She had a gift for arranging flowers, decades before this art became fashionable, and on this occasion, her arrangement of abundant roses set among deep green graceful ferny leaves was particularly admired. "I explained that the roses were for Rosie, and the greenery was composed of carrot tops in honour of Willie Elkin's red hair. There was a roar of laughter. No one had recognized the leaves, till I told them."

She liked to be abreast of her times. At the first dance she gave, soon after she was married, she arranged the flowers in the new Japanese fashion, a very few in each bowl. Her kind mother-in-law remarked, "Netta, dear, everything was so well done except the flowers. If you had told me you could not afford to have more, I would gladly have helped you!"

Netta's social activities at this time were typical of the more seriously-minded young people among the privileged classes. Thanks to forceful individualities like W. T. Stead and Annie Besant, there was a growing consciousness of the more acute inequalities in English life. Dinner-parties were often an occasion when philanthropic plans were discussed and consciences awakened.

Her father was a Liberal candidate for a London constituency. In a speech to the Liberal Council in 1885, he had announced his allegiance to full Manhood and Womanhood Suffrage, the Reform of the House of Lords, Local Administration, Free Trade, the Abolition of Entail and Primogeniture, and facilities for Land Purchase by Cultivators.

A letter from her mother, written to Netta in the year after her marriage, a little laments these political activities. "Papa continues to come home very late at night. I sit up generally, as sometimes he has a few minutes' chat, but generally he is too tired. Oh, these horrible politics!" An earlier passage in this letter refers to the great difficulty he had had in obtaining sufficient carriages to provide the populace with transport on the occasion of some polling day or rally. "Mrs. Singer we also asked, but she has not been able to secure any. I think Papa has about twenty-five. Aunt Clara and Mr. I. Hyam both think the carriages should be disinfected after the day."

The same letter is full of praises of Netta—"You are very good to write so many letters to all of us, you would be repaid if you were here to see how we all devoured them round the table." It concludes "With love to Ernest," and then this philosophic postscript: "As regards your spots, I daresay they will disappear again in a week or so."[6]

If the strong-minded Netta worried a little about her spots, she showed considerable patience and fortitude under a much greater affliction, that of very severe headaches. There are continual references in her diaries, "In spite of headaches I had frequent guests for lunch and dinner." "I was still suffering from continual bad headaches which did not seem to hamper my activities."

Netta needed not one but numerous friends to satisfy her hospitable instincts. All her lifelong friends were to be a revivifying influence. Old friends meant as much to her as ever. New friends were continually being added to her list. She found it the easiest thing in the world to make personal usefulness a predominant passion. She would have been of less value as the wife of a self-absorbed sculptor or a languid poet. She could never have placed herself at the disposal of a single lame duck. She must have a whole farmyard of them so that when one had finished quacking, she could pass quietly on to the requirements of the next. If the earlier years of her married life were turbulent—and rumour has it that at times they were—it may have been partly because Ernest was not really made for this farmyard life and had to get gradually accustomed to it.

She encouraged him to widen his horizons. It has been said that Netta first gave him his interest in art and architecture, but this is disproved by a letter to one of his sisters written while on his honeymoon. It is on very thin paper, stamped with the maiden initials of his bride—

---

6 She suffered from acne and had, in the past, managed to squeeze a few drops of philosophic comfort from the reflection, 'Well, if anyone ever marries me it will be for myself and not for my looks.' Despite this modesty, both she and her sister Lily were beauties.

H.M.
BAYERISCHE HOF. MUNICH
22 OCT. 1885

My dearest Edie,

Which is worse? That you and all your brothers and sisters have scarcely written us a letter since we have been away, you who have scarcely anything to do, or that I, who am fearfully busy enjoying myself and causing others to enjoy themselves, should have only written about twice as many letters as I have received? Netta has, without exaggeration, received ten times as many envelopes as I, and each envelope has contained two or more letters. However, we still manage to keep ourselves supremely happy.

We rose in the middle of the night and groped our way to the station whence we took the midnight train to Augsburg (I call 7:35 the middle of the night even if you don't). We arrived at that interesting and quaint old town at 8:43. We spent the morning wandering about looking at churches, the Rathaus, and the houses. The chief attractions in this town are some fine pictures by old German Masters, notably Holbein Senior (our Holbein's papa), fine wood carving, and best of all magnificent works in wrought iron. The churches contain most of this work; it is chiefly of the fifteenth and sixteenth century and excels in design and execution even Huntingdon Shaw's celebrated Hampton Court Gates in the Kensington Museum. The finest specimens are the inner gates of St. Ulrich's Church. These, although their surface is quite flat, from a distance appear to be in perspective. The design is somewhat like this, only if possible still handsomer. [Line drawing of ironwork.] The houses in Augsburg are mostly, almost universally, sixteenth or early seventeenth (century) buildings and besides their quaint appearance, are frequently adorned with old-world signs and screens made of the afore-described wrought iron.

We left Augsburg at a quarter after one and immediately on our arrival here endeavoured to show the Kosher restaurant proprietors that English appetites can sometimes rival even those of the Natives. "By the bye," we saw some very extraordinary peasants' costumes (inhabited of course) at Augsburg, quite like they are represented in pictures. I would like to have bought some, but they were too expensive unless I left out the live portions, but as these are the most interesting parts, I did not care to waste my money.

Last night we saw Les Femmes Savantes in German. I don't think

I told you how we have both been taken under the wing of the Kosher restaurant domestic; she speaks so prettily to us. Yesterday she said it made her heart quite happy to look upon such a lovely pair as we are. We are, of course, not a lovely pair, but we are simply seraphic compared with the other frequenters of the restaurant.

We intend, as you know, leaving here for Salzburg Saturday evening en route for Vienna, but our next address for letters will be the Imperial Hotel, Vienna. Our meals at this hotel are a joke; this evening we have ordered for dinner nothing but a plate full of tomatoes. Not much for a hungry pair, is it?...

I remain your ever-loving brother,

Ernest.

You will notice a budding economy in me by my using Netta's spinster paper.

Ernest had taken painting lessons at his school and had a natural endowment of good taste. When, later in life, he became rich enough to indulge it, his purchases of pictures and *objets d'art* would testify both to his judgment and to his individual courage. Years afterwards, he put on record his regret that he had not possessed equal courage in his early twenties, when his father had taken him to an International Exhibition in Paris. "We came to a room full of Impressionist paintings—Degas, Renoir, Manet, etc. My father said that these were very poor stuff and we had better come and see something really good. To this day I am proud of my reply, 'You know, I rather like them.' My regret, however, has always been that I never backed my judgment. It would have required a very small outlay." Oliver St. John Gogarty used to tell a similar story of how, when Hugh Lane brought the first Post-Impressionist Exhibition to Dublin, he could have had any Van Gogh he liked for forty pounds, but, like Ernest, he had lacked the necessary courage.

When eventually he did start buying, Ernest bought just what pleased him, a number of fine bronzes by Epstein, Chinese ceramics from the collection of Goerges Eumorfopoulos, a Sickert, a very lovely Stephen Bone, a Vlaminck, a Boudin, and a Utrillo. He commissioned Sargent to paint his wife and Glyn Philpot his two sons. Because he pleased himself and never bought speculatively or for snob reasons, his collection, although extremely varied, was nevertheless homogeneous with the homogeneity of genuine personal preference.

Netta encouraged her husband in the study of art. She also encouraged him to take up golf. Before long, Ernest was complaining that golf was used as an excuse to send him to Sandwich to get rid of him. To prove that this was not so, Netta, on one occasion, transferred the whole family holiday to St. Andrews. She cannot remember now whether Ernest's golf benefited or not, but she can remember vividly how, in her prevailing enthusiasm of the moment—which was conchology—she visited the local museum, and, leaning on the glass top of a showcase to admire particularly beautiful specimens of the blue-rayed limpet and to get the names for her collection, her elbows crashed through the glass, a mischance which embarrassed her beyond measure and showered havoc down upon the delicate exhibits. "I was forgiven. The curator wouldn't even let me pay for the glass."

Her first-born, Sydney, had been born in 1886, followed by a daughter, Marjorie, in December 1887. In London, she was kept busy in a multitude of ways, beside her duties as a mother. At her weekly At-Home, it was quite usual to find as many as thirty callers. "There were luncheon parties and dinner parties, and I used to go to the theatre every Saturday evening and also to a number of first nights. There were art exhibitions, and I remember my delight standing in front of Burne-Jones's recently painted *Briar Rose*. One August, the artist Solomon J. Solomon stayed with us. He painted a head of little Madge, using her own paintbrush for the purpose."

Ernest took a house at Walton-on-the-Hill for the summer and amongst the guests who came to stay were Netta's parents-in-law, her ex-pupil Herbert Samuel, Willie Elkin and his wife, Laurie Magnus, Willy Raphael, Matthew[7] and Maud Nathan, and Walter Cohen. Ernest was able to go up and down daily to business, and from this summer home, they explored the surrounding countryside in a pony-trap which Netta drove and from which she could indulge her passion for wild flowers. When the Jewish New Year came, they spent the Holy Days with her uncle and aunt, Sir Joseph and Adelaide Sebag-Montefiore. The changing or double-barrelling of names has always been a favourite target for relatives, both with Jews and Gentiles, and this one had not been overlooked in the limerick book by Ernest.

---

7 Afterwards Sir Matthew Nathan, Governor of the Gold Coast, Secretary for Ireland, etc.

> Uncle Joe—so methinks goes the story,
> Being anxious to add to his glory,
> When his old uncle died
> His own name magnified
> From Sebag to Sebag-Montefiore.

Netta's multiple interests can be deduced from the following extracts from her diaries. "We took a little house at Birchington so that the children might have more sea air." "In October I began Greek lessons with Mr. Vigniols." "My son Geoffrey was born on May 11th." "For some time I had been giving Hebrew lessons to Tottie, Gilbert Samuel, and Laura Franklin. I gave them an examination in April." "My daughter Olive was born on March 14th." "I heard Hall Caine speak on Russia." "In February I started a course on Geology at the Natural History Museum." "On the 28th April I went with my father to South Stoneham for the weekend, returned Monday morning, met the children who had come up from Birchington, and then went to a dance at Flo Beddington's."

South Stoneham in Hampshire had been bought by her father in the year that she was married. From then on, there were frequent visits to it. There must have been much packing and unpacking in Netta's early life, for besides the variety of her summer residences, there were also holidays abroad with Ernest. They made a tour of the French cathedrals, beginning at Rouen and going on to Caen, Bayeux, Tours, and Amboise. One January found her at Grindelwald with Ernest, Sydney, and Marjorie. They stayed there for a fortnight, long before winter sports had become fashionable. This was the Grindelwald known to Arnold Lunn as a boy, before the Bear Hotel had been burnt, the Grindelwald where the English style in skating still prevailed on the rinks, with the arms kept grotesquely close to the sides.

Netta was married and the administrator of a home. But she had still to find herself. Today she would probably marry much later, after a university career and several years of independent activity. She herself had wanted to matriculate. But in the 1880s, her life had followed the pattern of many a young Frenchwoman's: an extremely sheltered youth and then early marriage. Her younger sisters had never seen a man shave, and when they came to stay with her at Pembridge Gardens, one of the greatest treats of their visit was to see Ernest perform this daily ritual.

Minding her home, entertaining her relatives was not enough. She enjoyed social contacts; she enjoyed motherhood. But even it did not furnish an adequate outlet for her idealism and her abundant energies. She still lacked self-fulfilment. The great moment of her life had still to come, "the moment of truth." Only when it came would she be launched on the full tide of her destiny.

6

IN 1887, AFTER A MEETING held in Bradford at the house of a Mrs. Francis Steinthal, Charlotte Maria Shaw Mason, a young schoolteacher, who had published a book on the principles of education within the circle of the home, was asked by a number of earnest-minded parents to found a union which would help them cope with the parental problems which confronted them. It was soon in existence under the title of The Parents' National Education Union and presently it had its own monthly, *The Parents' Review*. Four years later, Miss Mason founded the Parents' Union School, originally a correspondence school to provide a syllabus of work and examination facilities for the home school only. This proved so successful that before long its programmes were being adopted by schools and classes all over the world.

Daughter of a Liverpool merchant, Charlotte Mason had been in a training college at Chichester and had had varied teaching experience before she became an educational reformer. Many of her holidays had been spent in the Lake District; she moved there in 1891 and in 1892 she started a training college in Ambleside called the House of Education, which was to provide teachers for home schoolrooms and, eventually, for many schools.

Her educational principles are set forth at length in the five volumes of the Home Education Series and in her last volume, *An Essay towards a Philosophy of Education*. Quite early she had taken as the text of her mission these words of Benjamin Whichcote, "No sooner doth the truth come into the soul's sight, but the soul knows her to be her first and old acquaintance." The motto of her Union was, "Education is an atmosphere, a discipline, a life," and the earlier portion of her excellent synopsis of aims and standpoints—which is too long to quote in its entirety—reads:—

1. Children are born *persons*.
2. They are not born either good or bad, but with possibilities for good and for evil.
3. The principles of authority on the one hand, and of obedience on the other, are natural, necessary, and fundamental; but—

4. These principles are limited by the respect due to the personality of children, which must not be encroached upon, whether by the direct use of fear or love, suggestion or influence, or by undue play upon any one natural desire.
5. Therefore, we are limited to three educational instruments: the atmosphere of environment, the discipline of habit, and the presentation of living ideas.
6. When we say that *"education is an atmosphere,"* we do not mean that a child should be isolated in what may be called a "child-environment" especially adapted and prepared, but that we should take into account the educational value of his natural home atmosphere, both as regards persons and things, and should let him live freely among his proper conditions. It stultifies a child to bring down his world to the "child's" level.
7. By *"education is a discipline,"* we mean the discipline of habits, formed definitely and thoughtfully, whether habits of mind or of body. Physiologists tell us of the adaptation of brain structures to habitual lines of thought, i.e., to our habits.
8. In saying that *"education is a life,"* the need of intellectual and moral as well as of physical sustenance is implied. The mind feeds on ideas, and therefore children should have a generous curriculum.
9. We hold that the child's mind is no mere *sack* to hold ideas, but is rather, if the figure may be allowed, a spiritual organism, with an appetite for all knowledge. This is its proper diet, with which it is prepared to deal, and which it can digest and assimilate as the body does foodstuffs.

Netta encountered P.N.E.U. in the early 1890s through a friend, a young mother, Mrs. Whitaker Thompson, who showed her the last number of *The Parents' Review* and told her that she ought to subscribe. She was immediately interested and began to read it regularly. Wanting to know more, she persuaded Ernest that they ought to take a short holiday in the Lake District. "We stayed at Lowood Hotel, and I made my pilgrimage one afternoon to visit Miss Mason. Years afterwards, she used to say, 'I looked out of the window and I saw a young person in a holland frock approaching the hall door.' Only that it sounds silly, I would say that we fell in love with each other at first sight. Miss Mason did say quite often that with my arrival she had found her long-awaited and predestined 'chela.'[8] If that

---

8   Pupil or future initiate.

was true on her side, it was still truer on mine. I had found the 'guru,' or sage and teacher, of whom I stood so much in need. I can only give you a very faint idea of the inspiration of her personality. She was quite small, rather frail, obliged eventually to plan her life as carefully as an invalid. But she burned like a clear flame." That first afternoon, they talked of some of the many things that interested them. Netta persuaded Miss Mason to say that she would stay with her the next time that she came to London. She did not hold out much hope of a speedy visit, but actually, she was to come quite soon, as a crisis occurred in the affairs of the P.N.E.U. Certain members of the Committee—including Lady Isabel Margesson and Lord MacNeil—were anxious to make the Union a sort of amalgam of Froebel, Pestalozzi, Charlotte Mason, and half a dozen others. But the others felt that they had their own prophetess and did not want a hodge-podge of all the great educationalists. Charlotte Mason had her own educational message to give to the world. The minority resigned when they found they could not get their way. Netta was asked to become Honorary Organizing Secretary. She agreed and has been secretary ever since.

Asked by someone once what she considered Charlotte Mason's greatest and most characteristic contribution to the educational thought of the nineteenth century, Netta replied, "I would say respect for the individual child. In her relations with children—friends' children, village children, children from schools all over the country—there was a really beautiful reverence and courtesy. She had a great sense of humour, too, and that helped her to understand children."

To Miss Mason, parents were very far from being omnipotent and omniscient delegates of God Almighty. She could write, "The authority of parents, though the deference it begets remains to grace the relations of parents and child, is itself a provisional function, and it is only successful as it encourages the *autonomy*, if we may call it so, of the child. A single decision made by the parents which the child is, or should be, capable of making for itself, is an encroachment on the rights of the child, and a transgression on the part of the parents."

Charlotte Mason, when Netta first met her, was in her early fifties. With the publication of her first book, the discerning had seen in her a living force for good in the lives of the young. After her death, Sir Michael Sadler wrote, "She threw 'a shaft of light across the land.' She loved England and therefore had at heart the upbringing of the children of England.

She longed that they should have what to her had been beyond price—the habit of reading great books which disclose the mind of man, seen in the light of 'a far-off divine event.'"

Undoubtedly, Miss Mason is amongst the great educators. And, where the teaching of literature is concerned, one feels inclined to say that she remains the only one with any inkling of the matter. Her contention was, "Let great literature speak for itself; an author is his own best expounder, and all attempts to interpret him, to impose explanation, gloss, annotation, or paraphrase at first encounter only make the child wince and turn away when he should be enjoying direct communication with the master. The poet, the philosopher, can all speak direct to the soul of the child and, when they do, the pedagogue should remain silent. What cannot be understood directly can well wait for another time. Children can understand quite a lot, if we will only remain silent." Miss Mason had a planned technique, which would keep the teacher's mouth shut, perforce: There was to be one reading of the poem or passage, and *only one*. Then, before attention had had time to wander, or been distracted by commentary, some child in the class must "narrate" back as much of the passage as he remembered. The rest might not interrupt during this narration, but they were allowed to make their own additions later.

H. W. Household has pointed out that she was not, strictly speaking, the inventor of "narration." A century before her time, Dr. Johnson had said to Mrs. Thrale, "Little people should be encouraged always to tell whatever they hear particularly striking to some brother or sister or servant immediately, before the impression is erased by newer occurrences." All epitomes in print, all pre-digested versions, were anathema to Charlotte Mason. She considered them an insult to the creative artist. Difficult words were not to be expounded unless a direct question was asked. They could be left until such time as the child—by meeting the word in a number of different contexts—would understand it for himself. To ungag the teacher at this stage can turn the whole lesson into a lecture on etymology.

A great author writes, not that he may be expounded, but that he may ring a bell in the secret chambers of the heart.

Charlotte Mason poured savage scorn on any technological or scientific approach to literature. It was part, she felt, of the over-exaggerated Herbartian educational philosophy. One could not teach the humanities as though they were part of an exposition of chemical process. They belonged to a different domain altogether, a different level of being.

Some of Charlotte Mason's earlier volumes are written with an almost Wordsworthian simplicity and *naiveté*. Perhaps living in the Lake District contributed to this effect. Furthermore, one needs to remember that she was born in 1842, almost Fairchild Family vintage herself, and had early fallen under the deep influence of didactic writers like Carlyle and Ruskin. The language of Isaiah or Ezekiel, the language of real moral uplift, is amongst the most poetic and the most moving in literature. But the language of conventional moral uplift is embarrassing, and we instinctively shrink from it. Charlotte Mason could write, "As you know very well, it is not pure water that causes drunkenness. Men long ago discovered how to prepare a substance called alcohol, and this it is that ruins thousands of men and women. Many good men and women, and children too, make a solemn vow that they will never taste ale or wine or other strong drink, unless a doctor order it by way of medicine. They do this, not only for fear that they should themselves become drunkards—though there is no knowing who may fall into that terrible temptation, or at what period of life such a fall may come—but because every little good deed helps to stop the evil in the world by setting a good example to somebody, and perhaps there is never a good example set but someone follows it, though the person who set the example may never know. This is one reason why it is well to keep one's taste for cold water, and to know how delicious it is."

All this is in the best tradition of pious Victorian resolution, and is all good advice, if your grandfather died of *delirium tremens*. But how much less than the whole truth it is. It needs biblical annotation, the psalmist's "Wine that maketh glad the heart of man," and the gospel's "Verily I say unto you that I shall not drink again of the fruit of the vine till I drink it new with you in my Father's Kingdom." Hilaire Belloc and G. K. Chesterton would have been infuriated by Miss Mason's views on the subject, and Chesterton would have quoted with a stupendous roar his own line from *Wine, Water and Song*, "I don't care where the water goes if it doesn't get into the wine!"

Nevertheless, the Charlotte Mason doctrine, despite the phraseology of the earlier books and despite a possible caveat from Chesterton on the subject of alcohol, has stood the test of time. Eton's famous headmaster, Edward Lyttleton, could call her teaching "the greatest practical discovery ever made in education," and a quarter of a century after her death, the Essex Education Committee would be giving support to her theories by banning homework for children under twelve and warning teachers that children must not be crammed for the admission examination to secondary schools. In these days of changed conditions in the home and huge classes at school, linked to a standardized system of teaching, we would do well to remember her views on the relationship between parent and child, and between teacher and child. Children must, she said, establish relation with God and man, the past and the present, with science, art, music, and nature. Life must be taken as a whole, and religion was part of that whole. The twentieth and last section of the *Synopsis* reads: "We allow no separation to grow up between the intellectual and 'spiritual' life of children, but teach them that the Divine Spirit has constant access to their spirits and is their continual Helper in all the interests, duties, and joys of life."

7

NETTA HAD JOINED the Pioneer Club, one of the first women's clubs, where she listened to debates between well-known people, and presently became Chairman of its Debates Committee. Towards the close of the nineteenth century, women began to emerge from subordination. Men had been hobnobbing together in clubs for a long time. It suddenly occurred to women, why should they not have clubs, too? And, as well as group association, women discovered how much individual friendship, as free equals, no longer under the iron dictate of husband or father, could mean to them. Netta had also joined another debating society conducted by Madame d'Esterre at her friend Ella Glover's house. Ella had come into her life at the time of her marriage. Musical herself, Ella used to play daily, good but quite simple music to her small son aged three. In no time, he would bring her the book containing the particular piece of music he wanted. Netta happened to take Charlotte Mason to tea with the Glovers, and she saw this and begged Ella to write an article on musical appreciation for The *Parents' Review*, the beginning of a crusade which accounts for whole symphony concerts being staged today specially for children, with a running commentary by an expert.

Ella Glover was only one of many friends. There was Mrs. Clement Parsons, authoress and lecturer; and Lady Campbell (Nina Lehmann) who arrived one day at 9 Pembridge Gardens with her husband, Sir Guy Campbell, to consult Netta about a preparatory school for their small son, and who were to entertain Ernest and Netta frequently in their beautiful home at Thames Ditton; and Mrs. Devonshire, writer and lecturer on Eastern art and archaeology. All her life, right into its tenth decade, Netta would continue to make new friends, while holding steadfastly to the old. Like Claude Montefiore, she can say, "I do not wobble in my affections." She gets on well with men, but she was born into the great age of women friendships and the majority of her friends are women.

At the age of fifty-five, Charlotte Mason could write to Netta, who was in her early thirties, "Happily you are like me, a woman who loves, and you have lovely friends and one at least who holds you very close but will probably not tell you so again, but will expect you always to trust her."

Charlotte Mason, with the instinct of a successful general for perceiving where a particular individual was most likely to be of service in her campaign, had realized immediately the potentialities of her new recruit. Netta was a born propagandist. Though she had not founded the Movement, it was she who established it. She was young, she was wealthy. She was tireless. Whenever she saw her opportunity, she blazed the trail. H. W. Household, the County Education Officer for Gloucestershire, could write to her many years later: "I can see for myself what you are doing that no one else could do—always keeping the Movement before the world in the best and wisest way. You have been the great organizer throughout. You knew Miss Mason's mind as no other living being knew it—the letters tell that: and had an influence with her, as well as with the world, without which her own generation would never have been won to knowledge of her." That was written in 1927 and, in 1951, when he was an old man of eighty-one, he would write to her, "None of the great things could have been without you."

She not only preached, she practiced. In 1892, she started the first P.N.E.U. class for children in London. She wrote a letter to the *Parents' Review* and pointed out that however valuable the syllabus and examinations and guidance of the P.U.S. might be, children needed companionship. She asked for the names of those who would like to join. A gymnasium was erected specially in Linden Gardens for the class, and a Miss Allen took charge of it. Later, Miss Faunce began to teach another class at the house of Netta's sister, Mrs. Waley, and from it grew the famous day school in Queen's Gardens which Miss Lambert now runs, and which has numbered amongst its pupils many girls who have distinguished themselves in public and social life.

Periodically, Netta went to Ambleside taking the two elder children, Sydney and Marjorie, with her. At one time, Charlotte Mason thought of making her the official Visitor to the House of Education in succession to Mrs. Dallas Yorke, mother of the Duchess of Portland, who had been Miss Mason's friend and lady Visitor since the foundation of the College, and who had just died. But she changed her mind, "because I would not for the world let your visits have even a nominal official character—they are too personal and dear for that." Netta had received the nickname of

"Lady A," a joking counterpart to Sir Augustus Harris, who was a great organizer of entertainments at that time. Miss Mason would have liked all her supporters to be as vigorous. Too well-mannered to call the lukewarm amongst them "rabbits," the Biblical alternative came to her rescue, and she writes after one of Netta's visits, "I am better, but still feel that the conies are a feeble folk. Lady A. has left all sorts of sweet impressions behind her." She could go further than that and become downright gushing, "I have read with great stirrings of heart your eloquent, cultured, strong, just and wise paper. It should be read in all the Branches. If P.N.E.U. had only made *you*, it has done a truly great work. Of course, you would have been clever and good anyway, but the *direction* you have taken is so good for the world!" And then she adds, with a touch of her hero Ruskin's epistolary playfulness, "There's a dish of sugar plums for you!"

Something deeper united these two women than mutual adulation, or even a sense of common purpose in education. Netta has said, "I think it was the intellectual and religious side of her teaching that attracted my young, eager mind. Without the religious basis, her teaching would have meant nothing to me. Though she was an earnest Christian and I a no less earnest Liberal Jewess, she accepted me with her wide tolerance and often said how glad she was that the Bishop of London (at whose Palace the P.N.E.U. was launched) had altered the word 'Christian' to 'religious' in the Constitution. 'Otherwise,' he had said, 'you would never get Jewish members.' 'Nor,' Miss Mason added, 'would I ever have had you.'"

In one of her letters, Charlotte Mason writes: "Dr. Knittel[9] said some deeply interesting things about the Jewish people—considered that they stimulated thought, intellectual activity of every kind—the Jewish people are for the education of the rest of us. Behold my Lady A. is but fulfilling her mission after all! I think I must have Jewish blood, if I could trace it, or I should not be so bent on bringing up the world at large." When in 1923, after Charlotte Mason's death, her successor, Miss Parish, as head of the House of Education, opposed the admission of a Jewish candidate on the ground that the Movement "could only really be understood by Christians," it was not to be expected that she should know of this letter,

---

9 The publisher of the Home Education series in German, his interest having been awakened by a speech of Netta's at the Conference of International Council of Women in Berlin in 1904.

but she had apparently overlooked the dedication in one of Miss Mason's own books[10]—

<blockquote>
TO
HENRIETTA FRANKLIN

This volume is affectionately inscribed in very grateful recognition, not only of her generous life's labour given to the spread of certain educational lines, but also of her singular apprehension of those ideals.
</blockquote>

The affection between them was the deep affection of an older woman who sees in a younger the fulfilment of some of her ideals. Netta was the pupil, Charlotte Mason was the teacher as well as the well-loved and trusted friend. She writes in May 1897, "I have been thinking very much of 'my child' and wish to make you promise to run down to me once a month or six weeks for the soothing and the calm of this sweet world and of your friend's love; yes—I feel rich in the possession of you, dearest, but you will find me very exacting, not at all in the way of affection, that goes without saying, still less in the way of exclusive affection, which thing is not lovely, but in the way of having you more and more God-fulfilled, ever more of your best beautiful self. I could not let you be less than yourself."

When, years later in 1951, the P.N.E.U. celebrated its Diamond Jubilee, Netta would write of these early days, "Sixty years ago there were no magazine articles, lectures, or radio talks to help those in whose hands was the training and teaching of the child. 'How shall we order the child?' was echoed along the ages in many a mother's heart since Hannah first uttered the cry. Many mistakes were made, battles of will, spoiling (which can be brought about by over-severity as well as over-indulgence) were all too usual, in spite of love and earnest endeavour. Charlotte Mason put the psychological teaching of the day, often to be found only in heavy and difficult tomes, into language which all could understand, and added her own interpretation of the laws of habit formation, inspiration of ideas, and the way of reason and will."

Children taught in their own home-schoolrooms, she has pointed out elsewhere, were often far from happy. "Most mothers seldom attempted to do more than teach the three R's and governesses, being untrained and often

---

[10]   Home and School Education, a new edition of which appeared in 1953.

with little understanding or love for the children, became bad-tempered, objected to being asked questions and even, when taking children for walks, were known to make the children keep in step with them, so little did they realize the needs of childhood."

The P.U.S. syllabus and programmes were to change that for many homes. Netta has related how Miss Mason encouraged not only a more stimulating diet for the schoolroom but also frequent contacts with living nature. Her first published book, incidentally, had been upon rambles through the counties of England and was called *The Forty Shires*—"Miss Mason taught us that we and our children must have a knowledge of living nature, and know birds and flowers as friends. So rambles were arranged from London and provincial towns, in the neighbouring county or even in parks; and Natural History Clubs were formed whose members received teaching by correspondence from Mr. Rowbotham, a great naturalist. In this work Miss Mason's friends Mrs. Hart-Davis in the Reading Branch and her sister Mrs. Anson in London, as well as Mrs. Henry Perrin, were our chief supporters. Nature notebooks and collections were exhibited."

In addition to these official gatherings, there were country rambles with her own children, which found their way into her diary. "I began taking the children for country walks and looking for wild flowers." "In March, Ernest, Sydney, Marjorie, Maud Schlösser, and I stayed together at the Swan Hotel, Leatherhead. We found many wild flowers and a scorpion beetle, and Marjorie tried to milk a cow." "I took the children to picture galleries and museums once a week." "We now owned a boat, which we kept at different points on the river and to which we invited many of our friends on Sundays. The children also went with us." "The children, Charlie Elkin, Annie Bussé, and I went hop-picking." "We found seventy-seven flowers on our walk and we made patterns on the beach, with the children." "On the 17th, I went with the children to their gymnastic lesson, then on to a botany lesson, and a meeting of the P.N.E.U. at Ella Glover's." Life was packed with activities. She would write to her sister-in-law Edith, "I am at Birchington and I am very busy. I have ten letters in front of me and about as many down to write, and I was up at 7:45 this morning, and I feel as if I should never get through my work. But then it is true, I have really got an absurd lot of irons in the fire. Ella Glover has inveigled me into joining a debating society she is forming, and I have actually to open the Debate and talk for ten minutes. She won't let me *read* a paper, and I, not knowing

I should have to do it, consented to a most idiotic subject, 'That we are happier than our Grandmothers.' I am simply haunted day and night by my grandmothers. I never knew them, and it is cruel of them to treat one thus. Certainly, they never worked half as hard as we do."

Her interests were multiple. The diary tells how: "Miss Matzke gave a lecture on the Art of Breathing. In the evening, I left for Mr. Underhill's[11] school, where Sydney now is. I talked till nearly 1 a.m. On Saturday morning, I had prayers with Sydney, attended a French lesson and one on English. In the evening, the boys gave a concert and Sydney played duets. On Sunday morning, I took Sydney for Hebrew, went for a walk, and found green hellebore. I lectured to the boys on natural history." "The children started skating on the artificial rink just opened at Prince's, Knightsbridge. Reading Malory's *Morte d'Arthur* to the children, found many wild flowers, fifty in a day quite common." "Visited Canterbury Cathedral with much interest, arranged for a brush-drawing class for the children."

Her energy and her zest for life were unlimited, but her headaches had continued and she consulted a doctor about them. He told her that she was anaemic and that she should take prairie oysters daily. Netta replied shyly, "We are Jews and do not eat oysters." Whereupon he laughed, left the room, and returned with eight raw eggs, which he made her swallow there and then. These were the prairie oysters. Thereafter, for a time, she had to take two daily.

In one respect, Netta's generation lay at a disadvantage. Sir Richard Burton might return from the Orient, steeped in Persian literature, and might, to the horror of his friends, assert, in his outspoken way, that most young English brides were ill-equipped to hear of, much less experience, the transports of passion. But Burton was a very shocking individual who said things that no one else would dream of saying. From the tragic reticence of the 'eighties and 'nineties, England and America have now rushed to the other extreme and in a burst of psychological reaction stress the physical relation to such a point that one finds *The Reader's Digest* making a valiant effort to try and right the balance. Sex is not everything. It is only one of a number of things.

---

11   He was one of the Oakfeld visitors, since turned schoolmaster. His knowledge of wild flowers, given him by his mother, had helped to inspire Netta with the determination to fit herself to do the same for her own children. By getting him to one of her meetings she had converted him to P.N.E.U. and he had introduced it into his own preparatory school for boys.

Nevertheless, many marriages need to be seen in their historical context; and perhaps, not least, Netta's. It was to last for a matter of sixty-five years and may even carry some lessons for a younger generation. Ernest adored his handsome young wife, he was immensely proud of her, and his light verse of the period bears witness to the pleasure and pride he took in her many abilities. Yet his youngest son, Michael, remembers as a child his mother in bitter tears daily upon the sofa. Ernest would lose his temper, he would storm and rage. He would say that he should never have married her. It is a tribute to both parents that in spite of these painful scenes, they each retained the deep affection and loyalty of all their children. They were to bring the boat of matrimony, eventually, and after many storms, into calm water. In later life, Netta was definitely the dominant partner, but not by any means to the extent that Field-Marshal Montgomery implies that his mother was. Ernest never gave the impression of having sacrificed the smallest part of his essential personality.

He was becoming prominent in the affairs of the bank. He had been a little inclined to hypochondria until Dr. Helen Webb sent him to take out a life insurance and they declared him a first-class life. He possessed to a much greater degree than either his father or his father-in-law all the more characteristically Anglo-Saxon traits, and to these were added the courtesy and charm of a Frenchman. Michael Franklin can say, "Father was always desperately anxious not to be ostentatious. He would talk to everyone, a farm worker or a peer, with exactly the same grave attention." One of Ernest's younger friends remembers that grave attention well himself. Intelligent, shrewd, an able businessman, and a specialist in his own branch of it, Ernest was asked to contribute the articles on Arbitrage and Foreign Exchange in the *Encyclopaedia Britannica*, and did so very effectively. A keen golfer, he played at Sandwich regularly, in a bright red coat with green lapels, and had got his handicap down to eight. Buckle, Editor of *The Times*, was often his opponent, and they arranged a match for their fiftieth, sixtieth, seventieth, eightieth, and ninetieth birthdays, many of which fixtures were kept. Indeed, Ernest would have kept even the last had his opponent still been on earth to play. His other hobby was bridge, and the Savile Club saw him fairly regularly playing a sound, prudent game until the car came to collect him and take him home.

Ernest was witty in his own completely spontaneous way. His best gems were reserved for his own family. Netta would arrive back from some Scandinavian conference and tell with approval how at a committee meeting, when the ardours of debate were over, the Queen had insisted on taking the head of the table and pouring out tea for everyone in the most friendly and homely fashion. Whereupon Ernest's instant comment would be, "Ah! I see, she never reigns but she pours." He loved punning. He loved innocent absurdity, like the story of the neophyte golfer narrating his morning's experiences. "Well, I began fairly well. I took fourteen for the first. And then I managed to do the second in sixteen. And then the next three were—let me see—twenty, twenty-four, and twenty-two. But after that I don't know what happened, I simply went to pieces!" Or the Frenchman's opinion of the English Channel after a very rough crossing, "C'est magnifique, mais ce n'est pas la terre." Another favourite golf story was of the individual persuaded to try his hand at golf, having never made the attempt before. Holding his club in the most unorthodox fashion, he took a tremendous swipe. The ball spun through the air, reached the green—it was a short hole—ran across it, and just managed to trickle into the hole. The beginner turned to his companion with a face radiant with relief, "You know, for one awful moment I thought I was going to miss."

Ernest's children loved it when he told stories like these. He would take them curio hunting, old door-knockers, link-holders and balcony grilles. When they asked him for some special boon, he would keep them on tenterhooks for a little time, with a twinkle in his eye, and then grant it. Though he might storm at Netta and even occasion bitter tears, he adored her, was immensely proud of her, and voiced his pride in her in periodic sets of occasional verse. His son Michael remembers as the phrase most often on his lips, "Oh, it pleases Mother," and adds the comment, "Half the things he did in life were because they pleased Mother." As time went on, he would come to accept her leadership. She was the instigator and the planner. She mapped out his life for him, as well as everyone else's; but on lines which suited him very well. His youngest son's only indictment is, "Like all wealthy Victorians, he was mean about trifles and generous in big things. He would give a sixpenny tip reluctantly, and yet sit down and write a cheque for one hundred pounds without a murmur. He liked to keep his best wines always for better occasions, until eventually they went sour. On the other hand, it used to horrify him when a brother-in-law put water into his wine."

8

IN 1896, A LADY DOCTOR came to give a course of lectures to the Belgravia branch of the P.N.E.U., and Netta formed the second great friendship of her life. Helen Webb had been an original member of the Ambleside Council who, as early as 1891, was lecturing to Hampstead parents on the making, storing, and conservation of nerve force and to others at Reading on the formation of habit.

She was a woman of many parts, not only a physician, but also an artist, landscape-gardener, and highly efficient housewife. She came of Quaker stock. Her book *Children and the Stress of Life,* which was based on her P.N.E.U. lectures, and later published by the Movement, is a study of the acquisition and conservation of nervous energy and moral force in an age which Matthew Arnold described as one of "sick hurry and divided aims," but which, compared with our own, seems a serene, unperturbed backwater. Many of its contentions have long since passed into current acceptance. Besides warnings like "Do not over-stimulate; do not over-educate," she could counter excessive Victorian seriousness with, "Too strong temptation is a stress which we ought carefully to keep out of the lives of our children"; and even write, "Let us not consider ourselves the owners of the children but the servants of Someone, Who being their owner, has the direction of their circumstances more absolutely and continuously than we ourselves," a sentiment which anticipates the Syrian mystic and poet, Kahlil Gibran's, "Your children are not your children. They are the children of life's longing for itself."

For nearly thirty years, Helen Webb was to be Netta's closest friend. She was to spend every summer holiday with the family, to be their counsellor and landscape architect when they came to live part of the year in Ireland, and to leave a vivid image of herself in the memories of all who knew her. In fact, it might be said that Helen Webb, or "Wai," as she was nicknamed by the younger children, became an honorary member of the Franklin family. She shared in all their enthusiasms, and she helped to determine the direction of their lives. To the younger children, she was the perfect fairy godmother. Indeed, with a shawl round her shoulders, she looked the part. She taught them many things, including the art of folding paper frogs. Years later, when in his teens, traveling third class to Ireland with his mother, who disapproved of extravagance, Cyril was able to put this art to good purpose. In their carriage was a squalling four-year-old, who despite every cajolement refused to be comforted. The situation was only saved when Cyril remembered Wai's paper frogs. At Holyhead, the grateful working-class mother pressed a shilling into the palm of his hand. Cyril demurred and said he would like it to be used for sweets for the child, but the mother insisted, and so Cyril accepted the shilling.

After her death in 1926, Michael Franklin wrote a lengthy appreciation of Wai for *The Parents' Review*. In the course of it, he said: "I don't think, except upon solemn occasions, I ever saw her face without a smile. She seemed to radiate joy and brightness. She was wise beyond fathoming. Her counsel was always invaluable. On every aspect of morality and ethics, she had a wise and true word to say. Amongst her most precious gifts was her power to bring out the best in others. She loved a witty story and she saw more real fun in life than anyone else I have known. Her beautiful freckled hands were a perpetual marvel. Her embroidery, which she did at incredible speed, was of exquisite quality. She could make things, too, out of almost nothing, out of matchboxes or hairpins, carve a head in an orange, or make exquisite bee-hives with the pith of a rush bound round an eggshell. She had a spinning wheel, and spun her own yarn—writing to me with great glee, that she had bought a whole sheep's skin in a market. She taught us how to make frogs and ladders, cocks and wheelbarrows out of paper. She was never stumped. Her ingenuity never failed. We were to perform a scene from *Madam Butterfly* in a local hall and were at a loss to know how to represent cherry blossom. It was, of course, Wai who solved our difficulty by herself sewing on countless silk blossoms to beech twigs."

Helen Webb might have been called teh Grand Vizier of the Franklin caliphate. Netta would have made a good Roman matron of the first century, wisely directing her huge household in all its varied activities. Or one can see her as the grandduchess of some little German state in the eighteenth century, surrounded by her miniature ducal court, intensely interested in the education of her offspring, a patron of the arts, and with her competent finger on every small detail of the state régime. It is true that her daughter Olive says, "We really saw very little of our mother. The house was full of domestics and governesses and bosom friends and protégés, and we were quite a little jealous of them. There were too many dependants, governesses, nurses, and housemaids. What we would have liked was an intimate family life. What we got was a public family life." And her sister Marjorie partly confirms this when she writes, "In Victorian and Edwardian houses, nurses and governesses were more in the picture than they are now, though my mother was a very vivid presence."

But the diary proves how much time, in the midst of all her activities, Netta actually gave to her children. She took them to their various classes, she went to galleries with them and on nature rambles. Her great joy was to read aloud after lunch, and owing to the various ages of the children, this practice was continued for nearly twenty-six years. It was called "half-past-two-ing." One of their favourite books was Malory's *Morte d'Arthur*. When Sydney and Marjorie played tiddleywinks on the floor, they used to name the various coloured pieces after the Arthurian heroes! Malory required a certain amount of skipping, and though Netta became very adept at this, Marjorie caught her out one day, and said, "I do believe you are skipping, Mother, I can never say I've read that book."[12] There were readings from Shakespeare's plays, in which even the youngest joined.

In London, she would try to give the younger children fresh air while the nurse was busy with nursery chores, taking them out in the park, and when Cyril had outgrown the perambulator, she used a long invalid chair to push him in. "It was wonderful to enjoy the absolute emptiness of Kensington Gardens, and I noticed so often by coming out at 8.30 I had got the best of the day and that fogs and mists occurred only much later in the day."

London had brought her many friendships. One of these friends was the Indian poetess and nationalist Sarojini Naidu, a remarkable person, at that time still merely on the threshold of her remarkable career. Born in Hyderabad in 1879, the eldest of a doctor's extensive brood, she had asserted herself even in childhood by refusing to speak English, which was the accepted language in her home, although her family were patrons of Sanskrit learning. She received on this occasion the only punishment that she ever remembered. Being shut into a room alone for the whole day, she came out, a full-blown linguist, thenceforward refusing ever to speak anything else, and replying to her mother in English even when the latter

---

12   According to the strict Charlotte Masonic tenets, this is a most dire offence.

addressed her in Hindustani. Because she had expressed her intention of marrying against the wish of her parents a Dr. Naidu, who was not a Brahmin, the Nizam of Hyderabad sent her to England with a scholarship in 1895, in order to separate her from him. She remained until 1898, a student, first at King's College, London, and then at Girton. Arthur Symons tells how she brought him her verses to the Inner Temple, "all the life of that tiny figure seeming to concentrate itself in her eyes." Netta remembers her as perhaps the most brilliant orator she has ever heard. Mrs. Naidu believed in woman's growing part in world affairs. She became a prominent Indian politician and the first woman to head a principality in India when it achieved independence.

Netta had some friends like Lady Frances Balfour who, it has been said, was notable for "her outspoken indignation at the existence of prejudice and discrimination and her impromptu, witty squashing of foolish rejoinders," but her greatest friends were often quiet persons of earnest outlook—for example, the Glovers, in whose house family prayers would still be conducted when they had ceased almost everywhere else. Another home in which she had found family prayers was the Cadbury one in Birmingham. Here she stayed in 1902. Her hostess played the organ daily at prayers. Long afterwards, when Dame Elizabeth Cadbury died, Netta wrote of her, "She was by no means beautiful in feature, but to her could be applied the old saying, 'If you are ugly at sixteen it is your misfortune; if you are ugly at sixty it is your fault.' She had the quiet mind and great ideas which had fashioned for her a really beautiful countenance with an engaging smile. Her courtesy in the Chair and in private conversation was entrancing. She was always ready with the right word. She never lost her temper. She suffered fools gladly! Her vitality to the end was indescribable. Possibly her early morning swim and cold bath gave her the strength." Netta's own cold baths would continue until she was seventy.

Pembridge Gardens was becoming too small for an increasing family and all her guests. There was a large mansion in Porchester Terrace which had been bought by Netta's father-in-law, Uncle Ellis; but, because it was an inconvenient house, with many small rooms, and would require a very large staff, it had remained empty for nearly ten years. Porchester Terrace, at right angles to the north side of Hyde Park, was said to be the longest in Europe. Various civil and military processions would form up there before proceeding to the Park. In 1888, Ernest's father offered to sell them the house. They went to view it with Mr. Flockhart, a brilliant architect, who had lately altered a house for Herbert Samuel's brother[13]. He produced a scheme which simplified the whole lay-out of the house, turning the staircase round, altering the entrance, and knocking various smaller, upstairs rooms together. A few days later, and it was all settled, and a dinner to celebrate the occasion was given at Pembridge Gardens to Flockhart and a dozen other guests.

This house remained their home for fifty-five years. The houses at the Hyde Park end of Porchester Terrace are rather charming, some of them with sloping, iron-roofed shelterways leading up from the pathway to the top of the flight of steps, so that no Edwardian debutante, descending from the carriage with Mama, could get wet *en route* to the doorway. The ironwork, the balconies, and the railings are delightful and suggest a period. No. 50 was a larger house than most of its neighbours, and with its porch set at an angle to the road. It had two gate-ways, and an extremely short, narrow curving "avenue" which led past the steps and immediately out again, and which caused consternation to any taxi driver who turned in too quickly, without ascertaining what lay ahead.

According to Jewish traditional teaching, one ought to share one's possessions. If ever a house was shared with friends, No. 50 was. It was nicknamed "The Henrietta Arms," and many people came to regard it as their London *pied-à-terre*. One of the advantages of Netta's frankness was that you could safely suggest yourself as a guest at any time, and, if it didn't fit in with her other hospitalities, you could count on her telling you so. A less outspoken hostess might make a desperate effort and squeeze you in, while at the same time resolving that this should be your last visit. But with Netta, it was different. Because one knew that she would not hesitate to reject your suggestion, it made it all the easier to ask.

Soon after they had gone to Porchester Terrace in 1898, Ernest decided to have his wife's portrait painted by Sargent. The result was a fine painting, quite worthy to hang beside the famous *Wertheimer* series in the Tate.[14] We see a young woman in her early thirties, with jet-black hair and wearing a white ballroom dress, looking towards the painter with a certain diffident curiosity. She is seated in one corner of a great armchair with her hands

---

13 Sir Stuart Montagu Samuel, Bart., M.P., a prominent Jewish philanthropist.
14 It hangs now, after many years' residence in the big drawing-room of No. 50 Porchester Terrace, as a loan exhibit in the Walker Art Gallery, Liverpool.

THE SARGEANT PORTRAIT

joined idly in her lap. On the small, round table beside her, which the artist sent for from Italy on purpose to include in the picture, lies a book. The portrait was painted in Sargent's studio in Tite Street. Netta's recollection is of the tall artist, very shy, smoking cigarettes incessantly and sometimes, during a rest interval, sitting down and playing movingly on the piano. His efforts to make conversation were anything but successful. Presently, he suggested that someone should come and read aloud during the sittings, an arrangement which worked very satisfactorily. In his recent biography of Sargent, Mount gives a slightly different version of the matter, which is nevertheless corroborative in its own way. There he writes that Sargent got on swimmingly with a few sitters, but there were people with whom he found little in common except a mutual shyness. When that was the case, there was none of the ease of conversation that has been mentioned. His portrait of Mrs. Ernest Franklin gives the impression of a woman of withdrawn nature, with a certain innocent charm. The fact was that she and the painter were so shy of each other while in the studio that neither of them spoke.[15]

When the portrait was finished, Netta's friends said it wasn't in the least like her. "Far too restful!" However, Ernest approved it.

She had a protégé of her own in the art world. This was Fred Yates, who had arrived in London from Honolulu with his American wife. They were neighbors of Dr. Helen Webb in Nottingham Place, and when their little girl Mary became ill, they called her in. A friendship followed, and one of its results was that they soon met, first Netta and then Miss Mason, who had come down to London to stay with her. Yates had already done delightful charcoal drawings of various members of the Franklin family and had been particularly successful with Olive and with Netta herself. Charlotte Mason now invited him to come to Ambleside and to paint her portrait. He explained to her that he could not really afford the long journey. Her reply was, "My dear man, pawn your boots and go." He went, liked the Lake District so much that he settled there, produced a portrait of Miss Mason which is familiar all over the world in P.N.E.U. classrooms, and was to do paintings of a number of famous people, including President Wilson.

---

15   John Singer Sargent by Charles Merrill Mount, p. 219.

9

THE HOUSE IN PORCHESTER TERRACE became a haven of refuge for innumerable friends who might want a night, a week, a month, or even several years in London. German expatriates lived there, as did an Irish schoolgirl whom Netta was sending to a London day school. It was also, because of its large reception rooms, an ideal place to hold meetings and gatherings. The Coal Commission, presided over by Lord Samuel, even used it for its sittings during the General Strike in 1926; and during the Second World War, the Greek Refugee Society had its permanent headquarters in the basement for more than a year.

Indeed, the house started its career of usefulness before the family had even moved in. Netta used it for a P.N.E.U. natural history exhibition while it was still being prepared, and its empty rooms resounded with the steps of boys and girls. To that exhibition came her eighteen-year-old brother Edwin, whose interest in nature she liked to think was thus fostered. When he died in 1924, he was part owner with Lord Grey and Bron Herbert of a bird sanctuary on the Broads and a trustee of the British Museum.

A still more significant meeting—perhaps the most significant and far-reaching of all in its effects—was held at No. 50 in February 1902, when a resolution was carried which officially launched Liberal Judaism in England. The occasion and the events which led up to it are worth outlining.

In 1878, a young man named Claude Montefiore went up to Balliol at Oxford. He came of a very wealthy Jewish family, his mother being a daughter of Sir Isaac Goldsmid, who had helped to bring about the emancipation of the Jews. She was a person of very considerable force of character. Claude's brother, Leonard, had already preceded him to Balliol, where he had a brilliant career and was said by Jowitt to have a touch of genius. He numbered Arnold Toynbee and Alfred Milner amongst his closest friends. When he left Oxford, he took up social work, but in 1897 he died suddenly while on a visit to America. Claude was considered too delicate to go into residence at Balliol, and so he became the guest of his tutor, Baron Paravicini.

If one liked to exaggerate, one could make Benjamin Jowitt, Master of Balliol, the originator of Liberal Judaism in England. Claude was one of Jowitt's most brilliant pupils. His letters are full of references to Jowitt and Bradley, and he helped to persuade Jowitt to publish his sermons, showering specially bound copies of the book on his friends. After taking a First, he went to Germany to pursue biblical studies with the idea of becoming a rabbi. This idea was presently abandoned; he became interested in education, was elected twice to the London School Board, and, at the same time, continued his work as a scholar. When in 1883 his father died, Jowitt wrote to him, "I cannot advise you for or against the ministry, but I would certainly advise you to lead an ideal life, by which I mean a life not passed in the ordinary pleasures and pursuits of mankind, but in something higher: the study of your own people and their literature, and the means of improving and elevating them. No life will make you as happy as that." In 1888, Jowitt sent for him and invited him to deliver the Hibbert Lectures on "The Origin of Religion as Illustrated by the Ancient Hebrews." He demurred, thinking himself too young, but eventually he accepted. The lectures were a great success and were later published.

In a letter of Jowitt's to Montefiore sent in September 1892, while the lectures were still being written, one can trace clearly the whole problem before liberal-minded Jews at that time. Jowitt foresaw, clear-sightedly, the difficulty which confronts all so-called "modernist" movements, whether Roman Catholic, Anglican, or Jewish: how can one introduce new ideas into religion without weakening too much the solidity and cohesion of the old, and the loyalty they inspire? He writes:—

> "The difficulty of Reformers is how to attach themselves rightly to the old. In some imaginary dawn of liberty, they cut the cord and find themselves helpless and isolated. The Jewish problem is not really different from that of other religions; they all belong to a former age, and they have separated themselves from one another by outward tradition. But that is no reason why they should not have the same reformed spiritual and moral faith, while in other matters they are determined by country, habit, or education."

A year later, we find him writing to Montefiore, after the delivery of the lectures:—

"You seem to me to have done a really valuable piece of work: it appears to me that there is good work to be done in Judaism; Christianity has gone forward; ought not Judaism to make a similar progress—from the letter to the spirit, from the national to the historical and ideal? The Jews need not renounce the religion of their fathers, but they ought not to fall short of the highest, whether gathered from the teaching of Jesus or from Greek philosophy.

Did you ever think of devoting yourself to the Jewish race, as the task of your life, first as a student, bringing before them and impressing upon them the Rabbis and other great Hebrew teachers; secondly, by endeavoring to raise the manners and ways of their teachers and educators? I should never attempt to convert a person from one form of religion to another. But I think that all persons are greatly the better for having a universal form of religion as well as a national and particular one."

Here we have the whole germ of Claude Montefiore's life work. He was a man who, like Von Hügel—who made him one of the very first members of his Synthetic Society and whose letters to him in the *Selected Letters* are of great interest—combined scholarship, simplicity, and a most genuine sanctity. H. A. L. Fisher wrote of him after his death, "Nothing is so uncommon in this world as a religious genius. Some few only, having this deep, inward grace of the soul, are known to me, and one of them was Claude. Despite great affluence and famous lineage, and though he was always much involved in practical affairs, he was a saint."

Claude Montefiore himself always disclaimed having been the founder of English Liberal Judaism. He consistently maintained that it was the work of a woman, Lily Montagu, Netta's sister. It was she, he always said, who had prodded him forward. She was the gadfly who had goaded him into action when he would have much preferred to have remained immersed in scholarly researches. She forced him out into life; she made him preach; she made him the central figure in a movement which was to bring many lapsed or lapsing Jews back to religious practice.

Lily was only seventeen when, with the approval of its rabbi, she had started English services for children in the New West End Synagogue—services in a language intelligible to them and to which many of the mothers also came. This was the first step from which all the others would follow.

Religion in the Montagu home had been, to some extent, a matter of formalism. Lily has written in one of her books, "Our parents gave us by example rather than by precept an insight into Orthodox Judaism as a great and wonderful inheritance which must be held in the utmost reverence and which would exist for all time." Yet it seemed to her that, despite all their piety, Judaism was, in her parents' view, not directly connected with the problems of everyday life, and that obedience in certain observances had come to be regarded as the supreme act of religion. When their brother Edwin had a severe headache on the Day of Atonement, a day of complete fast, and Rosie, their old nurse, becoming alarmed, sent for the doctor, the latter promptly ordered him to take food. His father was terribly distressed and later reproached the doctor, "You ordered a son of mine to eat food on this day, and it was not a question of life and death! How could you?" As children, each of the family used to read in turn, according to age, every Saturday morning, the long grace. "It was an exercise in Hebrew, and if we stumbled we were not criticized. Our parents were satisfied that the exercise was hard for us and that we did our best. Gradually, as we grew older, our dear father read the short grace for us. But we never associated prayer with these readings." She had to visit a Presbyterian home in Scotland to realize that the saying of grace was a prayer. Lucy Cohen is another who remembers the graces in the Montagu home[16]: "I remember dining there at a large party, and the long Hebrew graces before and after meals, when the men, if they had no hats with them, covered their heads with napkins and when the law of not eating at the same meal milk (comprising also butter and cream) and meat was strictly enforced."[17]

The effect of formalism upon a younger generation is always unpredictable. But in eras of a loosening of the bonds, it tends to defeat its own ends, like the effort to control a political situation with a regiment of soldiers whose loyalty is already impugned. Netta, Lily, and Marian would all reject Jewish Orthodoxy in favor of a form of Judaism whose appeal was not to religious observance but to the spiritual nature. Even as a boy, Lily tells us, her brother Edwin, "who was sincerely religious in the deepest sense of

---

16   Some Recollections of Claude Goldsmid Montefiore.

17   Mary Kingsley has also left a record of a dinner party in that house, confessing at the same time to 'a weakness for the nation of Israel, their idealism, their vast commonsense and their love for beautiful material objects'. She does not mention grace, but she describes Lady Montagu as 'an angel, persecuted by devils in the form of servants. This time it was the cook with a pain in her inside, hysterics outside, and Lady Montagu worrying herself over both phenomena'.

the word and who suffered more than any of us through being a Jew, was very observant and very impatient with all forms of traditional belief." It would have caused their father considerable anguish had he known it, and still more did the actual schismatic defection of one of his daughters, which came while she was still in her teens. "For the last year or two before his death," Lily writes, "my father felt that his 'Lilchem' (his special term of endearment for me) was divided from him by a wall of disapproval which even great love could not break down.[18]" The intermediary between them was her mother, who seems to have seen both points of view and to have been a most saintly character. Family affection triumphed—as it would triumph again and again in the succeeding generations—even over this grave divergence. But the first Lord Swaythling's will made it clear that he would allow no money of his to be diverted to the cause of Liberal Judaism or to go to any child who should marry a Gentile. To Samuel Montagu, intermarriage meant first the loss to their numbers and then—as an inevitable corollary—the loss of religion.

Netta and Lily grew up in a predominantly, if not exclusively, Jewish circle. They could see its defects, and their earnestness was shocked by the combination of orthodoxy and irreverence. The bias of their minds was thoroughly Protestant, and, like those pious Protestant tourists who used to be horrified to see members of the congregation spitting in a Roman Catholic cathedral in Italy, so they were shocked by some of the indifferentism they witnessed. Lily writes: "My father read the Seder service to all his children and a large family of nephews, nieces, and a few stray friends. He read every word from beginning to end, and many of his hearers behaved as if nothing was going on which was even remotely connected with religion. "They joined in the singing without even the slightest reverence; they joked and laughed, and my father went on reading, and, at the end, with unquestioning faith, asked God to accept the divine service. I remember rushing up to my eldest brother after one of these Seders (Passover) and expostulating. 'I feel ashamed,' I said, 'at the behavior of many of the people. How dare they think they are praying? If that is religion, I hate it and would rather take the religion of __' (mentioning a rigid Christian of my acquaintance). 'You don't understand,' he said. 'It is the Jews' bank holiday; they should be jolly.' 'But why *pretend* to pray? I would gladly join

---

[18] *My Club and I* by Lily H. Montagu.

in comic songs if people want to break loose, but let the service stop.' He laughed, but my cheeks were very red and hot, and I began to wonder about the funny religion which permitted such crass irreverence."

Religious reform starts from a consciousness of the present hollowness of long-accepted custom. But the mental distress of the teenage Montagu girls can be related to the whole trend of thought in the latter half of the nineteenth century, when all the various bastions of accepted religion were being fiercely attacked from a number of different angles. At the same time, social usage was changing. Jewish exclusiveness, which to some extent is the result of Jewish ostracism, was becoming a thing of the past. His success in life had forced Samuel Montagu out into the general arena; politics and travel brought him many non-Jewish contacts. The visitors' names at the beginning of the Limerick Anthology are Jacobs, Jessel, Ben Elkin, Moses, Stiebel, Schloss, Cohen, Spielmann, and the names of Gentiles like Jackson and Underhill and Davis are in a minority. But this closed social community was vanishing at the very moment that extreme religious Orthodoxy was also weakening. What was perhaps an inevitable result took place. Netta's generation did not weaken on the essential religious issue, but they took their own independent line. For Netta herself, to be a Jew has always meant not the racial factor but the religious alignment. It was her heartfelt wish that her children and grandchildren should marry, not necessarily members of the Jewish race, but persons of the Jewish monotheistic faith. At the same time, she is very far from being a bigot. She has been with me to service in the little Protestant church at Glenalla. As a young married woman, it pleased her to go wherever great preachers were to be found, so that she heard Moncure Conway at the Foundling Hospital, the Rev. Mr. Houghton at Lyndhurst Chapel, Hampstead, the famous Evangelical preacher R. J. Campbell, Stopford Brooke, and many others. Two-thirds of her friends, I imagine, are Gentiles. Jewish character is a highly concentrated essence—dynamic, vital, self-assertive—and I have noticed that highly intelligent Jews themselves seem to prefer it a little diluted in their social life. But the moment it is diluted, it is threatened. Netta has lived to see two of her six children and two of her numerous grandchildren marry Gentiles, and one of her grandsons marry a coloured American. Though deep in her heart she may not approve, once the thing is done, she accepts it; she is too tolerant and too philosophic to waste time in vain lamentations and welcomes loyally the newcomers into the family circle. Her own steadfast faith upholds her, and she can still believe that all things work together for good to them that love the Lord.

In November 1901, Lily sent out from 12 Kensington Palace Gardens a 'Private and Confidential' letter which would have horrified her father (who approved her philanthropic activities but fiercely deprecated her advance into the field of religious controversy) if he had seen it. In it, she says—she was twenty-eight at the time and had been engaged for some years in social service, running a Club Settlement for girls in the West Central district of London—'The belief has forced itself upon me that if we care sufficiently for Judaism to desire its continued existence, we must re-formulate our creed and express more clearly the claims which it justifiably may make upon our actions and our lives.' The February meeting under Netta's roof was the result. Out of it arose a series of services, mainly in English, held at the Wharncliffe Rooms on Saturday afternoons for Jews who, for some reason, were either unable or unwilling to keep the full Jewish Sabbath. Greater innovation still, other services were later arranged to take place on the Christian Sunday, a day when all business was suspended. For a time, Orthodox Jewry looked with favour on these experiments, especially the English services for children. But little by little, the innovators found themselves increasingly disposed to grow impatient with the more niggling insistences of Orthodoxy and to stress the spirit of that 'universal form of religion' which Jowitt had praised to Montefiore as being necessary, 'as well as a National and particular one.' To Lily Montagu—and to her sister Netta too, one imagines, daughters of their epoch—it seemed absurd that men and women should have to sit in different parts of the Synagogue when they worshipped together. At one moment, it looked as though the new body, the Jewish Religious Union, were going to come to terms with the West London Reform Synagogue, where they had many friends, and that the Synagogue would concede them the right to a Saturday afternoon adult service. Agreement had almost been reached, but it broke down on this question of where the separate sexes should sit, more than on any other single point. In any case, Lily Montagu had always been in favour of the Union maintaining its independence and, at the meeting which considered the amended recommendations of the Joint Committee, she strongly urged that the conditions made by the Synagogue should be rejected. The Union preferred to remain a small evangelical body of enthusiasts with Montefiore at their head, even if this meant that they had to remain for a time without a Synagogue.

GLENALLA ACROSS THE CORNFIELD

GLENALLA POND AND GLENBERG

Netta was closely involved in all this. The trend of her mind and all her religious sympathies lay with this cause in which her sister was playing so great a part. What was happening in England was being paralleled—indeed, had been anticipated by many years—in Germany and America. At a conference held at No. 50 in 1908, Dr. Seligmann, Rabbi in Frankfurt, described the emergence from the medieval ghetto of modern Judaism in Germany, and the Rabbi of the Liberal Synagogue in France told about the work there. There was no formal constitution of a new and separate congregation in London until 1909, and no Synagogue was acquired until 1910, when a Mr. Mendelssohn found a suitable little building in Hill Street. In the following year, a manifesto was issued announcing the establishment of the Synagogue and saying that they hoped to get the legal concession to solemnize marriage—a hope which was speedily fulfilled—and to support a minister of their own as soon as a suitable one could be found. Montefiore went to America to look for him, and with the help of Dr. Stephen Wise, founder of the Free Synagogue in New York and one of that city's most famous preachers, discovered him in a town with the appropriate name of Far Rockaway. He was Israel I. Mattuck. A coloured reproduction of a portrait of him by Pam, the painter of Churchill and Smuts, seated at his desk, eagle-eyed and intellectual, hangs on the wall in the drawing room at Glenalla—a memorial to a man whom Ernest and Netta so much admired and from whose ministry they were to benefit for half a lifetime.

Some of the earlier supporters of the Union, like Sir Isadore Spielmann, later withdrew for private reasons of conscience. They considered that too much was being thrown overboard and too independent a spirit shown. Others, like Laurie Magnus, the author and publisher, remained.

Like all reform movements, Liberal Judaism stressed the spirit against the mere letter. The Liberal Jew does not hope to save his soul by refraining from pork or lobster. He has shed a number of the observances. Proud of his monotheism, he is a little scornful of salvation by atonement or mediation, yet fully conscious of the value of the New Testament, thanks to Montefiore's great book on the Four Synoptic Gospels. In the words of Sir Basil Henriques, Claude Montefiore 'has given to Jews an understanding of Christianity and an appreciation of Jesus which can only enrich the lives of those who imbibe what he has written. And he has given to all men, regardless of nationality and creed, a glorious example of the beauty of holiness, a vision of God, his Master and his King.'

10

WRITING ABOUT THEIR YOUTH, Lily implies that Netta was even more liberal in her religious sympathies than she was herself. Though she supported the movement and went weekly to Hampstead to give religious instruction to a small class of children, Liberal Judaism had not quite the same exclusive claim for her that it had for her sister. 'Netta left our parental home too early to recognize fully how Orthodox Judaism created a form of obedience which meant holiness in daily life. Therefore, perhaps, she has been impatient with any form of rigidity in religion. She herself feels the nearness of God, but her chief concern in religion lies in making Judaism to be understood and fairly reverenced by society in general. Her special work has brought her innumerable non-Jewish friends, and she likes to understand their point of view. She thinks, I believe, that my view is far narrower because I feel that we Liberals have a definite message and that no consideration, even of friendship or tolerance, must be allowed to weaken it. In short, the missionary aspect, to which I am devoted, appeals less to her. But though our lines of work are parallel and can never be merged, she is touchingly ready to give me infinite encouragement and is most generous in material help.'

There speaks the prophetess. In her attitude to this younger sister, Netta has always given the impression of being conscious of Lily's prophetic role. On Saturday mornings at Glenalla, at the small service in the drawing-room for her children, grandchildren, and such house-guests as care to come, it is nearly always a printed or typewritten sermon of Lily's which is read aloud. In matters of comfort and material detail, Netta is the protector where Lily is concerned, but she is also the devout disciple, proud that her sister should have been the first woman to preach publicly from a pulpit.

In her public work, as was natural, the majority of the friends that Netta made were Christians. But in the vast family circle and on the fringes of it, there were many persons of her own faith. One great friend was Dr. Schorstein, with whose sister Claude Montefiore had fallen in love in the 1880s. He proposed—despite some alarm on the part of the very wealthy

Montefiore family, to whom the idea of his marrying the granddaughter of a Polish rabbi had come as something of a shock. After she had completed a course at Girton on Claude's suggestion, he married her.

Her brother was a brilliant consultant at the London Hospital and a charming and cultivated individual who was a frequent visitor at Netta's house. There one night, he met another of her friends, the American Mr. Earl Barnes, who was prominent in the educational world, and the two men talked poetry, politics, and art far into the night. Then they walked back together to Schorstein's house, where they continued their discussions into the small hours. The next day, Schorstein told Netta how they had each written down the name of their favorite picture, which, by an extraordinary chance, turned out to be the same. It was the lovely St. Anne with the Virgin cartoon by Leonardo da Vinci, which hangs in the Diploma Gallery at Burlington House. At that time, very few people were aware of it, and Netta and Helen Webb set off at once to see it. They, too, fell immediately under its spell, and it was they who persuaded a firm of art photographers to go to the gallery and photograph it.

Dr. Schorstein's life was to take a tragic turn. His sister, Thérèse, who had married Montefiore, died in childbirth. The child, a boy, survived and was immensely dear not only to his father but to his uncle. When he developed pneumonia at Clifton College, it became necessary to have an operation, and Schorstein was asked to perform it. He said to Netta, 'I have to plunge a knife into the flesh that I love best in the whole world.' The operation was successful, but the shock and responsibility on that occasion may have aggravated the diabetes from which he was already suffering. Schorstein became rapidly worse. His sight began to go. Claude Montefiore would visit him and read Greek aloud to him, and Netta was another constant reader at his bedside. He had been offered a professorship at Oxford but had refused it because of his health, recommending the famous Osler in his place. Not long afterward, he died.

From 1900 onwards, Netta's commitments—religious, parental, social, and educational—were continually increasing. She enjoyed them, but a number of them were undertaken primarily from a sense of duty. A photograph, taken early in the 'nineties, when Netta cannot have been more than twenty-seven or twenty-eight, shows her with high-piled black hair, a firm chin, and inexpressibly sad and steadfast eyes. It suggests seriousness rather than self-confidence. When in 1921 *The Times* came to write the obituary of her brother Edwin, they referred to 'his lovable and complicated character and the deep melancholy of his race joined to gaiety and a most individual wit.' That phrase, 'the melancholy of his race,' instantly suggests the young, earnest-eyed, velvet-robed Portia of this photograph. But whereas the brilliantly successful Edwin, who became Secretary of State for India, never believed in his own destiny, and was always saying that he would die young—which in fact he did—Netta, with her more devout outlook and greater faith in her star, moved steadily towards increased self-confidence. She has gone through life saying to herself what Danton murmured on the scaffold: 'No weakness!' Even in Donegal, the cottagers in outlying districts, who know that she has a title but not what it is, and who therefore always insist on calling her Lady Franklin, are well aware that she is dauntless. One of them said to her daughter Olive recently, 'And Lady Franklin, how is she? She's a warrior, she is.'

She *is* a warrior. But we know nothing of the campaigns she may have had to fight against despair. She is silent about all physical ills. She voices her impatience with people and her scorn for their minor stupidities; even her own sister Lily refers to her harshness in this respect. But if she is hard on others, she shows even less indulgence to herself. She has never been prone to self-pity, and it is the rarest thing to come across in a letter from Charlotte Mason to her, dated 12 June 1911, a hint that her firmness and resolution have been only slowly and hardly won. 'Thank you for opening to me the secret, sacred Peace of your life,' Miss Mason writes. 'Your letter is deeply interesting, and I think very important, and I do not think you morbid, nor necessarily ill of you for concerning yourself with the things that matter most. We can at any rate understand one another, for your malady is my malady, and I believe that it is the secret, eating malady of our time, and that you have given voice to it (so bravely!) means, it seems to me, that you have received a call to help.'

There must have been heart-searchings of this sort, but she was too active a subject to yield for long to depression. Instead, she threw herself into her many commitments, social and otherwise. The redoubtable Lady Magnus complained one day that she had never lunched at Porchester Terrace, and was duly invited. But when the day came, Netta had forgotten all about her. There was a large gathering at luncheon that day, including Edwin Montagu and a Mrs. Jarinzoff, mother of a school friend of Geoffrey. Everyone was at the table when the bell rang loudly, and the hostess suddenly remembered her forgotten guest. The parlourmaid was intercepted and told to delay opening the door. Edwin begged that he might remain anonymous. He was tired, and besides, Lady Magnus was deaf. Netta had her own plate taken away, a fresh place laid, and decided to make the excuse that the rest of her guests had started because the children had to get back to school. At last, into the room sailed Lady Magnus, exclaiming, "Even when you do invite me, it is like the siege of Mafeking to get into your house!" The meal continued, Netta making an entirely fresh start; and, in due course, Edwin made his escape. But later, in the drawing-room, Mrs. Jarinzoff was tactless enough to refer to him by name. "Edwin Montagu? Was he here? And no one told me. Why weren't we introduced? I thought he was the tutor to one of the children!" exclaimed her indignant fellow guest.

An old friend and valued colleague, Evelyn Whyte, gives an amusing picture of No. 50 in the first decade of this century: "Certainly the morning-room at Porchester Terrace was an enlivening place in those days. Perhaps there is a Russian lesson going on. Mrs. Franklin is being taught by a dark, sad-looking Russian lady, but the housekeeper wants to know if there will be two or four extra for luncheon, and Michael and his governess must say goodbye before going for their walk—and Michael has a great deal to say. Then the telephone goes, someone must speak to Mrs. Franklin herself, and the two staying visitors come to say good morning and to hear what the plans are for the day. An old friend calls to borrow a book, which cannot be found for the moment. The Russian lady looks darker and sadder but keeps up a ground bass of Russian grammar in spite of everything. One thinks of *The Cherry Orchard* and realises that, after all, it is not so unlike what she has been used to at home."

It has been said that the Central European Jew is not a Jew at all by race but is descended from a Caucasian tribe who were converted to Judaism.[19] This would explain the slightly Mongolian traits to be found in the features of Edwin Montagu and several of Netta's children. Whereas Ernest's father looked a typical rabbinical Jew of patriarchal countenance and was, in fact, descended from a long line of rabbis, a number of the Montagus, including Netta herself, have a quite different caste of countenance, much

---

19   Jowitt writes to Montefiore, "I dare say that you are aware that the Jews made numerous proselytes in Russia about the end of the fifteenth century."

less Hebraic in the accepted sense, and one which might easily be made to link up with the Caucasus or Turkestan.

Netta's children were very far from being cast in a single mould, although four of them—Marjorie, Geoffrey, Cyril, and Michael—began life with one similarity: a prodigal wealth of curly and intensely black hair. A photograph of Sydney, taken as part of a whole series by Ernest when they came to No. 50, shows a serious-visaged schoolboy, seated reading with legs stretched out in a cloth-covered armchair in his father's study. Marjorie is a lovely seventeen-year-old, seated by the fireside in her pleasant, well-lit, recently acquired bed-sitting room. A Japanese fan rests on the mantelpiece, and Marjorie, who has her black hair piled high on her head like her mother, has a slightly Japanese look. Geoffrey, Marjorie's junior by two and a half years, is a sturdily built teenager. At four years old, he had been a huge-eyed, wistful, astonishingly beautiful Jewish version of Little Lord Fauntleroy. In a velvet jacket with a wide, frilled collar, he sits with folded arms and seems already to be contemplating, with tender solicitude, the anomalies of human existence. His life was to bear out the earnestness of those sad eyes. Olive was a distinctly handsome schoolgirl, typically English in appearance and with a flair for a becoming blouse and a well-cut skirt. She was one of the three children who, by Netta's own account, were never argumentative. The other three, however, made up for this in rich measure. Olive, from the first, seems to have been quietly resolved to go her own way and to find her own happiness.

Cyril, born in 1898, just after they had moved to Porchester Terrace, became another curly-haired angel for whom Marjorie had set the pattern. At the age of six, he had an awkward habit of demanding people's names. At an educational gathering, he asked Lady Aberdeen hers. She bent down and said sweetly, "Ishbel, my dear." She could not know then how unsympathetically and contemptuously that Christian name would be used by Unionists throughout the length and breadth of Ireland when her husband became Viceroy under a Liberal government. On another occasion, Cyril had gone with his mother to one of his grandmother's Saturday afternoon receptions in Kensington Palace Gardens. The very large drawing-room was crowded. Presently Cyril was heard to say to an extremely shy young man, the last person in the room to wish attention to be drawn to himself, "What is your name?" "David," he replied. Whereupon Cyril exclaimed loudly, "Thank you, David, for writing those nice psalms!"

In one of the early photographs, Cyril appears wearing a dressing gown and propped up in bed against pillows, beneath Sir Joshua Reynolds' picture of the infant Samuel. This is Cyril at his gentlest and most acquiescent. In the rather anxious eyes of this sick, small boy, one sees certain gentle and kind qualities which the adult Cyril spends his life trying to conceal under a mask of superficial peevishness.

There remains the Benjamin of the family. Starting as a solemn, dark-haired, white-smocked, reverent attendant angel to that older brother with whom he would bicker happily for the rest of his life, Michael, in the photographic records of the time, soon becomes a dreamy-eyed, pensive creature from the Caucasus, with slightly closed eyes and a wide, humorous, already ironic mouth. There is one photograph of him holding a wide-brimmed Panama hat in his hand, which suggests a considerable degree of moral earnestness in this well-groomed ten-year-old and a determination to live up to the P.U.S. school motto, "I am, I can, I ought, I will."

These were the children round whom Netta's life would centre for many years to come, and indeed still centres. Of her role as parent to this large and highly varied family, the novelist, the late Kathleen Wallace, has said: "It is not to be expected that six children of pronounced and differing temperaments were easy or peaceful. The mutual devotion between them and their mother sometimes added to the stress. There was abundance of friction, of impatience and resentment from young, developing minds; of difficulty for a young mother and some bewildering heartache. Nothing out of the common lot, one may say. But it was the common lot raised to the *nth* degree, because here was a young mother with force of character and mental energy in superabundance, a terrific gift of capacity for organization, and a conviction deep as a creed that children were the most important things in Creation. No wonder that she set herself with her own to *mould them nearer to the heart's desire*."

She was not successful in the attempt. They were too much her own children for that. On all of them she had her influence—on two perhaps especially, Sydney and Geoffrey, in that she infected them with her own intense ambition to be of service to others. For a third, she has been the determining factor in life, without being actually responsible for the direction his life has taken. No one of very strong personality, no matter how considerate they are in their human relations or how much on their guard against any undue exercise of influence, can avoid dominating the scene to some extent. Netta, with all her intense affection, her ideals, her belief that reason must prevail with the young, probably denied her children one thing which might have been of much value to them—a little hardship.

Roughage is supposed to be a valuable and essential element in diet. In *The Rose and the Ring*, the Fairy Blackstick's wish which caused such consternation at the cradle-side of Giglio, when she came to the christening of her godson, was: "I wish him a little misfortune." Netta, however, loved her offspring too much—or not enough—for that. Her relationship with her youngest son, born when she was already thirty-seven years of age, has possibly been the closest of all. One must go to the recently published letters of Marcel Proust to his mother to find the perfect parallel for the relationship between Michael Franklin and his mother. Proust adored his mother. She adored him. Notes passed between them daily, even when they were living under the same roof. In just the same way, from the time that he went to Bedales until he married, Michael Franklin wrote daily to his mother when he was away from home. Proust quarrelled with his mother, was furious when she wouldn't have certain guests to dinner, and was annoyed when she protested that he was inconsiderate to the servants. But after three pages of angry remonstration, he will still end his letter to her with *mille tendres baisers*. In the same way, Michael bickers with his mother over mere trifles and yet is her fanatical adherent.

The whole later part of Netta's life has been lived in close relation to this youngest son. She has acclaimed his projects, condoned his faults, criticized him freely, resisted him, yet frequently bowed to his wishes in the end. It is difficult to be the Roman parent when one knows oneself to be as much loved as she knows herself to be. It is easier to put up with occasional inconsiderations and even to remain silent when one ought to speak. Michael's love and admiration for his mother are immense. He could never play the part of the "gay young lad" in Jean Richepin's grim poem, who obeyed the order of his mistress to bring her his mother's heart for her dog to lick. But if he did and, running with it, should stumble and fall, hers would be the mother's heart that, as in the ballad, cries out immediately from the ground, "Have you hurt yourself, my child, my child?"

In bringing up her large family, Netta had been lucky enough to have the services of 'Tot,' a friend's housemaid who had discovered that she had a vocation as a children's nurse. 'Tot' was as great a standby as the German nurse Rosie had been to an earlier generation. Much later, she would become a trained maternity nurse, and the hundredth baby brought into the world by her would be Netta's grandson, Damien. Thanks to 'Tot' and other equally loyal adherents, Netta could escape sometimes. She might take a two-day trip to Paris with Helen Webb merely to see Duse act. On her first trip abroad, at the age of twelve, the crossing had been so rough that she had assured her father he would never again be put to traveling expense on her account. But there had been many trips since then: with Ernest; with Ernest and the children; with individual children; and with friends like Helen Webb. With the latter, she went to Italy through the St. Gothard Tunnel. Their luggage failed to appear at the *douane*, and they left their keys with Cook's official and went on to Pisa. There, they ate figs and chestnuts and coarse bread on the steps of the Campo Santo before departing for Siena and more sightseeing. Their trunks had not yet been found, and apologies had to be made to their fellow guests in the hotel for not dressing for dinner. This only led to more speedy acquaintance. Avid sightseers where art galleries, museums, and churches were concerned, they enjoyed almost as much their drives into the hills, their efforts to establish some intimacy with the country people, and their search for wildflowers. They lunched on figs bought thirty-four for a penny, dispatched a daily diary to Ernest and the children on the back of picture postcards, and in the evenings read George Eliot's *Romola*, which fortunately had been packed in a handbag. At Arezzo, Helen Webb developed a bad sore throat and high temperature, and an English doctor had to be called in, who made them engage a nurse. Netta remained most of the day with her friend but paid flying visits to churches and galleries. When the invalid was better, they returned home by easy stages, and Netta resumed her life at No. 50.

At Christmas in 1903, Netta took her three elder children to Switzerland with her for winter sports. She had been there a week when she received a telegram that the baby, Michael, was very ill with pneumonia. There was not a moment to be lost unless she were willing to wait a whole twenty-four hours before starting back to England. She acted instantly. Friends she had made in the hotel were given money and the passports of the older children and asked to keep an eye on them. Within an hour of receiving the telegram, she was on the train and on her way back to England. When she reached Porchester Terrace, she found Dr. Webb there and two nurses. Dr. Webb had ordered that there should be a cylinder of oxygen in the house. The next day, the nurse told Netta, "Your baby is dying." She replied at once,

"You had better give him oxygen." But panic seemed to have overtaken the nurse, and it was Netta who dragged the cylinder from the next room and administered it. She had seen it being given to her mother-in-law when she lay dying. To this day, she is convinced that catching that train in Switzerland saved Michael's life and gave her the human relationship which, perhaps of all, has meant the most to her.

11

IN THE YEAR 1905, the Franklin family went for a holiday to Varengeville, near Dieppe. There, Netta, according to her custom, used to read aloud to the children in the evenings. Other guests in the boarding house would occasionally avail themselves of the privilege of 'listening-in,' and this led to a number of friendships. One of these friends, towards the end of their stay, remarked, "You all seem to love the beauty of the countryside and the simplicity of life here so much, you ought to spend a holiday in Ireland." There they would find, she said, everything they could want: freedom, lovely scenery, wildness, rare flowers, solitude. It would be easy to rent a place for the summer holidays. Netta got out her notebook and took down a few addresses.

All this was remembered next year. Netta and Sydney, the two spies sent out beforehand to view any Promised Land, were leaving next morning to visit a recommended farm in West Donegal when Ernest and Netta went to an evening reception at Toynbee Hall. There, they met Hugh Law, the Nationalist M.P. One of a number of Irish Protestants who, like Stephen Gwynn and Douglas Hyde, had espoused the cause of Home Rule to the great indignation of most of their co-religionists, he was a talented and popular individual, married to a daughter from one of the best-known Donegal 'planter' families. Lola Law was a Stuart, and the Stuarts had been in Ireland since the time of Elizabeth. Her father, who was a clergyman near Londonderry, owned Marble Hill, a wonderfully situated house on the shores of Sheephaven. Both husband and wife were very much in sympathy with the Irish Revival, and it was to Marble Hill that the poet AE (George Russell) used to come summer after summer to paint his pearly-hued pictures of angels and avatars and the people of the Sidhe, as well as the Law children playing upon the wide, golden beach in front of the house.

Lola Law insisted that her father, the Rev. W. Stuart, might know a still more suitable property than the one they were going to see. In any case, it would be absurd to go all that way merely to see one house. She would telegraph in the morning and ask him to wire to Netta at the Lough Swilly Hotel in Buncrana, near Fahan. At Buncrana, they found a telegram: "Hear that Colonel Symons would let Glenalla House."

It was on the far side of Lough Swilly, only four and a half miles from Rathmullen, which lies exactly opposite to Fahan. Nothing could have been more convenient. A sailing-boat ferry took them across next morning, and a jaunting-car conveyed them alongside the Lough as far as Ray Bridge. The house itself lay a mile and a half back from the bridge, beneath sloping woods. At that time, it was shut in closely by trees and buried by ivy. The long avenue was densely overgrown, and one had no view of the house at all as one drove up to it. The grounds were overrun with rabbits and magpies, which were never shot. Netta has put on record herself her emotions on this occasion. "The outside-car, the high wind, and the night journey had played havoc with my appearance, and I felt shy and nervous as I rang the bell. It took a long time before a sheepish-looking soldier-servant, accompanied by a barking of dogs, opened a chink in the door. 'I am told in this telegram'—which I thrust into his unwilling hand—'that Colonel Symons may let this house for the summer.' 'What's that, Mat?' called a voice from upstairs. I repeated my remark. 'Show them into the drawing-room.' We were ushered through a narrow, dark hall into a very shabby room with skins on the walls and floor. Sydney and I sat side by side on a sofa, and Colonel and Mrs. Symons sat opposite, eyeing us suspiciously. Suddenly, the Colonel began to speak. 'I know nothing about letting, and really you are lucky I didn't pepper your legs as you came up; I never allow trespassers. I have never done business with a lady, but if I do, I shall treat you exactly like a man.' (I wondered if that meant shooting me.) 'I shall not only want perfect financial references, but also social ones. I don't want just anyone in the house.'

My back was up, and I thought it just as well to impress them. 'I believe I can satisfy you. The Viceroy and Lady Aberdeen are friends of mine, and Sir Algernon Coote.' The latter was the premier baronet of Ireland.

'If what you say is *true*, then that is all right; why do you want to come here?'

'Well, to spend a happy holiday.'

'I don't allow any rabbit shooting, and it's no use writing to me that the drains are bad. I suppose you think this carpet goes to the end of the room, but it doesn't.'

He then took us over the house and repeated the remark, 'I suppose you think this is a dressing-table, but it isn't. It is a packing-case with a curtain over it,' and so on. We came down again, and he said to his tame little wife, 'What did I say to you on Sunday, dear? Didn't I say I didn't care if I let the house or not?' 'Yes, dear.' 'You will think it odd, but I really don't know what the rent is; I must go upstairs and look.'"

It turned out to be astonishingly moderate. The Colonel was himself a tenant and leased the place from the Hart family. Netta wired to Ernest to say that she had taken the house there and then. It was a little farther from a golf course than she would have wished, but its surroundings—which Ernest would be the first to appreciate—compensated for this.

Donegal had secured one more fanatical convert. It rains much in that county—three hundred days in the year, a cynic has said—but when the sun comes out, the sky becomes a deep azure, the mountain lakes become amethyst, the heather is a deeper purple than anywhere else and—most strange of all—the tiny, sloping fields of the small farmer, won with difficulty from the steep mountainside, become such a vivid green that the landscape seems lit from within, shining by its own inner effulgence. The color and radiance then are not of this earth. The sea is bluer, the fields greener, the bracken on the hills in autumn a richer, deeper, and more flaming golden brown than anywhere in the world. AE believed that the gods still inhabit Donegal. They had retreated to one of the few spots not yet ruthlessly exploited by man and moved there, stealthily amongst the hills, like the brown corncrake which still lurks in mountainy meadows, whose steep pitch and grey boulders make the use of a machine mower impossible.

To this earthly paradise, Netta now brought her flock. The journey *en famille* was even more desperate than they had expected. The three-year-old Michael was violently sick. The tiny train from Derry to Fahan had a breakdown, attributed in the district to the unwonted strain placed upon it by the Franklin luggage. Then there was the transfer to the Fahan ferry-boat and the reloading of the luggage on the stone pier at Rathmullen. Finally, they drove up the avenue. The caretaker at Glenalla had been told to have a meal ready for them; a great joint of rather greasy boiled mutton had been cooked, there were fresh green peas and Irish soda bread. But before Netta was allowed to put a tooth into it, the caretaker insisted on her accompanying him round every room in the house and completely checking the inventory.

The afternoon was spent unpacking. Ernest and Marjorie went out to explore and returned presently, having found nothing but dark, steep woods and dripping leaves. It had put them in anything but a holiday mood. The maids came down to report that there were holes in the attic floors where they were expected to sleep and that they would undoubtedly fall through and break their legs. The water supply seemed to require infinite exertion, pumping. Netta's heart began to fail. The younger children were put to bed early, and when they were safely off the scene, Ernest remarked firmly, "You undoubtedly meant well, but we leave for a hotel tomorrow."

Netta's own holidays in childhood had been generally spent at Brighton. As a pleasant change from an hour or two holiday lessons, she was allowed to walk up and down the sea front, wearing smart London clothes and button boots, with the German governess of the moment. She had brought her children to Ireland because she felt so strongly that what they needed, even more than button boots, was wild country in which to roam and find adventures. And now here was Ernest talking about instant removal to a hotel.

However, the next day the rain stopped, the sun came out, the woods shone with a green radiance, and the magic of Donegal began to work. There were little, rambling, mountainy rises all round, except where Lough Swilly revealed itself in the distance as a streak of silver. But these hills were small and uneven and were set sufficiently far back from the house to prevent one feeling shut in. In front of the house was a wide, sloping meadow and then the curving avenue; behind it, the woods rose up to form a most magnificent amphitheatre—the loveliest woods imaginable—whether in the early morning with the crests of certain, especially tall, firs standing out above the rest, caught already in the first sunlight and turned to gold; or at evening when the whole green circle became flushed and flooded with sunlight—beeches, pines, firs, larches, elms, or an occasional exotic tree like a monkey-puzzle or a eucalyptus—and, lower still, the dense avenue-border undergrowth of dark-leaved rhododendrons.

Today the house is bigger than when Netta first came there. It had its origin in the early eighteenth century. In the will of John Hume, Dean of Londonderry, who was born in 1771, a will made in 1817 and proved a year subsequently, we read: "To dearly loved wife Jane Hume, one annuity of £100 for her natural life out of the lands of Glenalla, which I hold by lease from my son-in-law, the Rev'd G. V. Hart"; and later, "To Captain and Mrs. Searle, the two last painted views of Glenalla." The Harts, one of the best-known English planter families in Donegal, had taken part in the Plantation of Ulster at the end of Elizabeth's reign after the suppression of O'Donnell's Rebellion. Fynes Morison says that the families of Samson, Brooke, and Hart alone brought to Ireland one hundred halberdiers at their own expense to aid the Queen and were rewarded later with extensive grants of land. "Samson had a vast tract of wild mountain range lying on the sea and now comprehending Horn Head and Ards. Hart was his neighbor at Doe Castle (at the head of Sheephaven), and Brooke, Donegal Town and Castle, and a fine acreage south of Muckish and Lough Salt mountains and near what is now the village of Letterkenny." At this moment in 1610, when the Hart family were taking possession of the Glenalla lands, the Franklin family was far away in Central Germany, soon to see the roof of their synagogue in Worms torn off by an angry mob and their cemetery laid waste while they themselves fled to Gernsheim on the Rhine.

This first Glenalla holiday was a happy one despite minor vicissitudes. There was no bathroom. One of the bedrooms had to be used as a bathroom, with hip baths and water carried up. The roof was not too sound. Ceiling drips occurred, a member of the household developed mumps, and one of the maids did actually put her foot through the top landing floor, an incident which she was induced to regard as all part of the hilarious fun of the holidays.

They were considered angels by the local cottagers, who normally were never allowed to pick up sticks in the wood or even to set foot in the place, whereas Netta now gave a school treat with sports and presented each child with a mug with their host's and hostess's name on it. Some of these mugs can still be found in local cottages. At the party, one very handsome twelve-year-old—Hughie Crawford—who had been overlooked, slipped in bare-footed and uninvited when the games began but disappeared when tea was served. He was hastily brought back. Hughie became known as "Apollo." He later went to America and was highly successful there. His daughter, a nun, visited Netta not so long ago.

In finding Glenalla, Netta might almost be said to have found half the future days of her life. The family went back to London determined to return.

Their great stand-by during the visit had been Davis's outside-car.

Most of their picnics were on foot into the hills, but for longer expeditions Davis and his jaunting-car were necessary. When on one of these, Netta was overtaken by one of her bad headaches, and she and Helen Webb had to take refuge in a small hotel in a remote inland town. There the dirt of their bedroom and the fact that they had come without slippers necessitated their spreading towels on the floor before they could walk on it. Wai was Irish herself, and despite such an incident, Netta was soon won over to the Irishry. Davis, the owner of the outside-car, liked the boys, gave them free rides and sweets, and it must have been a little of a blow to him when they reappeared two years later, accompanied by a Léon Bollée car. He need not have worried. The Léon Bollée was to leave plenty of opportunities for supplementary modes of transportation. The Donegal roads were desperate. There were practically no other cars on them, and a blacksmith's forge was the nearest approach to a garage. Hyson was the chauffeur. The Léon Bollée had been bought early that year, and there are plenty of references to it in the diary before they ever left England. 'We punctured at Guildford and again at Hindhead, and managed to get a new tyre farther on. We had great trouble with the acetylene lights on our way back and did not get home until eleven. Much excitement! Motor again out of order which prevented Ernest playing in the golf competition. Ernest and the boys motored to South Stoneham which took four hours and they had another puncture. The clutch went wrong and Hyson had to come up later, clutch out of order again.'

In Donegal, the Léon Bollée ran true to form. On one occasion, Hyson had to leave his passengers at a small country hotel, deep in the wilds, and trek back fifty miles to Glenalla on foot, carrying the broken part. When he arrived, he was so travel-stained that the maids took him for a tramp, screamed, and refused to let him in. The replacement, ordered from Paris, was long in arriving, and there was plenty of work for Davis and the outside-car meanwhile. Motors being practically unknown in the district, the appearance of the Léon Bollée on a road generally caused complete pandemonium. Donkeys fled away into the bog with their empty turf baskets flapping against their ribs. Men leaped hastily down from their low-backed carts and drew a nose-bag over the head of the animal between the shafts. Hyson became adept at leading trembling and snorting horses past the stationary Léon Bollée, their owners being too over-awed themselves to make the attempt. Often they themselves had fled into the fields.

Bicycles were another stand-by. Helen Webb's cousin, the Reverend Arnold Harvey, later to be a Canon of St. Patrick's Cathedral in Dublin and Bishop of Cork, arrived to stay on a bicycle, and did much subsequent cycling with Geoffrey and Geoffrey's undergraduate friends. This cleric was a very good amateur actor and mimic, and he had come to the right house for private theatricals, or even mere dressing-up and impersonation, which were highly popular with the Franklins. Other good friends were the rector of Rathmullen, Mr. Foote, and his wife, and 'the five toes' as Ernest called their children.

Guests accepted the vicissitudes of Irish life in the right spirit. One of the hostess's motives in taking Glenalla had been that it was large enough to receive formidable relays of successive guests. As her secretary for many years, Evelyn Whyte, has said: 'The most unlikely, nicely dressed, elderly people found themselves picnicking daily on hills which smelt of bog-myrtle. Often soft rain was falling, but Mrs. Franklin told them it was lifting and they forgot their good hats and enjoyed the strange experience. Each sat on a small square of mackintosh—named by Dr. Webb a "Demeter"—and ate with unusual gusto sandwiches made of soda bread and salmon caught in a mountain lough. Blue, white, and pink milkwort grew in the short, very green grass, and bog asphodel, butterwort, and cotton grass in "the dark places" as Mrs. Franklin's old nurse, Rosie, called the bog.' Netta was in her element, sharing her Irish Eden with her friends.

12

WOMEN WERE JUST BEGINNING to come into their own. The period into which she had been born stood to gain from the activities of Netta and her like. In one sense, they were typical. Liberalism was in the air, that liberalism in which her father, now in Parliament, was playing quite a considerable part. The protests of Shaftesbury and the eloquent if oblique pleadings of Dickens had begun to produce results. England was committed to a noble, if slightly roseate dream of universal social justice; a dream which, on an even wider scale, is the ostensible objective of all national and international policies today, their proclaimed purpose being to improve the common lot.

Some may argue that the dream has resulted in the greatest bureaucratic efflorescence ever known in history; that it has made industry and frugality a crime, and blackmail of the community a virtue; or that, after exalting personal freedom to the role of goddess, it promptly put her into doctrinaire chains and produced a new tyranny which makes the old resemble Eden before the arrival of the serpent.

But even when the partial truth of Newman's blackest croakings on the subject of liberalism run riot, has been indicated, and it has been brought home to us, once more, that Plato is right and that every form of government generates its own particular abuses, even then the achievement of English nineteenth-century liberalism appears a remarkable one. Only a cynic would say that it had emancipated woman and made her restless and unhappy; that it had removed the shackles of youth and prepared the way for the Teddy Boy. If other problems have arisen as the indirect result of certain reforms, that is only part of the inevitable human predicament. We are committed today to woman's equality and to a policy of enlightenment and understanding for the child, and this is in no small way due to the fervent idealism of Netta and her fellow enthusiasts.

The world of the young wife and mother who found herself mistress of 50 Porchester Terrace was a hopeful world, a world which believed that things could and must be improved. Netta threw herself into all her activities with ardour. She was too rational and too well disciplined to display either the virtues or the failings of the fanatic, to chain herself to railings or to strike a Cabinet Minister on the head with her umbrella. But she was willing to work tirelessly for any cause that she had at heart, whether it were Women's Rights, Education, or Liberal Judaism. Education was her foremost interest, but she had other irons in the fire as well.

She was a feminist. Ernest was against Votes for Women, but at least he had the grace to say, 'All the women I like best are suffragists, whereas the ones I definitely don't care for are anti-suffrage.' Netta's feminism showed itself practically rather than theoretically. A woman doctor brought her children into the world. A woman surgeon was called in when she had to have a major operation. It was a woman, Marie Shedlock, who gave her lessons in the art of reading aloud, and Netta was almost certainly the first private woman in the country to employ a woman secretary, and one of the very first to make use of a lady cook. She saw that women could be an important factor in civic life if they liked to exercise their influence.

Netta has said of that time, 'The early days were pre-eminently devoted to the struggle for opportunities for service, not for privileges, as we were eager to emphasize; we worked to bring about much-needed reforms, to open doors, to improve social conditions.'

Her public speaking had begun in dread and loathing. Her friends asked her why she did it if she hated it so much. 'Miss Mason says I must.' Once, however, she had overcome her shyness, speaking became easy enough. As early as 1904 she was chosen to go to Berlin and speak there at an educational conference in the big Opera House—since destroyed—to an audience of a thousand people. Her nerve failed her a little when she found herself on the stage confronting her huge audience, and she whispered to the Chairman, who was the strictest type of German schoolmistress, that she was afraid her speech was going to take twelve minutes instead of the allotted ten. 'Sei schnell, sei schnell' was the reply[20]. At the subsequent reception, a publisher came up to her and said that of all the speeches he had heard, hers interested him the most, and invited himself to the next P.N.E.U. Conference in London. He came and returned to Germany to have Miss Mason's books translated and published there.

At the outset of Netta's career as a public speaker, Charlotte Mason

---

20   'Be quick, be quick.'

had given her some good advice in one of her letters: 'One word states our theory and practice, but attack nothing—be indignant at nothing. When people's minds are on the defensive, they have no power to receive new ideas.' Both Netta and the clever and eloquent organizing secretary of the P.N.E.U., Amy Pennethorne, were persons of very wide sympathies so that they needed the advice less than most people. And even Miss Mason herself could show impatience with fellow educationalists, as when she writes, 'There is another futile article on Education in *The Nineteenth Century* this month—quite, quite futile, and I get cross about it.'

Netta had her own difficulties to surmount. She gives this account of a visit to St. Leonard's School at St. Andrews. She had gone there in the hope of converting the famous Miss Dove to Miss Mason's method. 'It was sixty-seven years ago and I was very shy. I began nervously to say something about the Parents' National Educational Union. But I had no sooner reached the word "parent" than back came the crushing rejoinder, "Don't talk to me about parents. I can't bear them!"' This is paralleled by the reply of that other famous headmistress, Dr. Mulvaney, when asked which kind of children she liked best, 'Orphans!'

Once Netta had got over her initial shyness, she had no difficulty in voicing her ideals and aspirations. 'We want our children to become seers of visions, as well as practical workers, persons who will stem the world's evil, and in whose presence and under whose influence immorality must vanish. They too must have learnt faith, known pain, and grown in an atmosphere of love—love of home, love of their fellow-beings, love of God. Such an atmosphere implies a spirit of unselfishness and of service, and where it really and truly exists, immorality of any kind is impossible.' And later, in the same address: 'Perhaps there is nothing more striking to those who love and watch young people than the way in which their minds seem to work in watertight compartments. This, to a certain extent, is true of us all. Very, very few of us act up to our highest conviction, just because one set of thoughts does not entirely permeate another. If it were not so, war and a low standard of public opinion could not exist. The whole trend of life would be toward perfect righteousness. The older we get, the more homogeneous our whole personality becomes, but the young and the less developed have not yet organized their interests, nor have these become part of themselves.' Her own life was to be a striking example of the gradual achievement of ever-increasing homogeneity. She never succumbed to the highly prevalent failing of the good pagan of those days, abstractionism. 'As regards the direct teaching of ethics, I have never been in sympathy with the attempts to divorce moral from religious teaching, and I have heard with much interest that the former secretary of the Moral Education League has come to a like conclusion. I confess I shrink from seeing "moral lessons" as a separate item on the school timetable. Leaving aside the question of Bible teaching, surely our literature and history lessons and every other lesson of the curriculum will afford us ample material for lessons in the moral virtues, without manufacturing self-satisfied prigs by giving them lessons on "honesty," "courage," "truth," etc.'

On practical matters, she was equally clear. In an address given to the International Women's Franchise Club in London on 'The Training of Citizens,' she said: 'To begin with, we must give our children habits of self-control, so that they do not worry others by temper, or lower themselves by greed. We need not too carefully study their likes and dislikes in food. They must be able to control their desires as children, or how can we expect them to resist the temptation of their appetites when they are grown men and women? Parents who never say "No" to the child who cries for a bit of anything that is going, must expect that the man should be unable to say "No" to himself. We can see the beginning of the choleric Briton whom we know at the Customs House, or of the nervous, fussy individual when facing any of the minor ailments of life, in the over-petted, over-soothed nursery child. When we teach the little child to help others, we shall have to steer warily between the word of encouragement and over-praise. We are training our children in citizenship, not turning out self-righteous prigs. We must be careful that the help is given in a spirit of love and of service, and not allow any idea of self-satisfaction to spring up in the child's mind. The child will say, "Am I not kind to help so-and-so?" and it will be well for us if we too are helpful, serving people as far as in us lies, and then our answer will be easy, "We all help; that is what we are here for."'

As a mother, she could overcome even her own apprehensions if she thought that this was her duty. 'I believe one of the stumbling blocks in the way of parents toward giving their children such opportunities as country rambles, tea-parties with Club girls, visits to their maids' homes, and so forth, is the ridiculous fear of infection, a fear which hardly seems to occur to people when it is a question of sending children to dancing classes. The gain involved is surely worth the risk.'

She was probably speaking of this maternal failing from personal experience. Another thing that she had had to fight in herself was her dread of heights. She hated them, and in middle life, she went to Dr. William Brown, Professor of Mental Philosophy at Oxford, in the hope of a cure. He hypnotized her and asked her, 'What do you see?' 'I see myself and my sisters sitting on the balcony at Lancaster Gate. My mother is saying, "Don't lean over too far or you'll fall, like Princess Alice's son."' He had run out of a drawing-room onto a balcony, overbalanced, and been killed. It is possible that this incident had increased Netta's phobia, but she may also have learned from it the danger of over-emphasizing fear in a child's mind.

Those who have known Netta only in middle or later life may find it hard to believe that she could ever have felt diffident and at a loss. But to the really perceptive, even the dominating tones of her fifties are revealed as partly a mask for a highly sensitive and sympathetic nature, and, still more, the result of her relentless determination to drive herself forward along the path she has chosen, in spite of every difficulty. She is not a tyrant or a matriarch, but a resolute idealist who shows occasional impatience with people. She makes abundant concessions to her closest friends, but very few to mere acquaintances. And to some extent, this may have lost her certain contacts that might have been enriching. Friendship has got to be on her own terms, but even here, one probably has to reckon with a hidden diffidence that prevents her from being at her best with people of different outlook and a different range of interests. In any case, she is far too forthright ever to play a part successfully.

When it came to her work, however, she had certain gifts which were highly valuable. Her manner might be forceful, yet she could display tact. She never set her heart on mass conversions; she was quite content if she could address a drawing-room of ten people and make one convert in the course of the afternoon. She was like one of those enthusiastic Men of the Trees, who always carry a few seeds, an acorn or two, in their pocket, ready to drop it if opportunity offers.

The fact that she could entertain on a large scale, as well as be unfailingly hospitable to individuals, meant that she could smooth the road for the P.N.E.U. in various ways that might be precluded to others. Also, she was the ideal committee member. That is to say, she enjoyed committees while at the same time scorning impatiently their indecisions, their verbosity, and their love of wasting time. No one could bring the meeting back so relentlessly and yet so good-humouredly to the point, and she had Florence Nightingale's gift of sizing up a situation at one glance and seeing instantly where the need for action lay. A letter had never to be read twice—a single reading photographed its essential features on her brain. Basil Marsden-Smedley, the present Chairman of the P.N.E.U., tells how at the very first meeting which he attended in that capacity, when his predecessor arrived without the prepared statement which he intended to read aloud and whose contents now escaped him, Netta, who had read it previously and who was already ninety at the time, was able to reproduce it promptly from memory.

13

NETTA HAD BEEN an early member of the National Council of Women. She was soon elected to its Executive, and in 1909 was chosen as a delegate to the Conference of the International Council of Women to be held in Canada. The first of June found her making a contour map in sand on a tray to enlighten Cyril and Michael on the shape of that country. Next morning, she was packing, and that night there was a farewell dinner party to certain relations and friends. On the day of her departure, she had 'a long talk with the children,' at which the seventeen-year-old Olive was the only one to dissolve in tears. This is all the stranger since Kathleen Wallace, who was at Girton with Olive, describes her as the rebel of the family, ruthless on occasion, and inheriting more of Netta's force of character and pioneering temperament than any of the other children.

Netta's mother, Ernest, Lily, and Rosie Elkin all saw her off at Euston. Geoffrey travelled with her as far as Liverpool. He was now nineteen, very quiet, very solid and reliable, and devoted to his mother. 'They were chums,' Olive could say after his death. With his quiet, steadfast temperament, he could enjoy her friendship without the relationship ever becoming oppressive on either side.

The voyage started well—a day to dream about, with opal sky and no motion. Read and talked, saw porpoises and birds. Next day, she gave proof of her eclectic tendencies in religion by attending a Mormon service which was held on board. There were meetings too, presided over by their President, Mrs. Edwin Gray—a suffrage meeting amongst others—and an informal concert where it was discovered that they had enough musicians on board to produce an orchestra. Netta was up at half-past five the morning the boat entered the St. Lawrence so as to miss none of the scenery as they steamed up the river. At Montreal, the delegates assembled on the quay opposite a corresponding group of hosts and hostesses who were to entertain them, and 'it was amusing to see the expression of slight anxiety on the faces of the hosts as the names were called out, wondering what prize they were going to draw in this lottery of hospitality.'

The conference which followed was strenuous. Before six o'clock in the morning, Netta was at her table writing letters and arranging papers and getting ready for the day. The day would be filled with meetings, organized sightseeing, and entertainments. On Sunday morning in Montreal, she went to the Cathedral service with her Montreal hostess, but in Ottawa, she was able to get to the synagogue, attending a reading of Bible lessons and psalms at a school for Jewish emigrant children, and study something of their living conditions, which disquieted her. Sometimes she had an eighteen-hour day—an early morning start to deal with pamphlets, a speech to be delivered on Children's Libraries, another paper to be read aloud on Music written for the conference by Ella Glover, a further speech at the Girls' Club Section, then a big party at the Governor's house, then a council meeting, and finally home at twelve-thirty. It was a red-letter day when she could write in her diary, 'We lunched in the garden, I wrote my paper and watched the birds. Found several flowers.'

In the course of this arduous tour, Netta had become increasingly conscious of a pain in one leg. She was used to pain. Since her school days, she had come to accept headaches as part of her particular mortal lot. Pain was to be endured; one did not trouble other people by talking about it. She had had a lump on her right leg since childhood, but the doctors to whom it was shown assured her mother that it was perfectly harmless. Now she began to suffer from throbbing in it. A woman doctor, delegate to the conference, wished to look at the lump, but she would not allow her. It was not the moment, she felt, to be laid up in a hospital far from home and from her family who needed her. The only step which she took was to write to Helen Webb and tell her of this throbbing.

She landed at Liverpool on Saturday the 10th July at six o'clock. Geoffrey met her there, bringing letters from Ernest and the children. The letter broke the painful news to her that their Glenalla holiday, planned for the coming August, was off. A stone thrown at the dining-room window had broken it, and Colonel Symons had promptly fled from the district. Ernest had written to Mr. Foote to know whether it was safe to come. The latter had replied that it was perfectly safe for the Franklins, who were popular visitors; but in an unguarded moment had added a facetious postscript that it might be better to bring a revolver. That decided Ernest; he said the only thing he would be likely to hit with the revolver would be Michael running about the lawn. Sydney and Marjorie were dispatched forthwith to Scotland to discover accommodation there, and the Glenalla visit was cancelled.

It was Saturday. And normally Netta did not travel on a Saturday. But all this news was upsetting. And the pain in her leg continued. She decided to go straight on to London. Ernest met her at Euston. But it was still the Sabbath, and whilst her parents were alive, she did not drive on the Sabbath. They walked together the whole way back to Porchester Terrace.

Next day, she visited her mother and father; and Helen Webb came in the evening, greeted her with all the warmth which a six-weeks' separation warranted, and immediately inquired about the throbbing lump which she had mentioned in her letter. Her face became grave when she saw it, and she insisted on Netta making an early appointment with a surgeon.

It was characteristic of Netta that her faith in her own sex even extended into the realm of major operations. She saw Miss (later Dame) Louise Aldrich Blake, whose bust is to be seen today in Tavistock Square. The latter had an X-ray taken and arranged for an exploratory operation to take place at No. 50 on the Saturday. Netta would have preferred to postpone it until after the holiday in Scotland, but the surgeon thought it unwise for her to be dependent upon the ministrations of some village doctor far from a town.

She was still leading her normal life, welcoming Helen Webb and other friends to dinner in the evening, watching Morris dancing in the garden, attending the P.N.E.U. committee, and making all the arrangements for packing for Scotland. On the Thursday, she dined in the evening with friends in Inverness Terrace to meet Miss Gray of St. Paul's School, and did not get home till midnight. To Miss Gray, she seemed to be in great pain and looking very poorly. Saturday morning, she stayed in bed in preparation for the operation. It was unlike her to give in to temperament, but on this occasion, she permitted herself a very slight lapse from the standards of stoical acceptance. She did not like the look of the nurse who had been sent. The lady had decorated her apron with artificial flowers. This seemed to Netta an inappropriate addition to a nurse's uniform. She protested that she would prefer another nurse, and another nurse was provided.

The minor operation was carried out. She came to after the anaesthetic, noticed the operating table in the room, and furthermore, noticed that Helen Webb did not come to her. That in itself was a little ominous. The nurse mentioned that her daughter was in the house. But Marjorie had a meeting that afternoon. If she had not gone to it, then it must mean that all was not well. Some time elapsed. Then the door opened and Sir Victor Horsley, to whose laboratory the suspected tissues had been conveyed, came into the room. Instantly, she realized that the matter was serious and that he had been chosen to break it to her.

'I suppose it's cancer?' she said to him.

'No, sarcoma. But your leg must come off.'

'I'd almost sooner lose a leg than an arm.'

She asked for a reprieve of a few days so that she might put her affairs in order. Again it is typical of her courageous, positive outlook on life that the arrangements made were for living and not dying. She wrote to her secretary, told her what had happened, and asked her not to allude to it in any way when she came on Monday morning, and when she would be given final directions about the P.N.E.U. Conference, which was to take place at Birmingham in the autumn. Then she wrote a letter to the readers of the *Parents' Review* telling them what had happened, but saying that she hoped to continue her work for the Union even though she would be on crutches for a time and the meetings would have to be held at her house. That letter in the *Review* was to bring her numerous messages of sympathy, including one from a completely unknown correspondent who gave her the name of the agent for a newly-invented American artificial limb. The agent came down from Yorkshire and was able to give her the limb in three months' time instead of the six which was the best that any London manufacturer could promise.

It is Netta's contention that Helen Webb not only saved Michael's life and Marjorie's life when the latter had a very serious illness but her own as well. It was she who had pressed for immediate action, it was she who had helped to give the courage necessary to rule out all foolish dallying with palliative measures. Had she not been a friend as well as her doctor, Netta would never have consulted her till probably too late. The operation was most successful, and the various suppliers of artificial limbs have commented on this. But such was the prejudice of the day that poor Ernest could not bear to think that a woman had performed it, and even went so far as to tell his partners and many friends that his wife thought that Miss Louise Aldrich Blake had performed the operation, but it was really Sir Victor Horsley who had operated. This fact reached Netta's ear and was too much for her. She therefore wrote to Sir Victor Horsley and told him that, as she was of course unconscious, she would like to know what part he had played in the performance of the operation. His answer, which she had typed and circulated to the partners, ran as follows: 'I asked permission to be present and watched from the bathroom a most skilful operation on the part of Miss Aldrich Blake and her assistant, Miss Chadburne, and Miss Brown, as anaesthetist—I didn't even wash my hands.'

But the operation not only deprived her of such joys as country rambles and cycle rides; at first, the conspicuousness was a sore trial. She was still only in her early forties, careful of her general turn-out, and she felt greatly the new difficulty of movement and the attention that her handicap must draw to her.

Three weeks after the operation—an amputation at the thigh—Netta was able to travel in an invalid coach up to Scotland to join the family holiday. Sydney went with her, and Dr. Webb and the nurse, and when the train stopped at York station, Dr. Mary Murdoch, the new friend made during the conference in Canada to whom she had been afraid to confide her troubles lest she should order her into hospital, paid her a flying visit. 'The stone through the window at Glenalla was a blessing in disguise, so far as I was concerned. If the family had gone to Ireland I could never have joined them there.'

Those who refuse to be underlings to the less favourable stars in their destiny are like a trumpet-call to the rest of us in life. It would have been easy to shrink from the ordeal, to postpone action, or like the French poet, Rimbaud, to leave it too late. Or, having accepted it, it would have been easy for Netta to decide that for the rest of her days she must be an interesting invalid. She was well off and without financial anxieties, and she could allow her friends to minister to egoism by an unfailing flow of sympathy. But, to her, such a course would have been utterly abhorrent. 'Danton, no weakness.' It is significant that I knew her for a number of years without ever being certain whether she had an artificial leg or not. 'They say that she has a wooden leg,' someone had whispered to me, before we ever met. But her disability was never mentioned in the family when I stayed with them, and I was willing to leave the matter a mystery. It might be an artificial leg or it might be just a stiff leg, but, whatever it was, it was obviously not a topic of conversation.

Such resolution in days before war had made resolution upon the part of the maimed a commonplace, and in a woman, gives an epical touch to Netta's behaviour. She could not know then that, nearly half a century later, she would still be making her own progress along the Glenalla flower-beds, leaning on a stick, while studying the fate of certain tenderlings; or that she would have been transported above the clouds, only a few hours before, in order to reach them. It is a curious trait in man's character that only the unachieved and unapprehended seems wonderful to him. What can be depended upon is commonplace. If a fairy had whispered in the invalid's ear as the train carried her northwards to Scotland to Ernest and the children, 'Take heart. A day will come when you will look down on earth from a height of ten thousand feet. A day will come when on the slopes of a Donegal mountain Cyril will be able to draw music for you from all over Europe as though out of the heather, like that music of the Sidhe made by invisible dwellers in the hillside. A day will come when you will be able to sit in the drawing-room at Glenalla and watch what is happening on a tennis court in Wimbledon. Life has still quite a lot of surprises for you, yes, quite a lot of surprises, and many of them pleasant.' If she had heard all this in her ear she would have thought that she was raving. Yet it would all come to pass.

When she was ninety-two, by which time the topic had come within occasional terms of reference, I asked Netta had her leg been more of a nuisance to her than she liked to admit. She said 'No.' What was a nuisance was that the amputated nerve gave her quite frequently acute pain from a leg which no longer existed. From the first, she had determined to make as light as possible of her handicap. Late in 1909, she and Dr. Webb and the nurse stayed at the agent's own house in Keighley in order that he might give her instruction in the use of the new limb. Afterwards, she took lessons from a Miss Tomlins of the American Physical Culture Institute. On two occasions in her life, she was ready to admit that it had been a handicap. But on each of these occasions, she had been equal to the emergency. Once, after she had been lecturing in Derby, the taxi failed to arrive to take her to the morning train. It was most important that she should not miss it as she had an engagement in London that afternoon. She was reduced to going out into the street, hailing a baker's cart, and explaining her predicament to the driver. Would he drive her to the station? He drove her to the station. But it had not been easy to get hoisted onto that baker's van. The other occasion was at Crewe station, and a porter had conducted her and her luggage to the wrong platform. Suddenly he realized his mistake. There was exactly one minute in which to get back to the right one, on the very far side of the station, if she were to catch the express. She explained to him that there was only one thing to be done if she was to catch the train. She could not run. He must allow her to climb on top of the huge truck-load of luggage, and he must then trundle her down the platform with the rest of his load, as though she were a hat-box or another portmanteau. Fortunately, he saw the force of the argument, and she caught her train.

By lessening her physical activities the loss of her leg may even have helped to lengthen the span of her life. It is amazing how much she has been able to do notwithstanding. Charlotte Mason visited her in London soon after her return from Scotland. When she entered the room and saw her for the first time on crutches, such a look of consternation and sympathy flashed across her face that Netta realized the degree of pity which she inspired in her friends. But she refused to indulge in self-pity, and, thanks to this refusal, people soon ignored and even forgot about her disability. At the Birmingham P.N.E.U. Conference, less than three months after the operation, she forced herself to make her way on crutches up the hall and to speak from the platform. It needed courage. But it made all subsequent ordeals easier. A few weeks later, she was able to put in an appearance at the Conference for the National Council of Women at Portsmouth. Invalidism was altogether outside her line. She could not run upstairs, but she could do most other things. She could walk to the Liberal Jewish Synagogue at Hill Street; she even walked as far as Ella Glover's in Hampstead, and she would often walk to her mother's in Kensington Palace Gardens and back. Later, she would travel all over the Continent alone; and, with a single escort, would tour America and South Africa. The unknown correspondent who had told her of the appliance, at a time when such things were still really in the experimental stage, had done her a striking service.

14

BY THIS TIME there were ten servants at No. 50, 'including a tweeny'. Only one of the ten was male, Hyson the chauffeur. Later, there was a man-servant, Harris, a general factotum. On one occasion when Ernest had returned from abroad, Harris carefully removed all the hotel and place labels from his portmanteau. Ernest was furious. Harris explained that the situation was not irremediable. He had not thrown the labels away and would replace them. He did so, and returned to exhibit the result with great pride; whereupon Ernest could be heard shouting at the top of his voice, having glimpsed a familiar brown label between two Côte d'Azur ones, 'Guinness! Guinness! I've never been there, you jackass!'

Netta's own journeys had in no wise been curtailed. She used to take Michael with her when she went to stay with Charlotte Mason. On one of these visits he remarked to his mother thoughtfully of their seventy-year-old hostess, 'Miss Mason works too hard. She should marry and have a daughter to help her.' When there was a celebration for members of the staff, teaching trainees, and children in the Practising School, he came to her and said, 'I don't want to desert you, but I am going to plead that I may be allowed to go with the children and I hope that I will not hurt your feelings.'

On the long train journey up to Ambleside he would subsist on water biscuits in a usually unsuccessful attempt to avoid train-sickness. But on one occasion the journey back to London, owing to a railway strike, was particularly long and tedious, and he succumbed to his bugbear. 'I am so sorry to be such an unpleasant companion,' was his disarming apology. Small wonder that a seven-year-old as courteous and as companionable as this should secure a place of very special affection in his mother's heart.

Ernest had had the two youngest boys painted together by Glyn Philpot as a birthday present for Netta, a huge painting, as large as the Sargent, and in some ways a more successful one. They stand side by side, with Cyril's hand resting lightly on Michael's shoulder, and the artist has caught Cyril's reserved diffidence and Michael's dark-eyed Mongolian air of mystery.

Years later Glyn Philpot at his own suggestion painted an excellent head of Michael as a twenty-first birthday present for him.

The relationship between the two brothers was a curious one. One can detect in it from the very start a loving-hating factor, a power complex, and a distinct degree of rivalry. Did Michael supplant Cyril at the critical age of four as youngest and best-beloved? Did each of them, dominated unconsciously by their mother's force of character, strive to assert his independence by establishing a dominion over the other? 'When we were small,' Michael says, 'I was Cyril's slave. My name was Unkhase, from some story we had read, and I had to do whatever he bade me. When Cyril went to school I became an only child. But I was still Cyril's slave. Cyril used to send me messages in his letters from school. "Tell Unkhase he is to run three times round the nursery table and then open and shut the centre drawer of the sideboard three times." I would do it promptly. "Tell Michael he is to build a city upon the nursery table." Unkhase obeyed, ran round the table, opened the sideboard drawer and began the city forthwith.'

The education of her sons had all along been a problem to Netta. There had for years been religious facilities for Jews at Clifton College, but she favoured the co-educational policy of the more modern type of school. Michael's account of the matter is characteristic:—'Father would probably have liked to see us at a normal public school like Clifton or Harrow. Mother wanted Bedales, which was co-educational, although co-education, except at Quaker schools, was then regarded as fantastically advanced and modern. There were rows about this and dozens of other things. You know the story of the famous man who said that his wife and he had quarrelled all the way across the Atlantic on their way to America? "You see," he told a friend, "my wife wanted to go to New York first, and I wanted to go to Washington first, and we couldn't agree." "What happened in the end?" the friend asked. "Well, in the end we compromised and went to New York." In the same way Mother and Father compromised, and Sydney went to Bedales, probably because deep in his heart, and despite his innate conservatism, Father felt that Mother was right and that times were changing.

There was a Franklin at Bedales continuously from 1900 to 1919. Sydney went first, followed by Geoffrey, Cyril and Michael. The two older boys enjoyed it greatly, the two younger less so.

A strange, Tartar-faced little boy, full of trustful eccentricity which a family may tolerate, but which the members of a school regard less indulgently, Michael was still old-fashioned and ingenuous when he reached Bedales. Though the family indulged, as many families do, in a private jargon of their own, Netta had brought her children up to deprecate the use of slang expressions, and when she paid her first visit to Michael at Bedales she was much amused by his apology, in the course of a long saga upon school life. 'After dinner we go to see Esther[21]—I beg your pardon—it's a slang word that we use here for half-past two-ing.'

He was so little a success, even in the younger class at Bedales, that he, like Cyril before him, was moved for a time to a Quaker P.N.E.U. school run by the Hickson family in Swanage. The Hicksons were enlightened educationalists, but Michael remembers spending an entire afternoon seated in the dining-room, confronting a cup of cocoa, which he would not drink because it had skin on it. His powers of resistance were phenomenal. He remained seated at the table except for an occasional brief departure at the dictates of nature. Evening arrived and Mrs. Hickson gave in. Michael went up to bed hungry, but with his stomach still uncontaminated by that terrible mantling of cocoa-skin.

Cyril at Oldfeld had also furnished his problem. Like his brother, he displayed a surprising insensibility to punishment. Nothing seemed to have any effect. Then one day Mrs. Hickson fined him. She had found his Achilles heel, and his reformation began forthwith. When she told the story to Netta, all the latter said was, 'Oh, the pity of it, the pity of it!'

Olive was at Girton, where among her fellow-students Netta met the daughters of Count von Arnheim, that is, the grown-up babies of 'Elizabeth's' charming *April Babies' Book of Tunes*. Cyril had taken to brass-rubbing, and his mother accompanied him to All Hallows, Barking, and many other churches so that he might pursue his hobby. In November 1911 he had his Barmitzvah or Jewish confirmation. The night before, Netta heard him saying the Hebrew 'Grace after Meals' through in his sleep. When the day came he read his portion of the Pentateuch excellently, and everything went well.

The brief factual record of Netta's diary for 1911 suggests ceaseless activity—dinner at the House of Commons with the Prime Minister, Asquith, John Burns, her brother Edwin and his wife, who had been the

---

21   Siesta

Honourable Venetia Stanley; next day a motoring trip to Maidstone for a P.N.E.U. meeting; attendance at an At-Home given by the Japanese Society; attendance at an address given by Mrs. Besant, the Theosophical leader, on 'Self-Sacrifice'; attendance at a meeting of the Poetry Society to which Lloyd George had promised to come, but Alfred Percival Graves took his place. She was up at 5.45 a.m., and had left the house before half-past six in order to watch the Coronation procession of King George V from Sir William Byrne's room at the Home Office, with all the family except Geoffrey, who had gone to the Automobile Club. She watched a great suffragist procession at Prince of Wales Gate, and went on with her friend Ella Glover to the Portman Rooms to meet Mr. and Mrs. Haslam, the Irish suffragists, both nearly ninety, who had walked hand-in-hand in the procession. Most of the engagements are cultural and purposive. Poetry interested her; and sociology; and of course education; and art, and all its off-shoots, such as flower arrangement. But music never seems to have been a dominant interest, although she played the piano well enough to accompany Cyril on the cello and Michael on the violin; reading was always one; massive undertakings such as Romain Rolland's *Jean Christophe*, as well as unlimited reading aloud to her children.

She was often at her parents' homes, in London and at South Stoneham. Marjorie and Olive remember 12 Kensington Palace Gardens as a place of parties, family gatherings to inspect their grandmother's Court dress before her presentation at Buckingham Palace, and assemblies for the lighting of candles on Sabbath eve, and the great Jewish feasts of the year. South Stoneham house, the country seat near Southampton which, half a century before Samuel Montagu became its owner, had been visited by Queen Victoria and the Prince Consort who witnessed the netting of the famous salmon pool, had other and even more acceptable delights for the younger grandchildren, woods and wild flowers, and trees to climb, and a go-cart that looked like a miniature Daimler.

On the 12th January 1911, Lord Swaythling died. He had lived to see most of the ambitions and aspirations of his very modestly circumstanced boyhood fulfilled far beyond his wildest dreams. He not only owned a salmon pool, which had been one of his ambitions as a boy, but he owned a great collection of pictures, Constable, Turner, Gainsborough, Holbein, Ruysdael, Old Crome, and a collection of Queen Anne silver and of Paul Lamerie's work which, after his death, went to the South Kensington

Museum. He had made himself a force in the political life of his country and in the municipal life of London, the city of his adoption. It had been mainly due to him that the Royal Exchange had been roofed over by the City authorities. It was at his suggestion that a clause in the Finance Act of 1894 had exempted from death duties bequests to public libraries, museums and art galleries. According to his daughter Lily, he had 'based his political creed on Biblical authority, which seemed to justify his democratic principles. He found in the Old Testament the expression of his faith in the separation of Church and State, in the liability of employment, in the State responsibility for human life and health, in the limitation of hours of labour, in the laws against entail and primogeniture and the accumulation of lands. Here, too, he found the doctrine of "worth before birth" revealed, and this doctrine inspired his Liberalism throughout his life.' His philanthropic activities on behalf of his co-religionists had been multiple and had taken him to the continent in 1882 after the outbreak of violent Jewish persecution in Russia, sent there at the request of the Mansion House Committee for the relief of Russian Jews to control and direct the resultant stream of emigration. Two years later he went to the U.S.A. to help in the establishment of Jewish agricultural colonies in the Far West.

Michael can remember standing at the top of Porchester Terrace, seeing nearly two miles of carriages and hansom cabs pass down Bayswater Road in front of the Park. It was the cortège of his grandfather's funeral. There had been two memorial services for Lord Swaythling, one in the West End and one in the East End, and Geoffrey as an undergraduate set down his impressions of each of these: 'The West End service was fairly crowded; people felt they ought to go. The service was not very striking and to one of the younger generation not a great memory... At the end there was a certain amount of pushing and crowding to get home to tea; and then it was over. In the East End things were quite different. I arrived at the synagogue half an hour before the service was timed to commence. A great crowd, quite orderly, were outside the doors, and naturally we thought that the doors had not yet been opened. We were led in by the back door and what was our surprise to find the inside of the large and stately building crammed full of people, men, women and children. They had come to pay their respect to the man they had revered; this, they felt, was the only way that they could show their esteem. Men with just enough clothes on to make themselves look decent. There was no possible room for anyone else to get in, as all standing room was taken up, right up to the gallery. A hushed buzz and that was all was heard, quite faint and restrained. The building was supposed to hold a thousand people and about five hundred more crammed in.' He went on to compare the consideration of this crowd for the eight relatives present, after the service was over, with the jostling and pushing at the West End Synagogue, and to reflect with all the earnest sensitivity of youth, 'Here was a rich West End peer, who had gained the hearts and souls of his poorer brethren to such an extent that a service was held under the circumstances I have tried to describe. How was such greatness attained? Was it simply by giving money away however it was earned? This man must have *done* something to get himself into the hearts of these men. He must have given up something that was his, some of his own flesh and blood, his very self to make them happier.' When Lord Swaythling's will was published, the clause in it disinheriting any of his children who should marry a Gentile and directing that no money of his should be used to aid the Liberal Jewish Union, caused something of a sensation. But his dread of intermarriage was in some degree justified from the religious angle. The Vatican's corresponding dread of intermarriage between Roman Catholic and Protestant found expression in the *Ne Temere* decree about this time. If parents hold a different faith there is always the danger that the children will end with no faith at all, or that they will grow up in an atmosphere of continual religious controversy. Parents who elect to leave the whole question open until the child is an adult have, as Sir John Wolfenden recently pointed out, really given the verdict against religion, since they have eliminated any encounter with it during the most crucial years.

Bernard Harris, commenting recently upon Jewish intermarriage, pointed out that there is Jewish blood now in many famous English families, the Rosebery, the Wellington, the Mountbatten, that of Lord Cholmondeley, and, he might have added, that of Lord Lascelles. 'Years ago,' he writes, 'these "mixed marriages" were found predominantly among families high up in the social scale. Indeed much of the strength of the aristocracy comes from the fact that Jewish blood is diffused among many of the oldest and best-known families of the land[22]'. But an increase in intermarriages at all social levels has meant a dwindling in the number of practising Jews. Despite

---

22 Second article in a series 'The Faith by which we Live' in the Sunday Express.

the arrival of 150,000 Jewish immigrants in England after Hitler came to power, there are, he points out, only 450,000 practising Jews in England today, of whom about 280,000 are concentrated in or around London.

Jewish influence upon the English national character exists, but it has nothing to do with the rise of certain great Jewish families in England in the nineteenth century. It came much earlier, at the time of the Reformation, as Laurie Magnus points out in *The Legacy of Israel*. 'The language of the Bible then became the daily speech of common folk,' and played no small part in the formation of the Puritan mind. Matthew Arnold called the governing idea of Hebraism *strictures of conscience* as against the governing idea of Hellenism, *spontaneity of consciousness*, and the Authorized Version of the Old Testament made the earnestness of the psalmist a part of English character. Moreover, the influence continued. Kipling's *Recessional*, written in 1897, is, as Magnus says, strongly Judaic in outlook and expression and stems from the 51st Psalm. And Wordsworth's 'Pure religion breathing household laws' is completely Hebraic in outlook and sentiment.

15

THE FRANKLINS had not been back to Ireland since 1908. There had been several holidays abroad meanwhile with different members of the family. Marjorie and Sydney and Geoffrey had 'taken' Netta to Italy the year after her operation. Sydney had done some wonderful organizing so that she should not be fatigued, and they had gone to Venice and read Ruskin there, and followed in his footsteps. The same two 'couriers' had accompanied her to Copenhagen and Stockholm for the International Council of Women Congress in the latter capital. Early in 1912 Netta inquired once more about Glenalla only to be told that Colonel Symons was no longer tenant, that there was no water available and various other difficulties. They decided to go to the Port-Salon Hotel instead. It was about twelve miles from the spot already so well loved by them. 'July 18th. Left for Ireland via Fleetwood and then to Letterkenny. Luggage sent in advance—three bicycles and fourteen cases were all there. Stayed at Port-Salon Hotel, found fifty flowers on the cliff alone, learnt *Hound of Heaven* by heart, and worked at Italian. Went in outside-car to Knockalla; the family climbed up. Michael painted flowers and bathed. July 25th. Drove in car to see Glenalla and our peasant friends. Miss Wilcox was staying at the house. We lunched on the hill near the gate. Olive had learnt to drive a car, and she motored us back. In the evening talked to Mrs. Dowden, the wife of Professor Dowden, poet and author of *The Life of Shelley*. July 28th. Wet all day long, worked at Italian and read Montessori in Italian. I took Professor and Mrs. Dowden to Kindrum and had tea on the hillside. Michael had his first golf lesson. Professor Dowden read his poems to us—also some of Robert Bridges and Yeats.' The diary entries are trivial yet illuminating. 'Took a stray dog from the hotel, which had hurt its foot, to the vet. Marjorie had motor lessons but not very successful. He heard Marjorie had passed first part of second medical. Cyril read *Our Mutual Friend* on the beach and in the evening. Marjorie out for a lesson in car, ran into a post, cut her hand, and Hyson cut his face. It was a marvellous escape and Cyril was badly upset by hearing it.' (Thirty years later she would observe that this post which had been so violently struck by Marjorie and her automobile was still awaiting repairs. In Ireland things like this cannot be done in a hurry.)

They were renewing friendships and making many new friends in the district. They drove over to Marble Hill to see the Hugh Laws and may have caught a glimpse of the bearded AE painting the Law children as they ran naked along the sands. They called on Miss Hart, the owner of Glenalla, who was living in her other family residence Carrablagh, overlooking the sea, quite near to their hotel. They had an Irish Literary afternoon, at which Helen Webb spoke on Seamus Macmanus. They even arranged a suffrage meeting at which Netta took the chair, and twenty-eight copies of *The Common Cause* were sold.

Then on 26 August Ernest and Olive went back to London, and Netta moved with Helen Webb, Cyril, Michael and a maid, Annie, to a farm guest-house at Castlegoland on the far side of the county. Here they met the Osbornes from Milford, future neighbours and friends, as well as Mr. Gullant, M.P. The latter took one look at Michael and asked was he any relation of Edwin Montagu, so great was the resemblance. There were lakes everywhere in the district, and Cyril fished with an adult friend whom he had made in the guest-house. Netta was reminded of her own childhood's Sabbatarian restrictions as she sat in the low-ceilinged parlour on Sunday, watching Mr. Slater—this new friend—arrange and re-arrange his flies all day. His principles did not allow him to fish. Such abstinence was thoroughly Judaic in origin and intent. In itself it was meaningless, like so many things which she and her sister Lily had discarded. Yet it revealed an ability to control the will, a willingness to abstain from a pleasure as a sign that one was ever alert to bow to the will of the Lord.

Ernest was contemplating buying Glenalla. While at the Port-Salon Hotel a fellow guest, Mr. Buchanan, an architect and surveyor from Derry, had told them that when Rosamund Hart came of age she would sell Glenalla and satisfy herself with Carrablagh. She was a ward in Chancery, but the Lord Chancellor might even allow her to sell it now. They drove over to see it, and soon negotiations were well forward. At the last minute, however, there was a hitch. The Lord Chancellor of Ireland had a paralytic stroke; no one could act for him if he was still on the soil of Ireland, and so the deeds could not be signed. At last in the summer of 1913, after a whole year's delay, it was decided to move him out of the country, and his deputy was then able to complete the sale.

The house had been in the possession of the Hart family for well over a hundred years, one of several out-lying residences acquired subsequently to the original grant of lands from James at the time of the Flight of the Earls. The Harts possessed plenty of drive and energy, and like many of the planter families made themselves prominent in empire-building. A number of them were to the fore in the Indian Army, and one of them was Governor of the Leeward Islands. Netta was not the first Henrietta to be connected with the house's history; a Maria Henrietta Hart had been born at Glenalla on 1 April 1837.

Rosamund's father, Henry Chichester Hart, had always preferred their other home at Carrablagh. He was a talented naturalist[23]. Many of the trees in the Glenalla woods were planted by him, although the woods themselves are primeval.

Wai, who was of Irish origin herself, had been to the fore in encouraging them to buy the house, and was a tower of strength now in planning the garden and the various changes to be made. She won praise from the architect for her suggestions for the two stone cottages known as the 'mill houses' up by the poultry yard, and for the grey stone gate lodge. Ernest had decided to have the whole Glenalla roof lifted to enlarge and give light to certain attic rooms; to add a covered terrace at one side of the house, and four bathrooms. Wai was insistent that the kitchen and scullery and servants' hall must be planned intelligently and with a view to pleasing the inhabitants thereof, not exactly a matter of general concern in 1913. No sooner had the deeds been signed than a builders' strike in Derry held up the work, and later, in the middle of raising the roof, drenching rain delayed its completion. As usually happens on these occasions, there was far more to be done than they had realized.

'Dr. Webb and Cyril and I', Netta writes, 'came over in the autumn of 1913 and stayed at the Pier Hotel, Rathmullen, going over every day and supervising the work and picknicking under the beech tree

---

23 He was appointed naturalist and botanist to Admiral Marsham's Expedition to the North Pole in 1875 on H.M.S. *Discovery*. After going on the Hall and Kitchener Geological Survey of Sinai and Arabia in 1884 he became lecturer in Natural Science at Queen's College, Galway, for a time, and he was made High Sheriff of Donegal in 1895. There are books by him on *Rare Plants in Donegal, Flora of Donegal, The Mountain Flora of Ireland, etc.*

on hard-boiled eggs and soda-bread brought from the hotel, and the delightful Glenalla peas and potatoes which had already made themselves appreciated and which were the only things grown in the kitchen garden. Whilst the building was proceeding, Mr. Buchanan wrote and told me that probably we were not aware of the existence of a very good little house in the grounds which had been built for the use of the land steward. Although we had spent two summers at Glenalla, this little house was so overgrown with trees that it had never been discovered. It proved a delightful extra house, and during the summer we lent it to many people. On one of the many visits that Dr. Webb and I paid during the building, I happened to mention whilst driving up that we ought to have a name for this house, other than land steward's house, which was no longer appropriate. She at once hit on the name of Glenbeg—"beg" means little—and so fitting was it that immediately I had announced it, the men were using it quite glibly.

One incident occurred which has always remained in my memory. We saw a very sleepy badger going along the stream, and the next minute the workmen from the roof were running down the slope with sticks in their hands. Cyril said, "Mother, they are going to kill it." And unfortunately he was right, and in two minutes they had beaten the poor creature to death. It was a very horrible occasion."

One problem, a good drinking-water supply for the house, was solved with the aid of a local water dowser, who located a spring quite near the house. Early in 1914 the Rev. Mr. Stuart of Bogay wrote to ask whether they knew that they had an extremely nice lake in the grounds. It had never been noticed, being choked with mud and reeds, and now it took all the men on the estate three weeks to clear it, after which it was stocked with trout from Derry.

The transformation of Glenalla took time and much wise planning. When Netta and Ernest came over at Christmas they had to stay at Glenbeg. But by Easter Glenalla was ready to welcome the family, and Netta could hold her simple little consecration service, according to Jewish custom. For years one could still find a tiny scroll fastened to the side of each doorway in Glenalla, in obedience to the injunction in Deuteronomy vi 'And thou shalt love the Lord thy God with all thy heart and with all thy soul and with all thy might. And thou shalt write them on the door-posts of thy house and upon thy gates.'

They had many guests that summer. From the first the Franklins tended to establish relations of genuine accord both with those who worked for them and with the country people around. But their spontaneity, their mild bohemianism and complete indifference to all façades lacking rational support, made them something of a nine-days' wonder in conventional circles. They attended local tea-parties; they were the greatest friends with the Church of Ireland parson and his family, the Hugh Laws had taken them to their hearts, and Lola Law's charming sister Mrs. Perry would do so when she returned from India. But to the prim, Franklin informality and Franklin scorn of mere appearances—all too evident even when they were doing their best to conform—were sometimes the cause of raised eyebrows and of the slightly malicious titter.

It did not worry them. They were too much themselves and they had too many good friends and too steady a flow of distinguished visitors from across the Channel to be distressed because their ways did not please everyone. Already they were doing wonders to the place, spending money on it to an extent that had not been done for years. The main door was moved to the north end of the frontage on to the carriage drive, and a wooden porch was added; a garage was built and a laundry and dairy adapted from existing yard-buildings, and a fine poultry yard created. Hot water was introduced, and lighting by petrol-air gas. The raised roof gave the house much greater dignity, and provided two large guest rooms and a number of servants' rooms.

Amongst the papers at Glenalla is a typewritten copy of a poem written by some local peasant wit who revisited the place about a year after the Franklins had gone there. She was evidently well acquainted with the names of the various workmen upon the estate. 'Written by a country woman, 1914' is all that the typescript says. I suspect that she was Presbyterian and that she retained a good deal of the dry Scottish wit. Occasionally—I may be wrong—it seems to make an oblique thrust at Jewish initiative and Jewish prosperity, without the writer really being fully aware of it. Either that, or else the laudations are genuine and she was so overwhelmed by what she saw that she could not refrain from giving voice to her wonder. The poem, which has an authentic touch of Merryman about it, begins:—

> Through Glenalla Woods as I chanced to stray
> I met a man upon my way.
> I asked him would he kindly tell

> If I was near where the Harts did dwell.
> He looked at me with a curious gaze.
> "Are you a stranger in this place?
> Or, surely, you would have heard the news
> Glenalla House is bought by Jews.
> The dear old place from cellar to tile
> Is all done up in modern style."
> I said I was glad to hear the fact
> For the Jews I held in great respect.
> The Book which we should oft peruse
> Was preserved unto us by the Jews,
> And every reader knows it's true
> Each sacred writer was a Jew.
> He says "If you come back with me,
> Some of the changes you shall see."

Nearly eighty animated lines follow, written with the same gusto and admiration for the new cottages built where the sawmills used to stand, for the haystack, for the new hen-run:

> It was composed of several pens,
> And they were full of Cocks and Hens.
> He said they kept an Incubator,
> Or some such artificial heater.
> But what do you think but, by the dickens,
> This spring it roasted fifty Chickens.

Glenbeg, the octagonal tower-house in the woods, had been completely renovated:—

> There was nothing old that I could tell
> But the Belfry and the dear old Bell.
> They could not make her change her tone
> Unless they broke her old backbone.
> She still gave out the same old chime
> To make the labourers keep good time.

Much that was unfamiliar greeted the poetess's eye:—

> The piggeries were there no more
> Where I've counted rats full many a score.

As for the garden, it overwhelmed her:—

> The Garden looked so neat and clean
> Not a weed was to be seen,
> The fruit and flowers did seem profuse
> Said I, 'Good luck unto the Jews.'
> The men were like a hive of bees
> Each one busy as you please.

Everything she saw earned her praise. She bade her various friends goodbye and departed nursing her inspiration:—

> I said again I will call round
> When I am passing through the town[24].
> If Mr. Franklin gives me leave
> A visit to the house I'll have.
> I now came down the Dirty Lane
> I thought they might reverse its name,
> The place was rid of all refuse,
> Another triumph for the Jews.
> I mounted my bike and thought how funny
> What can be done with brains and money.

The lady's admiration was perfectly genuine, and her poem was evidently taken in good part, for the records disgorge two further poems which are signed Hesther MacNutt and which are evidently from the same hand. The authoress was no fool. She had only to enter the house in order to grasp the essentials right away:—

> What struck me most about the house
> Was marked simplicity,
> Combined with elegance and taste
> In all things I did see.
> No gaudy pomp or empty show
> Did tempt the eye to roam;
> All things I saw were genuine –
> An ideal Jewish home.

---

24 Poetic licence. The nearest town is three miles away, but in Donegal 'town' is used for townland or parish.

Once again one gets an occasional impression that Presbyterian irony is at work:—

> Exactness, neatness ruled the house
> In every small detail.
> A master mind the plans designed,
> I noticed without fail.
> All was complete both in and out,
> There was nothing wanting there
> But a rabbi and a synagogue
> Where they might offer prayer.
> Perhaps next time I call round
> That too may there be found.
> Where'er a Jewish dwelling lies
> Is consecrated ground.

But the dominant impression is one of genuine approval –

> Now I will lay down my pen;
> The evening has grown cold,
> And I may say with Sheba's queen
> 'One half has not been told'.

The last of her three poems is perhaps the most genuinely poetic. Sir Walter Scott would have been quite happy to father many of its lines. It is a paean of praise in favour of the Glenalla woods, that great, green amphitheatre, towards which one looks from in front of the house and from the terrace at its side:—

> The nicest sight I ever saw
> Or perhaps I ever may
> Was the sun going down on Glenalla woods
> When coming down Orr's brae.
> The setting sun, with slanting rays
> By slow but sure degrees
> Did cast a flood of golden light
> Among the leafy trees.
> The sturdy oaks with spreading boughs
> Dressed in their summer green,

The silver firs with upturned leaves
Did variegate the scene.
And all the lesser trees each one
Their beauty did combine
Unto the wood from where I stood
It looked to me sublime.
The copper beeches every one
Stood queen amongst them all,
With darkest shades they filled the glades
Round Franklin's stately hall.
The cuckoo's soft and plaintive voice
Made music through the wood,
The small birds sang on shrub and tree
The pigeons loudly cooed.
The cawing rooks in clouds did fly
Belated to their home,
Whilst loud and hoarse the corn-crake cried
Amongst the waving corn.
The fields so green could all be seen
Where the cattle roamed at will.
From where I stood to view the wood
I could see McMahon's mill...

16

DURING THIS FIRST EASTER at Glenalla, Netta went down to Dublin to stay at Sir John Arnott's house in Merrion Square and to deliver a lecture at Alexandra College. The college gave a luncheon at which she had to reply for the guests; and her host gave a dinner-party at which Yeats and James Stephens were present. They, like Synge, Pearse, AE, and Lady Gregory already figured prominently in the long bookshelf devoted to Irish writers at Glenalla. While in Dublin, she lunched at the Vice-regal Lodge. She had long been a friend of Lady Aberdeen, President of the International Council of Women. Ishbel was a most remarkable woman. Her father, Dudley Coutts Marjoribanks from Scotland, was a partner in Coutts Bank, and owned a deer forest in Inverness-shire. At fourteen, Ishbel, riding in the Row, used often to have as her companion John Gordon, an Oxford undergraduate, ten years her senior, whose acquaintance she had made in Scotland. He was a third son, but accidents overtook both his elder brothers and he became Lord Aberdeen. A rumour started in 1877 that he had proposed to Ishbel, and whispered congratulations greeted Lady Marjoribanks wherever she went. Goaded into desperation by these, she wrote and asked the young man his intentions. He replied that his feelings were of the warmest friendship, but that he could not be sure that they were any more. He then retired to Haddo in Scotland, to be followed by a letter from Ishbel's mother telling him of the annoyance they had endured and concluding, 'What is the evidence of love but the seeking of companionship? Continual introspection is a fatal error. For your own sake I would not have you throw away a priceless blessing.' Alone in the wilds of Scotland, Aberdeen decided that she was right.

And she was right. It was the beginning of a lifelong romance which continued unabated for fifty-seven years. They departed in a sailing vessel up the Nile on their honeymoon, bought four kidnapped Sudanese child slaves in order to free them, and adopted them as their own children in order to have them baptised. When they returned to England they smuggled with them a young Moslem convert to Christianity whose family had vowed to murder him. This was only the beginning of a long life of public-spirited and philanthropic activities. Aberdeen became Governor-General of Canada, and was twice Viceroy of Ireland, in 1886 and again from 1905 until 1915. He and Lady Aberdeen had been joint presidents of the P.N.E.U. since its foundation, and Ishbel had written as early as 1887, 'I am very pleased with a new book *Home Education* by Charlotte Mason; really sensible, rather on the lines of Herbert Spencer.'

The Aberdeens did an immense amount of good in Ireland. Ishbel founded the Women's National Health Association. She laboured unceasingly, but was always unpopular in extreme Unionist circles because of her graciousness to the Home Rulers. Aberdeen himself was not too popular in the same circles and was considered undignified. He would come out to the doorway himself to call a cab for a visitor. When a shawled woman strolled in by some accident to a garden party at the Vice-regal Lodge he led her towards one of the tables and said to the waiter, 'Give this lady some tea.' When Netta arrived at the Vice-regal Lodge in Phoenix Park that day in April, she learnt that her hostess was laid up with some minor indisposition. She felt a little shy at the prospect of lunching alone with His Excellency, and an A.D.C.; but she need not have worried. Her kindly-eyed, bearded host spent most of the meal singing the praises of his wonderful wife, a topic on which she could give cordial endorsement, and after lunch she was taken off to Ishbel's bedroom, the Viceroy conducting her there and acting with schoolboyish glee the part of an attendant footman in the lift.

She had met Yeats in Dublin. She met his friend and fellow-poet, Sturge Moore, soon afterwards at a dinner party in London given by the artist, Lucy Kemp-Welch. There were as yet no thunderclouds on the international horizon. Next month she was in Rome, where she attended a Peace meeting, and witnessed the toe-kissing of the statue of St. Peter; as well as seeing her much-admired Duse act. 'Visited Montessori School, N.-I 113 the first I had seen, and was not impressed. Evening garden-party with Queen Margherita. Saw my first fire-flies in the garden.' A few weeks later she was back at Glenalla, sleeping in the open-sided 'chalet' built for her by Frank MacConighey, and known as 'Glenhutch', which had been placed on the far side of the meadow opposite the house; and arranging pictures and ornaments with Olive. Then back to England for National Council of Women and P.N.E.U. meetings; followed by a return to Ireland on 26 June. Glenbeg was lent to two maiden ladies, and other guests helped to fill the big house. "The children bathed almost daily. I went out in the donkey bath-chair with the girls and the children. Ernest golfed. Marjorie passed Pharmacology." Then come the significant entries. 'July 30th. War declared between Austria and Serbia. July 31st. Mrs. Devonshire and Antoinette arrived, also six Club girls for Glenbeg' (from Lily Montagu's Girls' Settlement). 'Aug. 1st. After prayers read *Richard III* with family and girls from Glenbeg. Aug. 2nd. War between Germany and Russia declared. August 3rd. Very wet. Ernest to London. August 4th. Ultimatum to Germany. War declared 11 a.m.

The family remained in Donegal until mid-September, and then returned home. The war had caught Charlotte Mason and her amanuensis, Elsie Kitching, at Bad Nauheim. Presently they were repatriated via Holland. In November the mistress of Glenalla was back in Ireland for a week and staying at Glenbeg, since for short visits and a few guests it was simpler not to open the big house. Netta had offered hospitality at No. 50 to Belgian refugees, and was rung up by the Committee to know would she take an Army captain and his wife and daughter. Their rooms were prepared accordingly, but when the daughter arrived she proved to be a small person of two and a half, and a cot and perambulator had to be promptly borrowed. Little Marthe Purnode became Netta's 'pseudo-grandchild' and her 'Belgian baby', and used to address her as 'bonne-maman'. Her initial entry into the morning-room at Porchester Terrace was disastrous; she slipped badly on the parquet floor and cried loudly. This embarrassed the mother, who was an exacting and rather spoiled young woman, and who hastened to explain that her daughter was really a very happy little girl and never cried. Netta turned the little girl's thoughts; and when, after a few days, she realized that the mother's educational methods were based upon the old-fashioned slap, she laid down an absolute rule that in her house there was to be no spanking, and that the family would have to leave at once if there was.

Marthe was a distinct character. On one occasion she was travelling to Donegal, and Netta took her along to the lavatory on the Irish train. Marthe took one look at the rough-and-ready accommodation and the condition that it was in. Then she shook her head and said firmly, 'Pas poieta, bonne-maman!' which was her version of 'Impossible!' After the war was over, she went to a P.N.E.U. school in Torquay, and became bilingual, although always with a marked French accent. Many years later, when she was secretary to the Speaker of the Belgian Parliament, she flew to London and back, in one day, in order to be present at Netta's ninetieth birthday party.

Another Belgian refugee family, father, mother, son and son's fiancée, were installed in one of the two small mill-houses at Glenalla, and three of Netta's sons went to the war. Sydney, who had gone up to New College from Bedales and was now in the banking firm, became an officer in the Pay Department of the Navy. He served on a sloop under Admiral Wemyss and was mentioned in dispatches. Half-way through the war his ship came unexpectedly into Lough Swilly. He was given shore leave, since he was only a few miles from his Irish home. He was on top of one of the hills, neighbouring Glenalla, when a telegram was handed to him, suddenly recalling him. He hastened down, collected his possessions, and crossed the lough, only to find that his ship had already sailed.

Later in the war, Sydney came on leave to London. He was looking extremely ill. Saying her prayers at night and praying for him, Netta seemed to receive a psychic message, "Don't worry; he will be operated upon for appendicitis and will come through all right." The next day, she drove by car to visit a friend, and dismissed the car at her friend's door, telling the chauffeur that she would walk home. But when she came out, the car, to her surprise, was still there. "I did go home," the chauffeur told her, "but I have been sent back as Mr. Sydney is very ill." Before going up to his room—always an effort since it was at the top of the house, and because of her lameness—Netta telephoned to Helen Webb to say that she was sure Sydney had appendicitis and asked might she give him a hot-water bottle. The doctor, when he arrived, pooh-poohed her diagnosis. "He has been eating cranberries, that is all. There is no sign of anything more serious." Netta begged for another opinion. Sydney was indignant with his mother since he was due back on his ship the next day. However, an X-ray was taken, and Netta's premonition was proved right. Perforation might have taken place at any moment. Only on one other occasion, when Marjorie was ill and when she felt the hand of her late friend Michael Fairless stroking her forehead and a voice assuring her that all would be well, did a similar psychic or semi-psychic experience befall her.

Geoffrey also went to the war, but not as a soldier. He had been a seriously minded youth at Bedales, had loved his time there, and, at the end of his school career, had remarked, "I have never been homesick, but I am now horribly school-sick." From Bedales, he had gone up to Lincoln College at Oxford in 1909. He refused to join the O.T.C. and was a pacifist before the war ever came. He left Oxford to go to work in the Woodbrooke Settlement in Selly Oak, Birmingham, and was there for several years. Soon after the war broke out, he joined the Quaker Ambulance Training camp at Jordans, which had been organized by the Friends War Victims Relief Committee. Before long, he was in France working under the aegis of the French Red Cross and in touch with the French War Office. He did excellent work, was popular, made many friends, among them Francis Birrell, the son of Augustine Birrell. But he was always keenly awake to the ghastly wastage of war. "Friends seem to go at a terrible rate," he wrote home, "it is all so tragic, and to me so useless—can't they see that the only thing that can happen is that more boys die and more homes are made miserable?" After the war ended, and when in 1920 relief work was transferred to Germany, Austria, and Poland, Geoffrey was given the task of winding-up the Paris office.

Cyril was too young to go before 1917. Then he joined the Honourable Artillery Company and, according to his own modest version of the affair, survived his career as a gunner merely by a combination of luck and good management. He was sent out to France in 1918 and found himself grooming mules at five in the morning in the base camp at Harfleur, an occupation that—as the author knows himself—can be almost as perilous as the front line. One day, he saw a notice on the board asking for instrumentalists for the camp band. He summoned up his courage and went for an interview with the bandmaster, gave a touching rendering of "Home Sweet Home" on a borrowed cello, and was accepted. Some weeks later, orders arrived that the band was to march in front of all drafts of troops going down to Le Havre for train embarkation. Cyril had a vision of himself being pushed in a bath-chair and scraping away furiously on his cello. The alternative was another instrument, and he elected for the clarinet, practising so assiduously that he was lucky not to become a casualty at the hands of his own men. After six months with the band, he was sent up the line to a unit of the H.A.C. at Loos, equipped with 18-pounders, and served with them until a very bad attack of boils on his neck took him first to the Field Dressing Station, then down to the base, and then, by a rather fortunate chance, home. There is nothing of Uncle Toby about

Cyril's war reminiscences. Characteristically, he insists on telling the story in a burlesque and self-deprecatory note.

Before Cyril went out to France and while he was still in training, Netta went up to Leeds to pay him a visit there. She was returning late at night and had just reached St. Pancras station when an air-raid warning was given. She could not go to the Underground air-raid shelter because of her leg. Miss Oakes, her housekeeper, met her and went to find a taxi. They then lost each other in the darkness. Netta sat in the porch of the station and waited—the very porch which was destroyed in a later air-raid. When no one returned, she dragged her suitcase part of the way to a hotel nearby and engaged a room. Meanwhile, Ernest, in a panic at No. 50, began to telephone the police and various London hospitals; no 'phone call to a private house was permitted during a raid, and so Netta could not telephone him. He eventually contacted Marjorie, who was working in the New Hospital for Women quite near to St. Pancras. She was dispatched to look for her mother and, walking through the hotel, suddenly came on her. When the raid was over, a taxi took Netta home at 9:30 a.m. to be at her place in synagogue later in the morning. Some years later, when she was driving past St. Pancras Station with her eight-year-old niece, Judy—who had lost her father Edwin Montagu in 1926—she pointed out the portico where she had sat and where, in a later raid, so many people had been killed. Judy always stayed with her when her mother was abroad, and Netta remarked to her, "I suppose God wanted me to live so that I could look after you." Whereupon Judy, with a child's relentless logic, added, "Yes, and I suppose He wanted the other people to die."

Meanwhile, Michael continued his education. He had left the school in Swanage and returned to Bedales. Many of the masters had gone to the war, and, with the staff depleted and discipline relaxed, it is perhaps not surprising that Bedales suffered a little in its running. Michael experienced something like Jew-baiting. And, by a strange irony, his biggest tormentor was a boy of Jewish descent, one day to be director of one of London's most famous art galleries. Michael's own account of his schooldays is that he was a butt and a buffoon—a buffoon because it was one way of turning aside the persistent attentions of his enemies. Of a nervous temperament, the continual petty persecution of the future art expert terrified him. One cannot live one's school life in a state of almost chronic apprehension and not be marked by it. One day, the Headmaster sent for him and told him that he was being removed at the end of the following term. He received the news with feelings of considerable relief. Strangely enough, his persecution ceased about this time; he became more popular his last term and produced a review (the school called it a 'Merry Evening') which had a big success.

He was whimsical, witty, capricious, talented. He had Edwin Montagu's Mongolian look; but his expression was more mobile, and he could transform the polyglot melancholy of his features into sudden simian mimicry. With a very quick sense of humor and, at the same time, a considerable inherited fund of P.N.E.U. earnestness, Michael's qualities were striking enough but hardly those that win instant approval from one's schoolfellows.

At the age of fifteen, at the side of a small mountain lake above Glenalla, he had written his poem 'The Scarecrow' upon paper not normally used for authorship. It won a prize of two guineas in the *Poetry Review*, was set to music and sung at the Albert Hall by Megan Forster, made into a record by Pemberton Billing, who 'forwarded royalties to the tune of four-and-sixpence,' and used in a song-sheet by the L.C.C. It has been reprinted in many anthologies. Recently, in the garden at Crawley, Michael's thirty-five-year-old gardener, discovering who the author of it was, announced that he had had to learn it at school and still remembered it, and began to recite it in the broadest Sussex dialect to the man who had written it many years before as a schoolboy. A charming, tender little poem, 'The Scarecrow' fully deserves its popularity. But its author, a born virtuoso in this as in so much besides, has never attempted to repeat the achievement.

> A scarecrow stood in a field one day,
>   Stuffed with straw,
>   Stuffed with hay.
> He watched the folk on the king's highway,
> But never a word said he.
>
> Much he saw but naught did heed,
>   Knowing not night,
>   Knowing not day,
> For, having naught, did nothing need,
> And never a word said he.
>
> A little grey mouse had made its nest,
>   Oh, so wee,

    Oh, so grey,
In the sleeve of a coat that was poor Tom's best,
But the scarecrow naught said he.

His hat was the home of a small jenny-wren,
    Ever so sweet,
    Ever so gay;
A squirrel had put by his fear of men
And kissed him, but naught heeded he.

Ragged old man, I loved him well,
    Stuffed with straw,
    Stuffed with hay.
Many's the tale that he could tell,
But never a word says he.

17

THE NUMBER OF THOSE who followed the P.N.E.U. programmes in home schoolrooms had increased enormously, yet the examination papers of every child were still read personally by Miss Mason. And by now, many private schools were using the syllabus. Halfway through the war, a further step forward was taken when a primary school in Yorkshire adopted the method, followed shortly afterward by the conversion of the Secretary of Education for Gloucester county, Mr. H. W. Household, whose zeal eventually introduced it to three hundred elementary schools in Gloucestershire. In fact, the whole county might almost be said to have opted for it. Soon the children of this rural population had become zealots for Homer and Shakespeare and Scott and Dickens. At about the same time, some Roman Catholic convent schools in the South of Ireland became converts to P.N.E.U. Yeats's beautiful poem 'Among School Children' was almost certainly written after a visit to a Waterford convent where the programmes were being used:

> I walk through the long schoolroom questioning;
> A kind old nun in a white hood replies;
> The children learn to cipher and to sing,
> To study reading-books and histories,
> To cut and sew, be neat in everything
> In the best modern way—the children's eyes
> In momentary wonder stare upon
> A sixty-year-old smiling public man.

In his life of the poet, Hone writes of this time when he was a senator: 'From Joseph O'Neil, he learned a great deal about the educational system in Ireland, and equipped with this information and with Gentile's theories in his head, he felt competent to take part in a tour of inspection of the primary schools, proposed by certain of his Senatorial colleagues. "I went," he wrote to Lady Gregory after his tour, "to study a very remarkable convent school. I was amused in one class when a child, on being asked to give the 'narratives' last learned (my visit was unexpected), repeated my biography out of *Who's Who*—poor intellectual diet—and another child, Sigerson's—disgusting diet. The children had no idea who I was. This, however, was not typical. The literary work, prose, and verse, was very remarkable.'

The expression 'narratives' almost certainly refers to P.N.E.U. 'narration.' But unless the good nuns had got wind of the visitation and happened to have a *Who's Who* in their possession, Yeats seems to have got things a little mixed. Or the children could have been reading the miniature biographies at the back of some school anthology and produced two of these from memory.

Netta went frequently to Dublin, sometimes on her way to Donegal, sometimes from Donegal, receiving hospitality in order that she might lecture or speak at some meeting. 'Spoke at Alexandra College, Dublin.' 'Spoke at Mrs. Wilson's house, Ballymena.' 'Spoke in Dublin Marlborough Road Training College. 300 present. Lord Frederick Fitzgerald in the chair.' And for every one Irish engagement, there were at least a dozen in England. In one year, she records that she slept in thirty-one different places. In another, in forty. Under war conditions of traveling, and with her disability, this necessitated considerable fortitude and resolution.

For a number of years now, she had been Chairman of the National Union of Women Suffrage Societies. Its President was her close friend, Millicent Fawcett, and other colleagues were Edith Picton Turberville, Mary Stocks, and Eva Hubback of Morley College fame. An entry in the diary for 1917 reads, "Went with Mrs. Fawcett to the gallery of the House of Commons. The Suffrage resolution passed Committee. Failed in the Lords." Forty years later, on the occasion of the centenary of the birth of Emmeline Pankhurst, Netta would write in the *Parents' Review* of that "small, gentle-looking woman whose militancy for votes for women roused so much enthusiasm, devotion, self-sacrifice, and even, in some cases, death," and would try and define what their aims in those days had been. "This generation of career women, and the men whose fathers so vehemently opposed the demand for equality of opportunity, wonder what all the fuss was about. Women craved the right to serve and the opportunity to train themselves for such service; they never asked for special privileges. As we look around today, those of us who have lived to see the gradual fulfillment of these demands are thrilled as new openings for such service emerge. We remember the alarm expressed by many that women who recorded their votes in the polling booths would thereby become unsexed and that dissension would arise in the home when husband and wife walked into separate booths! We now see how absurd these fears were and realize more and more how professional partners as architects, doctors, etc., feel that life is fuller and more worthwhile when common interests can be converted into common action."

The war ended, and a new phase in Netta's life began. Parents are, in some degree, re-born when their children reach the threshold of adult life, and they can share with them all their new-found enthusiasms. Netta had been thirty-seven when Michael was born; and, when he went to the university, she was still quite young enough to enter with zest into all his interests there. He was just at the age when his vitality and liveliness of mind and receptivity to her own ideals were especially welcome. He had become her travel courier and charming companion. His youth had been spent in a house where there were ten servants, but he had always been encouraged to love simple things, to show consideration, to travel third-class and to share some of his privileges with East End work-girls and East End Jewish boys. His mother and Wai had been the two great influences in his boyhood; Wai with her pince-nez and shawl; his mother in a full-sleeved blouse and dark skirt with cloth shoulder straps, rather like Swedish folk costume, and with a châtelaine swinging at her waist as she went about her business. Of Wai, he has said, "She seemed to set the very air aglow with her personality. I felt with her none of the awkwardness that is felt between youth and age; she was in sympathy with one's every mood, one felt the better for having been with her." It was her advice and care that had saved many lives, his mother's and his own amongst them. She was amongst the first to advocate open windows, cold baths, and the sleeping of children out of doors. And for the soul, she had equally good counsel.

His mother was even more of a heroine in his eyes. Netta had been beautiful in youth; but photographs of her in her mid-thirties tended to have knit brows and a sullen, almost dour expression, and do not suggest a happy person. Only as she has grown older has her face resumed radiance and animation. Twenty years later she would be a strikingly handsome woman, with searching black eyes and confident demeanor. But the Netta with the châtelaine, whom Michael remembers so vividly, was a Netta who perhaps needed him almost as much as he needed her. A certain strain—quite intelligible in those early days of her disability—shows in her face. Even after he had gone to school, her influence had remained paramount with Michael. He wrote to her daily. Sitting beside her in synagogue, when the time came to return after the half-term holidays, he would steel himself for the ordeal, though almost on the verge of tears, because it was for her sake. And now, after the First World War, his real companionship with her began. From Bedales, he had gone to a coaching establishment in Maidenhead, where he was coached for Responsions. Michael would cycle back to London every Friday to be present at the Friday evening family service and would return to Maidenhead on Sunday. As soon as he had successfully taken Responsions, he went off to Grenoble to a summer course. He was given an allowance for the first time, but it presently ran out, and he maintained his financial equilibrium by taking a job in the evening playing the drums in a local cinema. This was the first public manifestation of a versatility which was to be as much his enemy as his friend. Those who can do a lot of things well find it hard to anchor themselves patiently to one. Michael begged his mother to come out to Grenoble. She replied, "I cannot climb mountains and pick Alpine flowers." He promptly wired back that he had found a tramway into the mountains and that she must come.

This Grenoble visit was a great success. It was June. They picnicked in the fields, picked countless flowers, and Michael even produced an ice-cream pudding, which was something of a rarity in those days. A char-à-banc took them one day to Le Lauteret. There they saw soldinella; and Michael found a white pinguicula which had not been found before in that region and presented it to the Col du Galibier Alpine Garden. This was subsequently named *Pinguicula alba Franklinii*. It was very hot, and Netta had worn the lightest of dresses. Suddenly, they discovered that the char-à-banc was leaving almost immediately. They decided, in spite of having no change of clothes, to remain the night, not realizing how cold it would become as soon as the sun had set. They were extremely glad of the little stove in the inn, and of a hot brick, when they went to bed.

The Grenoble trip had been preceded by earlier post-war ones with different members of the family. Cyril had travelled with her to Norway and fished in Norwegian streams while his mother conferred with the International Council of Women and went to a tea-party given by the Queen. At the very moment that she was stepping on the steamer at Christiana to return home after the conference, Geoffrey, who had been visiting two fellow war-workers, was waiting on the platform at Frankfurt-am-Main to board a train. As he did so, he stepped between the train and the platform and was dragged for some distance. He did not lose consciousness, but to him it seemed the end. "I have broken my back and am finished," he said. When they had placed him in a shelter on the platform, he said to James Norton, his friend, "You had better go home; your wife will wonder what has happened to you and will be anxious. I am cold, there is a coat, put it round me."

Netta was met by this news when she reached London. Sydney had already procured a passport and gone off to Frankfurt. She followed him as soon as possible. She found Geoffrey in the City Hospital, still in terrible pain. He remained there for another seven weeks, but Netta had to return to London. To the friends who visited him there, he used to say, "Now, I, a pacifist, know something of the experiences of a wounded soldier." He had never been a combatant, but he had done the longest period of work for the Friends' Mission of any individual worker, and he received many letters now from his Quaker fellow-workers. When the doctors allowed it, Netta made arrangements for him to be brought back to England in a special ambulance carriage. But at the last minute, the German authorities refused to allow the ambulance carriage to go through Belgium without a guarantee that it would be returned. They were afraid that it might be seized as reparations. Geoffrey, who had already been carried down to the platform, had to wait a further two days while Sydney made frantic efforts in London to secure the guarantee. He had fractured the lower lumbar vertebrae below the level of the spinal cord, and there was temporary paralysis of the lower limbs. Back at Porchester Terrace, he spent weeks in bed, visited by many friends, and skilfully nursed by Sister Adelaide Berks, whose politics and general outlook were highly conservative, so that he could say later, "I know now that one can be great friends and live with someone for eight months with whom one disagrees on many points." It was Sister Adelaide who taught him to use his legs again, kicking a ball in the garden at the back of No. 50 under the peering eyes—or so he said—of all the maids. But when at last he was about again, Geoffrey, with something of his mother's attitude to physical disaster, would refer to the whole time of his illness as "a great adventure."

It was Geoffrey who, later in the 'twenties, brought Paul Robeson to sing at No. 50. Sir Arthur Bryant has called this great negro singer "probably the greatest interpretative artist of our time," and, although he disagrees with him politically, "the dedicated champion of an oppressed people." Robeson came to England in 1924 and thought he had never seen any land so beautiful, green, and companionable. "I longed to fling myself flat upon my face and hug the cool earth." A barrister and a *Phi Beta Kappa* man, he would soon begin to thrill English audiences by his acting and to enchant them by his singing of negro spirituals. There had been famous singers at No. 50 before, but none quite so arresting as the walnut-colored owner of this deep, wonderful, resonant, and golden voice.

The big house with the slanting porch used to see a number of celebrities in the 1920s. Sarojini Naidu, by now well known as a poet, came to stay. She amused Ernest greatly on one occasion by describing Gandhi to him as "the nicest little Mickey Mouse I've ever met." Netta herself heard Gandhi at a prayer meeting in the East End to which she went with her sister Lily. They stood at the back of the room, but the majority of those present squatted cross-legged, Brahmin fashion, on the floor around the great teacher who was one day to meet death at the hands of a religious fanatic of his own race.

Edward Lyttleton, another visitor, roped in to speak at a meeting, came and stayed the night before. Next morning, anxious as ever to demonstrate the worth of the P.N.E.U., Netta took him to Miss Faunce's and Miss Lambert's school, and into a class where the children were reading and narrating Bacon's "Essays." As Lyttleton was a trifle deaf, she handed him a book so that he could follow in the text. Presently she said to him proudly, "Doesn't that girl narrate the passage beautifully?" "Oh! I'm not listening at all," said Lyttleton, "I'm reading ahead. We don't read these books nearly enough, nowadays!"

Life was as full as ever. There were lectures to go to, poetry readings, art exhibitions; Edith Sitwell reading her poems aloud, Maude Royden preaching and soon to become a great friend, Maude Royden, who would come to cite Netta as "an example of basic Christianity." Another very close friend was the animated and amusing Lillah McCarthy. One relative to whom Netta was particularly devoted was her sister-in-law, Mrs. Freddie Franklin, daughter of Lady Magnus and sister of Laurie Magnus. Normally, to be a friend of Netta, one need not actually be a pioneer thinker, but one had to hold strong and independent views on life. But "Mrs. Freddie," gentle and talented and uncontentious, won Netta's devotion from the first by sheer charm of personality. Her animation and unfailing goodness of heart were her great attraction, and right into her eighties, she would remain one of the most loved and cosseted of guests at Glenalla.

Netta can endure conventional exchanges but only up to a point. After that, she begins to show her impatience. In her youth, she could enjoy a reception at Stafford House with the beautiful Duchess of Sutherland standing at the top of the stairs to receive the guests; but her real preference has always been for the smaller circle of wholly congenial friends. When she encountered less congenial personalities, her graciousness was so patently assumed for the occasion, and so liable to terminate abruptly when she thought she had done her duty, as though at the bidding of a stop-watch, that I doubt if any except very stupid persons were ever taken in by it. Even intelligence can only survive with Netta on her own terms. She is an idealist; for her mere verbal fireworks are not enough. Moreover, she very definitely tends to divide her own sex into sheep and goats. The goats are the people who let their sex down, who neglect their intelligence while wasting time and devotion upon their fingernails. The only trouble is that, occasionally, she classifies as a nitwit some young person who, with a little more patience and encouragement, might be able to prove that she did not deserve the title.

It is difficult to know how much purely social contacts mean to Netta. She has never, certainly, sacrificed the gracious side of life to any puritanical rejection of fripperies. Even now, she will take the long drive from the Glenalla wilds to Derry once or twice during the summer to keep an appointment with the hairdresser and likes to be suitably dressed for every occasion. She is fond of quoting Helen Webb's dictum that in youth one can carry off most things and need not trouble so much about one's appearance, but as one grows older one should pay greater attention to one's turn-out. Her jet-black hair remained dark till remarkably late; then it gradually became iron-grey. It is always perfectly set. For years, Madame Neville, half-sister to Max Beerbohm, was her dressmaker, using exquisite fabrics, like the one of blue, shot with gold, which Ernest brought her from Damascus, or hand-woven russets and browns by Mairet which blend harmoniously with the heather and bog-myrtle, asphodel and sphagnum moss of Donegal.

Her jewels, when she wears any, are carefully chosen—a long necklace given her by Kathleen Wallace of jade beads ending in a little silver flower which opens to the delight of children; an exquisite Cartier pink enamel, penny-thin, pendant watch set with diamonds; black and white onyx beads; and, in former days, the superb pearl necklace.

A few months before the end of the war, misfortune overtook this. She had been to the dressmaker and shopping and had then gone on to the P.N.E.U. office. From there, she walked to Queen Anne's Mansions, nearby, to lunch with her brother Edwin. Lady Diana Manners, whose friendship with Edwin and Venetia is related in her own and in her husband's volumes of reminiscences, was a fellow-guest. Netta was admiring her very beautiful pearl necklace across the table at luncheon when she put up her hand half instinctively to her neck, only to discover that her own pearl necklace was missing. It was the one which Ernest had given her on their wedding anniversary, and now it was gone. When lunch was over, she returned home and summoned the police. They decided that, as she stopped to put on her mackintosh when halfway to Queen Anne's Mansions, a thief must have come up silently behind her and skilfully unfastened it. Despite every effort of Scotland Yard to find it, it was never recovered. As it was insured, a new one was purchased, but the second one never meant quite the same thing to its owner.

18

THE GRAND-DUCHY in Donegal had become a well-ordered domain and was giving pleasure to more and more people. It had been exciting to discover that it figured in a well-known novel of the period, A. E. W. Mason's *The Four Feathers*. A crumpled note in the desk at Glenalla establishes this.

17 Stratton Street,
W.
5th November 1913

Ernest L. Franklin, Esq.
50, Porchester Terrace,
Hyde Park, W.

    Dear Sir,

    I am happy to answer your letter. The place called Glenalla is a village up in the hills to the north-east of Ramelton. The house to which I expect you are referring, and which I called the Lennon House, is, I should think, the one which you have bought. I am vague about its ownership, but I believe it was let to a Col. Symons. It stood off the road to Letterkenny, and it was the only one of its kind in that particular neighbourhood.

    Yours very faithfully,
        A. E. W. Mason

In the book, various passages suggest the real Glenalla, although Mason exaggerates the size of the stream. Years later, when a film was being made of the book, Michael proposed that the appropriate scenes should be shot in *situ*. But an *ersatz* 'studio' setting was preferred, perhaps because some rumor of the vagaries of Donegal weather had reached the producer.

    Netta dates her keen interest in gardening from the acquisition of Glenalla. She had long been interested in wild flowers. Now, with Wai's help, she began to create a garden and to think continually, even when in London, of the welfare of its varied inhabitants. Helen Webb drew up charts, and both the rock garden and the bog garden were inspirations of hers. Michael remembers the laying-out of the rock garden immediately below the terrace, with its narrow concentric paths and its modest central summit of rock, from which strikes out the oblique greenery of a creeping cotoneaster. "Every stone," she would direct to be put "just right," and gradually the whole would take shape under her guidance. The gardeners often thought her quite wrong, but she was always right. The workmen adored her. The water garden and big herbaceous border were created the same year, 1916. Two years later came the bog garden, the stepping-stones across the stream, and the miniature lake. The mountain stream, descending steeply from Peat Hill, pours over a waterfall in the wood amidst laurels, dark green rhododendron bushes, and the exposed and twisted roots of trees, like an Arthur Rackham fantasy; and then, bridged by the avenue, winds its pleasing way through a strip of meadow, under alders and willows, before branching out into the multiple channels bridged by narrow planks with rustic handrails. Finally, it empties its normally shallow waters over slippery stones and a reef of gravel into the "lake" itself, which was devised to provide not only a mud trap, at a spot which had been marshland and tangled waste, but, with the help of a flat-bottomed rowboat, an unfailing joy to a succession of child visitors.

Wai, because she was Irish, helped to give the Franklin family their understanding of and affection for the Irish character. She could make its shortcomings intelligible, if not immediately acceptable. The deadly-efficient Netta was not likely to tolerate a 'flochoola' attitude towards minor responsibilities. But Wai, reading Synge and Pearse, and Winifred Letts and Moira O'Neile aloud in the evening, acted as an interpreter of national temperament; and having successfully weathered her first contacts with it, Netta could go on to achieve the results she wanted. She trained a number of Irish maids who became superb examples of professional efficiency and, at the same time, genuine friends of the family. One of them, who was with Netta for many years, flung her arms round her on the day she was leaving to get married, kissed her, and said, "If I'm as happy in my married life as I've always been here with you, I shall have no complaint!" In the case of a stupid girl, Netta's temperament does not fit her for a role of unending patience; and, having once decided that a girl is stupid, she can be a little unfair in her subsequent judgements. But most girls respond quickly to her methodical rule. Just as Robert, the gardener, received a lengthy memorandum on the treatment in winter of the different plants, so a new maid was provided with a careful typewritten schedule of her duties:—

> *Biddy*: Drawing-room
> Hall
> Call rooms 1, 14, 15 and Miss Webb
> Unpack for them, brush clothes, and pack and take breakfasts
> Bedrooms
> Go to pantry at 12:30 and help for the rest of the day
> Tidy hall and drawing-room during lunch and dinner as convenient, and empty waste-paper baskets

One guest might want help in packing; another might need to be unpacked. But it was all down in black and white so that even a recent recruit could not go very far wrong. And her consideration for the guest is paralleled by her consideration for the staff. They are not asked to serve late meals to returning fishers who enjoy flogging a mountain lake in almost complete darkness. A collection of giant thermoses has solved that problem. Treats are arranged for the staff. Their holidays are a matter of genuine concern.

It was a big household to be looked after. Kathleen Wallace has set down some of her recollections of those early days:—

> Every spring or summer of the war, I went across to Glenalla. The journey was an adventure in itself, no flying in those days. I usually travelled with Olive, and we brought up the rear-guard of whatever was the current house-party. The boarding of the boat at Holyhead became a scramble as there were more passengers than space. We heard a stout, red-haired woman clutching a small boy by the wrist proclaim, "We've come from India, I'm telling you, and this poor child hasn't sat down since Calcutta."
>
> Sometimes we were in charge of young visitors who were children of Miss Lily Montagu's club members. One of these was a charming and very good little boy who wore a very handsome diminutive overcoat with an astrakhan collar. I said, "What a nice coat," and he answered with engaging simplicity, "Yes, my father made it for me to come in. My father's a tailor. It's got a fur collar because it's an *artist's* coat. I'm going to be an artist when I grow up." Anyone who has been to an

exhibition containing the paintings of Archie Utin will realise that, at six years old, he knew where he was going. Another and still smaller boy, named Teddy, had the face of a seraph, a mass of silky hair, and a shrill, importunate little voice, whose cockney accent didn't match his face at all. I have an entertaining picture of Teddy, who attached himself fondly to Mr. Franklin like a puppy, scampering down the lawn in pursuit of him, with shrill cries of "Uncle Ernest, wait for me!" And his long-suffering host, ejaculating to us, "I wish he wouldn't call me that."

Impromptu fancy-dress, dancing in the big hall, putting on a play, concerts—all these were an essential part of those halcyon days.

There stands out in the picture a figure who, while bringing to all these doings a humor which darted and gleamed like a veritable dragon-fly, brought at the same time a quality, an element, which raised them into a very different sphere. Madame Enriqueta Crichton, at one time prima-donna in the Carl Rosa Opera Company, came to Glenalla with her little son, John Vincent Print, aged eight. She came as a teacher of music, to work with Cyril and Michael at cello and violin. She became a much-valued guest, threw herself into the business of seconding H.F.'s schemes for amateur music and theatricals with a whole-hearted energy. Madame Crichton possessed intense charm and warm kindliness. Everyone loved her. Many people besides myself remember the summer when H.F. decreed a concert in aid of the funds of the little local church. Enriqueta Crichton considered the material to hand, to wit, the house-party, and set to work. It included a friend, Ruth Lowy (now Mrs. Victor Gollancz), a very pretty girl and a born dancer. Ruth, said Enriqueta Crichton, should devise a ballet—and dance it. It was entitled "*The Letter*," and I can still see the hall with the Steinway grand, and Madame Crichton improvising at the piano and reciting in her enchanting voice a letter conveying a swain's faithlessness, while Ruth, barefoot, skimmed about the great room humming, tossing her curly head, completely absorbed and unselfconscious. *Butterfly* had been one of Enriqueta's most famous roles; she had sung it across the world. "We will do Act Two," she said, "and you (to me) will sing Suzuki." The performance was to take place in the Ramelton village hall. "Gods," said Madame Crichton simply, "we must have gods. Plenty of gods." The vicar's little wife blinked and looked dumbfounded. When we went down for rehearsal, she had done her best; there were bamboo chairs and tables and paper fans, but no gods. I remember that the fans and bamboos were removed and that the stage was bare except for the little prayer-gong and kneeling cushions. The night came. The entrance fee was 3d; the audience crammed the hall and even sat on the high window-sills. I have seen *Madame Butterfly* in many parts of the world, from Covent Garden to Shanghai. But I shall remember always the voice of Enriqueta Crichton sending the ecstasy and the gradual mounting despair, pealing and whispering across a village hall, and see her standing waiting at the window in the desolate daybreak, child and hand-maid sunk in sleep at her feet, and the lanterns still faintly guttering. The stage was ankle-deep in fresh, strewn flowers and on the final long, high note of exultant joy she lifted her arms in the wide, winged sleeves, and bent her head, and I scattered basket after basket of fresh rose-leaves, Glenalla rose-leaves, over her and about her feet. She said to me afterwards, "this is the first time I've played the flower-scene with real flowers."

After this performance, Mrs. Macdermott, the local grocer's wife, came up to Netta in great excitement. "You cannot think what it means to me to hear Madame Crichton. I walked twelve miles into Liverpool as a young woman to hear her and have never forgotten it. It would be the greatest joy if I might shake hands with her." She was invited to tea, and to her infinite delight, Madame Crichton gave her one of her songs with her autograph.

It was in 1924 that I made Netta's acquaintance for the first time. A married half-sister of mine was a keen member of the P.N.E.U., and at her suggestion, I had sent a written sketch of one of my child friends in Jersey to the *Parents' Review*, and received back an appreciative letter from Miss Mason in her own handwriting to say that she would publish it. Some months later, at a dinner-party at my half-sister's, I met Netta, whose praises had already been sung to me by Amy Pennethorne in Jersey—Netta, who had founded the Rathfarnham branch of the Union seven years before and who had now come back to Dublin to address it. She invited me to Glenalla, an invitation that I was able to accept a few weeks later. My arrival is fixed in her memory because of the remark made on that occasion by one of her temporary maids. I had driven up from Dublin in a Baby Austin with a brother-in-law who was going to spend four nights at Rosapenna Hotel and who was invited to come for a night when he collected me again. As we drove up the avenue at about 3 o'clock, Netta remarked to this maid that if we had had no lunch she had better be ready to give us some. There was a scornful snort from the lady in question, and she turned on her heel and left the room, exclaiming, "Beastly hotel!" The phrase was less insulting than she imagined, for Netta has always rejoiced in the fact that both

No. 50 and her present London home, No. 88 Carlton Hill, have always been called "The Henrietta Arms" by her many friends.

Glenalla was, in the vulgar phrase, an eye-opener to me. I had never been in a household where so many people were so thoroughly being themselves. Perhaps the twenty-one-year-old Michael, good-natured as his mother but with a little more of the exhibitionist in his composition, took pleasure in introducing me to the household's mode of existence, and in seeing with what wide-eyed appreciation I responded to it. It was a place of refreshment and, at the same time, a center of storm. Life there was based on a single principle: Everyone must enjoy himself to the best of his ability and in the way which suited him or her best. But at the same time, everyone must also show a certain basic consideration for the modes of life preferred by other people. The generations overlapped, and there was a considerable gap of years between the oldest and the youngest. Glenbeg, which had been occupied by Jewish girls from the Club all July, was now housing Netta's sisters, Lily and Marian, and their life-long friend and companion, Miss Connie Lewis. This trio came down to Glenalla from time to time and mixed in a number of its doings; they represented an element of maximum *gravitas*, so that even Netta herself after half an hour in their company seemed to take on the aspect of a third Hebraic prophetess. After dinner one night, she, Michael, and I went up to Glenbeg to join in a Shakespeare reading there. I remember following Netta up the rather slippery and very steep flight of wet stone steps that Michael had made, and which wound their way up between the laurels to the little house where the three ladies awaited us. Our progress was slow, but there was no comment or protest in the darkness.

Next day, Michael was asked to take his two aunts and myself on a long motor drive. The car was a big, rather old-fashioned Hudson. A farmer's stray cart-horse, grazing along the hedgerow in a very narrow lane, did not seem to like it, whipped suddenly round, lashed out, and crumpled up our left front mudguard with a well-directed kick. But the real sensation of the afternoon was yet to come. Michael drove us out along a stony track, unfamiliar even to him, which presently brought us out onto a narrow ledge fronting the Atlantic about twenty or thirty feet above the black, storm-shaped rocks of this much-buffed coast. It may have been a mistake on his part, or he may have chanced his hand because it would give us an exceptionally good view of the distant Tory Island, but it was immediately evident to us, as to the Light Brigade, that someone had blundered. We could not go on unless we chose to plunge into the Atlantic. And the track along which we had come was so long and rough as to make reversing a problem. Michael decided to turn the car. He had a small square ledge on which to do this. Quite evidently, he prided himself on being a daring driver but with complete control over his vehicle. He proceeded now to put on an act deliberately calculated to establish this fact beyond any dispute. Movement was limited to about three feet in any direction. When we drove forward, the two front tires appeared to be projecting over the abyss. I longed to get out from my seat beside the driver. But shame forbade me. However, one of his aunts in the back of the car exclaimed, "Michael, this is really too much. You must let us out before you do any more." Maneuvers were suspended, and both ladies climbed slowly out of the back and withdrew to a corner of the ledge. As an imperturbable male, I felt obliged to remain beside the driver while he completed his *tour de force*. But I did not enjoy it.

The man was an exhibitionist, but what an agreeable one: versatile, witty, and with a magnificent reading voice—deep, resonant, persuasive, and slightly ironic. At times he delighted in buffoonery. But something of the Jew's sense of the tragic, an emotion that cannot actually be called self-pity but that shows itself keenly aware of other men's hatred down the centuries, had got into that voice and accounted for its deeper resonances. When he launched forth on a long declamation in Whitmanesque free-verse—"Because I am a Jew"—you felt that you were listening to one of the Babylonian exiles.

At one moment he would stress his Jewishness; at another, the similarities between Jew and Gentile. Netta had come to church with me in the tiny neighboring Glenalla church on Sunday morning. Michael would say, "Of course, we regard Jesus as a prophet, a great prophet, but only a prophet." It was impossible for him to forget this issue. He had already received a sharp reminder of it, for he had lost his heart to the pretty daughter of a Judge in the Indian Civil Service, and instantly, both families—his own and hers—had done their best to ensure that it went no farther. To be a Jew was to enjoy the favor of God and the disfavour of man. All those Biblical prophecies which that curious sect, the "British Israelites," so much covet and even appropriate as their own, were yours for the asking. You could go out with joy and be led forth with peace; the mountains and the hills would break forth before you into singing, and all the trees of the field would clap their hands. And, at the same time, you were despised and hated; regarded as the blood-brother of every slick-witted Sheeny in the umbrella trade. In fact, it was rather as though every Englishman were compelled to think of himself as the collateral of the bookmakers on Epsom Downs.

Netta, with her many non-Jewish friends, had long since ceased to feel any sense of separateness; she was an Englishwoman of the Jewish faith. But to every successive generation, the problem must present itself anew. Sooner or later, they must feel a compelling impulse to say to some new friend, "You know I am a Jew," or, "You know that I have Jewish blood," perfectly aware that, in about five out of every ten cases, this will prejudice them in some obscure, unformulated way. Their virtues will lose a little of their validity: "Yes, I suppose so, but then Jews find it so easy to be charitable." And their vices will have acquired an additional slur: "Typically Jewish!" For example, the Scots are mean; the English will haggle over trifles and pride themselves on having saved some quite negligible sum. I have known an old Frenchman, on whom I was billeted on the Somme, work himself into a white passion because, since I slept on my own camp bed, he was only receiving a halfpenny a night for me, as against a franc a night if the bed had been one of his. That halfpenny was brandished in my face until I thought the old man would have a stroke. But, if a Jew is mean, it immediately becomes a national characteristic: "He can't help it. He's a Jew, what do you expect?" And Jewish humor, which loves the jest against itself, stresses this more than ever.

The Jew is a marked man. Chronic insecurity down the centuries has made him apprehensive, highly solicitous for the welfare of his immediates, sensitive, quick-witted; alternatively obsequious and arrogant; for the precariousness of his position makes it difficult for him to strike a happy mean.

I had been brought up on Browning. If one has read his *Holy Cross Day*, or heard, as I had, Shylock's best speeches declaimed by a Hungarian-Jewish sixth-form master named Elischa, one is in little danger of even the faintest taint of anti-Semitism. Besides, I like quick minds—minds that anticipate your argument, minds that see immediately, exactly where it is leading. So, when Michael recited Edmond Fleg's moving defense of the Jew to me, he was preaching to the converted. But at the same time, I found Netta's own attitude to the religious side of the question reassuring, with its emphasis on shared acceptances rather than on differences.

One evening, Michael drove me down to Raybridge, a distance of about two miles, to show me Lough Swilly by moonlight. We left the car by the bridge parapet and got out. It was low tide, and, climbing the parapet, we went down onto the wide stretch of slightly muddy strand, which smelt faintly of decaying seaweed and the fragile shells of long-deceased crabs. On the far side of the silver-flooded stretch of water, one could see the shadowy outline of the low hills on the left bank of the Swilly estuary. Suddenly, Michael, who had just played the part for the O.U.D.S. at Oxford, remarked, "Would you like to hear one of my speeches as Polonius?" "Yes, very much." So there, by moonlight, crunching the sand and the razor shells when he moved at all, Polonius button-holed me and gave me his advice before I set forth on my mission to France. I became Laertes, and this old man with the crumpled Caucasian features was speaking not just because he liked the sound of his own voice, but because he wanted to give me, his son, whom he loved, the triple-distilled wisdom of six or seven decades—worth a fortune to me if I chose to take it—not that youth often accepts such charity, preferring nearly always to buy, highly expensively, what it needs for itself. The advice was excellent, and Polonius unloaded it, piece by piece, slowly upon me, like an old servant unloading and carrying the luggage indoors from a phaeton. He was full of quirks and oddities, and his only real folly, of course, is in imagining that youth would listen to him. But it is excellent advice all the same. When at last the speech was finished, we returned to the car, climbed into it, and drove back up to Glenalla. The unique performance was over.

I had to wait twenty years for another that would rival it. It was at Ray also, only a few hundred yards from the bridge, but this time indoors by a friend's fireside. The speech then was Biron's great speech in *Love's Labour Lost*, with Michael rolling out the slow periods —

> "A lover's eye will gaze an eagle blind;
> A lover's ear will hear the lowest sound"

with unequalled fire and sonority at a moment when at least three people in the room were peculiarly well attuned to heed them.

Wai was a fellow-guest on the occasion of this first Donegal visit, shawled and spectacled, and of a peculiarly soothing and reassuring presence. She joined in the play-readings; she read one of Padraic Pearse's stories aloud to us; she felt her way in the darkness with us up to Glenbeg; she was a typical Franklin dilutant, that is to say, a person who prevented the strong family concentrate from becoming too heady. The Franklins are impulsive, outspoken, a shade excitable, and absolutely tireless. In Churchillian phrase, never has a family argued so much about so little. Helen Webb was as restful as a cushion, tactful, whimsical, and with a touch of Irish brogue.

She died in March 1926, and in another house-party which I joined in September of that year, youth predominated. Nancy Samuel was a fellow-guest; Jean Farquhason, who afterwards married the publisher Ronald Boswell; Iris Lemare, the musical conductor; Allan Gwynne-Jones, one day to be Master at the Slade; all of them Bedalians; Archie Utin, Netta's artist protégé; Enriqueta Crichton and her son John, whom Netta was educating; and, representing the older generation, Netta's sister Florrie Waley. The various age-groups went their respective ways. We fished, we played tennis, we read aloud. At the end of my stay, I could echo the sentiments which Gilbert Samuel, Herbert's solicitor brother, had written in the pale, olive-green morocco-bound Visitors Book—"A happy visit. Sunshine inside and out. Glory be to (Glen) Allah!"

Nevertheless, a curious thing happened after I had left. I travelled back to Dublin with one of the Glenbeg guests, a girl of eighteen or nineteen, a member of the Girls' Club, who had been educated at a good school and was now being sent to Oxford by Lily. She came from a very modest East End home, and she was perhaps unduly conscious of this. At any rate, to my surprise, I found her savagely resentful of the behavior of her hostess. She had been bossed, ordered around, and, worst of all, she had been patronized. I would have liked to point out to her tactfully that people who would pay your fare from London to a remote corner of Donegal in order to give themselves the pleasure of patronizing you for a fortnight are distressingly rare. Besides, Netta bossed all her guests. Lord Samuel, the Cabinet Minister, had to walk up Peat Hill obediently when he was told the morning was suitable; and, when he got to the top and saw the still mist-wreathed beauties of Lough Swilly below him, he felt duly rewarded. Picnics were arranged according to the strictest principles of John Stuart Mill, "the greatest happiness of the greatest number"; the London working girls who then occupied the octagonal tower had expeditions arranged for them; and when Sir John Simon came over to tea from the hotel at Rosapenna, they were duly summoned down from Glenbeg to dance with him and the rest of the Glenalla house-guests. Perhaps it was all a little dictatorial. But if there had not been that guiding hand at the center of things, there would have been anarchy, and is anarchy, I longed to say to her, so much preferable to organization?

Of course, Netta was managerial. She was now in her late fifties, and her mere voice, raised on some point of importance, or if her family were being exceptionally argumentative, carried across the room or up the stairs all the thunders of the wrath of Jehovah. I could understand her seeming awe-inspiring to a new acquaintance; I could even understand her seeming brusque and impatient to a point of rudeness. Nevertheless, it seemed to me that a stranger must be singularly obtuse if he did not perceive very quickly how much kindness and consideration for other people lay behind the dictatorial manner. Lily could say of their childhood, "We rejoiced in her sympathy and understanding; but we rebelled sometimes against the domination she always liked to exert and her passion for managing other people's concerns, and organizing their lives for them with the sole purpose of making things easier for them." This has remained a trait throughout her life, but it has become more and more infused with tolerance and understanding.

19

ON THE 15TH OF JANUARY, 1923, Netta received a telegram summoning her to Ambleside. Charlotte Mason was already unconscious when she arrived. She sat up all that night and was present next day at mid-day when Miss Mason died. She was eighty-one, and as *The Times* said in their obituary, "Her personal influence was probably more widespread than that of any other educationalist of her time. The loyalty which she inspired was more than could be accounted for by the mere weight and force of her educational philosophy."

Of all her loyal devotees, Netta had probably achieved most. To her, Charlotte Mason was "that rare combination, an original thinker and philosopher, and a marvelous organizer and businesswoman." But she was far away in Ambleside, and it was Netta, Evelyn Whyte, and Amy Pennethorne, who had had to fight the daily campaign in London and the counties, and who were the mobile column without which the *generalissimo* might have been helpless.

Michael remembers Charlotte Mason as "small, round-faced and apple-cheeked. She had a coachman, Barrow, who was a sort of John Brown to her Queen Victoria. He would take her driving and stop periodically opposite some viewpoint on the roadside. Then Barrow would say to her, 'Now, miss, this is something for us to look at.'"

After her death, the Charlotte Mason legend would become a little oppressive in certain circles. She herself had said, when living, "There is nothing presumptuous in thinking or feeling that we are right. It is in fact necessary to get used to this kind of spiritual vigor. Otherwise, we lose all clearness of thought and are bound to go wrong." Such a sentiment is perfectly fitting in the mouth of an intellectual leader, but it is more dangerous when disciples begin to repeat it. In years to come, the Union would sometimes seem to outsiders a shade too complacent, and unreceptive to anything outside its own sacred code —

"Miss Mason always said this. Miss Mason never did that." But

Charlotte Mason herself had been anything but a formalist, as Elsie Kitching makes perfectly plain in her essay in the 'Memorial' volume. Miss Mason disliked any form of red tape. "In proportion as a piece of work needs organization, it lacks life," she would often say. "Don't make schemes for arranging the school work ahead. It must be fresh term by term or it will get stale." She never worked out of hours, nor let herself think of problems at night. She avoided expressions of personal opinion lest they should act like 'suggestions' on those who loved her. She distrusted personal influence as limiting and belittling the person influenced, and she steadily set her face against any form of personal influence over any with whom she came in contact. She laid down principles and waited for others to think along her lines of thought and find the right solution.

It was probably true, but by a strange irony, although she deprecated personal influence, her own personal influence amongst her immediate circle was to be overwhelming, and her very name became something of a shibboleth after her death.[25]

One can appreciate Charlotte Mason's spiritual stature more easily from casual remarks made to her amanuensis than from either her own letters or from the almost ritual loyalty of the utterances of her disciples. To Elsie Kitching she would say, "Always remember that persons matter more than things. Don't say anything that will leave a sting." Or, having coped with certain tiresome letters with a gentle graciousness, "Remember, no one is made up of one fault; everyone is much greater than his faults," and then, with a smile, "I find it much easier to put up with people's faults than their virtues."

General Sir Robert Baden-Powell has left it on record that the Boy Scout Movement was a direct outcome of Charlotte Mason's insistence that both teacher and child should use their eyes and ears. She had recommended the use of his small handbook for soldiers, *Aids to Scouting*, published during the Boer War, to her students at Ambleside, as being full of wise hints upon the inculcation of observation and deduction. One of these students, Sue, came as governess to General Allenby's home and was discovered one day playing scouting games with her small charge. "Father, you are shot; I am in ambush" (the General was riding home and had passed under the branches of a tree) "and you have passed under me without seeing me. Remember, you should always look upwards as well as around you."

---

25 See *The Story of Charlotte Mason* by Essex Cholmondeley

He told the story to Baden-Powell on his visit to his home, and from that germ was born his whole idea of scouting for the young. "From this acorn," wrote Baden-Powell, "grew the tree which is now spreading its branches across the world."

Even stranger is another example of its indirect influence. One of the many places to which Netta had taken the gospel was Oxford, and from a P.N.E.U. school there came the child who was to have the unique distinction of naming a planet. An early P.U.S. speciality had been the Nature Walk. On one of these, the Ambleside teacher, Miss K. M. Claxton, had made her class place the different planets at appropriate distances: Mercury a canary seed, Venus a small pea, Earth a larger one, Mars a bead, Jupiter an orange, Saturn a golf ball. The latter was exactly one thousand and nineteen paces from where they had first set out. It stuck in one child's mind, and so, also—in a wholly different lesson—did Bulfinch's Age of Fable with its wealth of mythological references.

One morning this eleven-year-old heard her grandfather, Falconer Madan, Librarian of the Bodleian, read aloud from the daily paper that a new planet had been discovered, "a dark one." She had been on that planet walk with her class. She knew her Bulfinch, and after ruminating for a moment or two, she said, "I think Pluto would be a good name for it." Her grandfather passed the remark on to his friend, H. H. Turner, of the University Observatory at Oxford, who promptly wired the suggestion to the Lowell Observatory in America, where the discovery had been made. It was accepted. Presently, The Times was congratulating Miss Venetia Burney on "perhaps the happiest of all essays in classical nomenclature." Planet-christening seems to have run in the family, for it was her grandfather who had suggested the names Deimos and Phobos for the satellites of Mars. This is obviously not the moment to quote the lines of the poet Francis Jammes:

> On a baptisé les étoiles sans penser
> Qu'elles n'avaient pas besoin de nous, et les nombres
> Qui preuvent que les belles comètes dans l'ombre
> Passeront, ne les forceront pas à passer.[26]

---

26 They have baptised the stars, and have not taken heed,
When dealing out their names that stars have no such need.
The figures that foreshow through some far night
The comet's patch can never force its flight.

The P.N.E.U. was given full credit on this occasion by Dr. Madan, who wrote to Venetia's schoolmistress, "The Royal Astronomical Society itself could think of no better name than Kronos (not Chronos), the father of Jupiter. I really believe that had Venetia been under a less capable and enlightened teacher than yourself, the suggestion of Pluto would not have occurred to her, or if made, would have been just a vague guess. As it is, her acquaintance with some of the old legends of Greek and Roman deities and heroes, and that 'nature walk' in the University parks enabled her to grasp at once the special elements of the situation and to be the first to make a suggestion so reasonable as to be accepted by the whole world of science."

Certainly, the achievements of her Movement have been remarkable. To Miss Mason, it had always been the child that mattered. And in this, she had Netta's wholehearted support. Children were the infinite potential. Netta did not think children perfect, but she thought them capable of harmonious and successful development. Handled the right way, they might become courageous and cultivated, cheerful and intelligent—like so many of her own valued adult friends. She, who can show such great impatience with people's triviality or weakness, is generally silent about their real faults. And children are excused still further, since so many of their faults can be traced back to adult influence. Kathleen Wallace has called Netta "the most undemonstrative and unemotional of human beings," and then gone on to say, "I do not think that she ever lavished fondness on any child. But she had a need of them; she would rather have them about her than not; she delighted in sharing their interests and their plays and their company. The infinite importance of the child was to be the mainspring of her greatest life-work."

This is a little misleading. She is incapable of anything in the nature of gush; nevertheless, Netta's behaviour towards children reveals a vast, if restrained, tenderness. She loves children. She loves their natural goodwill, their spontaneity, and the deviousness of their approach when they thought that it was a matter for courtesy. Years after the occasion, she will call to mind how little Hamish Noblett, the seven-year-old son of the rector at Rathmullen, came to lunch one day at Glenalla. The Franklin children were not allowed to drink at meals, and there was no water on the table. Presently, out of the blue, in bland tones and with just the slightest tang

Trans. by Thomas Bodkin.

of a North of Ireland accent, came this charming conversational gambit, offered in just the same way that one would offer any other interesting bit of information, "Mrs. Franklin, ye know I'm a great water drinker!"

Ernest was a child-lover, too. He was a Vice-President of the Children's Country Holiday Fund and President of its specifically Jewish branch. Marjorie remembers how, when he was already in his seventies, she made an appointment one day to meet him and some of his grandchildren near the Round Pond in Kensington Gardens. When she arrived to keep this assignment, she found her father flat on his back on the grass, with half a dozen children—blood relatives and otherwise—rolling over him. Later, as they were walking away, she said to him, "Who were those other children?" "Oh, let me see, there was Titania, and Maudie and Tony. Nice children. Very nice children." They were complete strangers, but previous encounters, when in the park with his grandchildren Roger and Joe, had put him on Christian-name terms with them. All his life he remained a teller of fascinating fairy tales in which he used all the accepted ingredients but favoured elder sons as against younger ones and made other minor changes in the recipe.

20

CHARLOTTE MASON HAD DIED at the beginning of 1923. Later in the year Netta permitted herself a holiday and went to France with Michael. When, at six years old, he had been made the witness of his mother's disablement it must have stamped itself deeply upon his childish imagination, and now he was the perfect travelling companion, one who even put tissue paper between her dresses and packed them for her when they moved from place to place. All his life it has been an obsession with him to find gadgets which would be an assistance to her. Netta herself adores gadgets; it is her delight to discover a new one, and to introduce it to her friends. But Michael is the gadget-finder *par excellence.* As a schoolboy he designed a special leather gardening belt for her with immense pockets so that she could garden without inconvenience. He found a picnic stick that she could thrust into the ground beside her, on to which were then hooked three or four plates as though on a cake-stand. He also got for her two sticks that she uses today, made of a wood as strong as ebony, yet lighter than matchwood.

They set forth for Paris and went on to Avignon. In the course of the next fortnight they visited Tarascon, went to Les Baux, saw Pont du Gard, Aigues-Mortes, Nîmes and Arles, and then went on to Carcassonne and Ussons-le-Bains. Wherever possible they searched for flowers but at Ussons the weather broke, which impeded their expeditions. In the course of one, *gendarmes* discovered that Michael had not got a passport with him. They interrogated him, and, when he maintained that they were there merely to gather wild flowers they became increasingly suspicious. As it was pouring with rain, they finally contented themselves with making him identify *Lilas in Petit Larousse Illustré,* and accepted these credentials, frail though they thought them to be.

Michael was now at Queen's, having gone up to Oxford in October 1922. According to my wife, who was at St. Hugh's at the time, he was already something of a celebrity at the University. Michael's own verdict is, 'I was not much of a force in my college, although I played hockey for it.

But I was fairly well known outside it.' He had been whimsical, impetuous and charming as a child, but of a highly tempestuous nature. He could remember how, when one of his mother's greatest friends died, his nurse had locked him into the night-nursery because he had been naughty. He wanted to go downstairs to comfort his mother, and in his rage he kicked through the panel of the night-nursery door and escaped. School life had done little for him. Now, in his early twenties, he came into his own. He was made Treasurer of the Union, and very nearly became its President; he was assistant Editor of *The Isis*, and Secretary of the Isis Hockey Club. He was also the founder of the first Liberal Jewish Synagogue in Oxford, and tells how they shared the same quarters as the Orthodox Jews whose service followed theirs. 'I used to read Claude Montefiore's sermons aloud, but I took care to put them always at the very end of our service so that Orthodox Jews who had come early would get the benefit as well, and perhaps be converted!' But what really made him widely known was his dramatic talent. It was a peak period for the O.U.D.S., among whose members were several young men who subsequently became well known as actors and playwrights. When J. B. Fagan produced *Hamlet* with the O.U.D.S. in the early 1920s, Ivor Brown wrote of that production, in which Gyles Isham took the part of Hamlet, that it was excellent in every way, but 'only of Polonius can we say that this is the best we have ever seen'. Michael was Polonius. He had joined the O.U.D.S., as a dining club, but volunteered for Polonius when it was discovered that the running Blue who had been given the part, moved so badly, that 'he couldn't even walk across the stage'. Sybil Thorndike and Basil Dean also raved about the performance of Polonius. Michael played eight parts in all during his time with the O.U.D.S., 'Nine, if you count the cock that crows in *Hamlet*.' He was Justice Shallow to Emlyn Williams' Dull in *Henry IV*, Part II; the Troll King in *Peer Gynt* to Robert Speaight's Peer; and Boyet in *Love's Labour's Lost*. And he appeared in Ayliff's production of Rostand's *Fantastics*. He was also top, two years running, in the British Empire Shakespeare Society's prize for character acting at the Haymarket Theatre. The Undistinguished Duckling of Bedales had become a university notability, and when Netta went up to Oxford to watch him act she must have been filled with pride.

Lillah McCarthy, now married to Sir Frederick Keeble, lived at Boar's Hill, and often invited Michael to help her run her parties. With his gift for sociability, he was a distinct acquisition. He met Robert Bridges and also John Masefield, another member of the Boar's Hill colony. Masefield read his own poetry aloud to him and others, in his drawing-room. 'His voice was like a cello, and in the middle of his reading a wild cat suddenly jumped out of the woods, in at the window, and on to his lap. As soon as he had finished reading, it leaped out of the window again and went back into the woods.'

Michael's own voice was often heard at the Union. He was a distinctly agile-minded debater. He had inherited his father's quickness for the spontaneous witticism. When a friend, Robert Figgis, told him over the dinner table of some society woman who had once remarked to him in quite good faith, 'Mr. Figgis, I wonder if you agree with me that *The Importance of Being Earnest* is the best play Shaw ever wrote?' Michael's instant comment was, 'Well, of course, you know what you should have said to her "A remark like that would make Shaw wild".'

Once in the Union he was briefed to support Sir Johnston Forbes-Robertson in a debate on 'The Stage is better than the Cinema'. At the last minute, however, he was asked to change his allegiance and to oppose the motion. His predicament was known to many of the Union members. He began, 'Mr. President, Sir, when I received your message tonight I felt myself in a trap. And driving along in this trap I met the great stage-coach'. The rest of his sentence was drowned in laughter. When it had quietened, the speaker went on to explain that it had really been quite simple to change sides, 'only a matter of reversing the "ands" and the "buts".'

Michael stood for the presidency of the Union but was defeated by Alan Lennox-Boyd by thirteen votes. Later, he was chosen as one of a university team of three which was being sent to America to debate against teams in thirty-six universities and colleges there. "I was the light-weight; I supplied the comic relief." This is a little too modest. Nevertheless, he probably owed his position in the team to his quick wit. Soon after he had started a postgraduate course in Comparative Religion at King's College, London, under W. R. Matthews, Dean of St. Paul's, there was a University of London centenary debate at the Guildhall, and the speakers to represent King's College at it were chosen by an eliminating contest. Subjects were drawn from a hat. Michael cannot even remember the subject which came to him, but he can remember what enabled him to capture the sympathy of the judges. He had observed in the lecture room in which the trials were taking place that there remained on the blackboard certain geometrical figures from someone's class. Pointing to them, he began, "You will notice that I have taken the precaution of drawing a plot of my opponent's speech. Here he was quite acute; here he was a little obtuse; here he drew a parallel; here he went off at a tangent; and here he made a circle, which, as you know, is an infinite number of points all equidistant from the center of the subject!" This piece of successful improvisation brought the house down and sent him to the Guildhall to represent King's College, although he had only just arrived there.

Stephen Wise, Rabbi of the Free Synagogue in New York, was one of America's most famous preachers. He had stayed at No. 50 in 1910 and addressed crowded meetings in different parts of London, and it was he who had found Rabbi Mattuck for Claude Montefiore.

Towards the end of 1923, Wise suggested and helped to arrange a P.N.E.U. lecture tour for Netta and Mr. Household in the U.S.A. and Canada. Netta brought her friend and secretary, Evelyn Whyte, and the tour was a success in many ways, although there were no large-scale conversions. Netta spoke at club luncheons, in private houses, in schools and colleges, at a Friends' Meeting, and even in a large Episcopalian church in New York. She stayed in Philadelphia with her friend Earl Barnes and his wife and made it her business, while there, to contact eight unknown relatives of workers on the Glenalla estate. After some weeks, Geoffrey joined her in the States, and she was able to see the Grand Canyon, the Yosemite Valley, Santa Barbara, San Francisco, and the Canadian Rockies, in his company.

Two years later, in 1925, Netta did another tour, this time at the invitation of the National Council of Women of South Africa. She was then President of the National Council of Women of Great Britain. She brought with her Daphne Gould, an Ambleside-trained teacher, and they visited every province of the Union, as well as North and South Rhodesia. In six weeks she addressed nearly fifty meetings, lecturing sometimes as many as four times in one day. She had stood up well to the strain of life in America and South African air was so stimulating and South African hospitality so cordial that she returned home, not tired but refreshed. What had delighted her most on her visit had been the grandeur and the beauty of the country, the sky, and the vast expanses, the birds and flowers, the color and the peace. On her way to Bulawayo—partly by goods train—she stopped at Plumtree to visit a large boys' school consisting of a number of thatched huts. Here she slept out under the many stars of the South African night, set in a deep blue sky, with the thought of her own little summer house far away in Ireland in her mind. It was a joy to her when she had an opportunity to address Jewish communities in isolated towns, although this activity had its own problems. "I had two Jewish meetings, but at the second, where a thousand were present, the pompous chairman muzzled me, and I had to change much of my talk while on the platform." She was not there to speak specifically on education but, whenever she could, she seized the opportunity to preach the P.N.E.U. gospel.

She visited Rhodes' grave at Matoppo, set on its flat hilltop amid enormous boulders covered with brilliant lichens, yellow, red, rust-colored, and bright green. At the top, they were greeted by what the natives have named "The World's View," a vast landscape where great outcrops of rock rise from amidst dense vegetation suggesting a time long since when man's presence upon the planet was an almost negligible factor. The temperature was 106 degrees, it took forty minutes to reach the top of the hill and as much to come down, and the going in places was quite difficult, but there were no complaints from the lady with the stick; and on the same evening, she kept faith with a small Jewish group whom she had promised to address.

They stayed as guests of Sir Herbert and Lady Stanley at Government House in Livingstone, saw the Zambesi River where it is a mile wide, and visited the Victoria Falls a second time, by moonlight, in order to see them under perfect light conditions. A letter home tells of a tremendous thunderstorm when they were traveling in a train by night and when the lightning made circles of fiery ribbon in the sky. It worried Netta when mails were delayed. Then a huge packet of forty-five letters arrived, but she had no leisure to read them until after midnight. "Elevenses," the South African custom of mid-morning tea, which she detested, was mitigated by "wonderful strawberries and cream, and the best figs I have tasted." The Premier Diamond Mine bored her as did going down a gold mine, which was also very tiring. But she saw with interest on the Bertram wine farm a huge willow tree grown from a shoot from one in Napoleon's garden on St. Helena; and it thrilled her to catch a glimpse of a secretary bird. Presently they returned to Cape Town and on Christmas Eve Netta gave a broadcast talk. Then they embarked for home on the *Windsor Castle* on Christmas Day. Technically speaking, the tour was over, but the voyage home gave plenty of further opportunities for propaganda.

Michael had decided on a career. He would become a rabbi of the Liberal Jewish faith. It may have been partly Netta's influence in his life which made him elect for this calling. Nearly two hundred years previously his ancestor, Rabbi Menachem Mendel Franckel, had died on 18 April 1761 and they had buried him in the new graveyard at Breslau, the site of which he himself had chosen not long before, by throwing a stone over his shoulder. They had put on his grave—which, by a strange chance, was the first to be dug in this new cemetery: —

> Here lies one who served his Lord in the sanctuary —
> Who was faithful in his innermost thoughts to Him who sent him.
> He loved his duty at all times,
> He subsisted from the work of his hands.
> He occupied himself with the commands of his Creator.

Five generations of Franklins had been born since then. But there had been many rabbis in the family before Menachem's day, and now there would be another, but in the new tradition.

Michael's novitiate lasted over two years, and it is a curious story as narrated by himself. He studied in New York under Dr. Wise, his parents' friend. He stayed first with a friend of Netta's, a Mrs. Moskowitz, and later he had an apartment of his own. He began his training with a genuine sense of dedication. "I believed tremendously in my vocation in the beginning. I felt that a Liberal Jewish rabbi was needed from a Liberal Jewish home. And there was no one else but me to do it. I studied in a small college—the Jewish Institute of Religion. Wise's own son was reading to become a rabbi too, and I saw lots of the family. I became a preacher, quite a good preacher. I was even invited to preach in a Christian church."

Stephen Wise was a big man, with a huge leonine head and magnificent dark grey hair. Netta and Ernest had been duly impressed by him when he stayed with them at Porchester Terrace fourteen years before. Everything about him was big, the tone and range of his voice, "A voice like an organ, and he would consciously pull the stops out! With that voice he could sway the multitudes to an ecstasy. Neither of the Billies—Sunday or Graham—could touch him. He was the greatest Liberal Jewish rabbi in the U.S.A., in my opinion, and certainly in his own. "Michael, if I had not had the misfortune to be born in Silesia, I would have been the first Jewish President of the United States." He had only one rival, in Cincinnati,

I think, a Rabbi Hillel Silver. It was rather like the two popes at Avignon and Rome. Fundamentally, Wise was a fine person, and a genuine idealist. He went into action against international wrongs on various occasions, in a splendid way. But sometimes the fortresses he set out to storm were only windmills."

This dynamic personality was a stimulating influence, without a doubt. But Michael's temperament did not need stimulation; he already had most of the qualities—at least the superficial qualities—which Wise could offer, even to the organ voice on which he was equally adept at pulling out the stops. What he needed far more was some of the saintliness of the retiring Claude Montefiore, a man who hated crowds, whose mission had been forced upon him, and who could refer to Lily Montagu as the "gadfly" without whom he would never have been stirred into action. If he had had Montefiore's seriousness and his sanctity, or if he had even had Wise's self-confidence and ambition, Michael might have made a famous and successful evangelist for Liberal Judaism. But a genuine sense of mission was lacking. Presently he began to doubt the wisdom of the step he had taken. "Do you know when I finally gave up the idea of being a rabbi? When I found that I was bringing tears to the eyes of my congregation. I couldn't go on. I realized at that moment that I was an actor, and not a preacher at all, and that I had no right to be in the pulpit."

Leo Baeck[27], the famous Berlin rabbi who refused to flee from Germany under the Hitler régime because he felt that his fellow nationals needed him, and whose heroism in a concentration camp, and subsequent pleas to the Russians when they arrived not to massacre the camp Nazi guards without trial, have been praised in such striking terms by Dean Matthews of St. Paul's[28], once set down what he considered a rabbi, and what a Jew must be:—

> A message is not the preaching of a preacher,
> But rather the man himself.
> He is the decisive element; only if he himself is a message can he bring
>   a message.

---

27 Elected President of the World Union for Progressive Judaism 1939.
28 'A Hero of Modern Judaism' by the Very Rev. W. A. Matthews, Dean of St. Paul's, one of several essays in In Memoriam Leo Baeck.

For only then will there go forth from him that reality which is con-
veyed in Dante's sentence:
'he speaks reality and you speak words'.
In the last analysis, therefore, only a pious man can preach.
One speaks today frequently of 'the affirmations of Judaism'.
The true affirmation of Judaism is always the Jew himself;
Precisely he, who through himself, becomes a message."

At the Institute of Religion there had been one rabbi, Rabbi Lewis, whose saintliness had kindled Michael's imagination, but he himself saw his own rabbinical virtues as solely rhetorical and the best thing to do seemed to be to admit that a mistake had been made and to turn back. Netta, like Hannah in the Old Testament, must certainly have felt deeply the disappointment of her hopes and aspirations for this son of hers. But her experience was in no way unique. It has happened to many.

> And you?
> And you?
> Look at me, gaze into my eyes and tell me
> How many hopes you buried in stark graves,
> In little narrow graves,
> Such as a dog has, or a pauper
> And you?
> What tender, delicate, graceful child was yours,
> In what grave lain?
> Sound, trump!
> Yield up your content, coffins.
> Re-integrate, pale ghosts.
> No. Earth, lie heavy
> Lest at that sound too many walk abroad,
> And mine amongst them.

21

THE NETTA OF GLENALLA was one person, engaged in what might be called a minor frontier campaign of making as many various people, relatives and friends, happy in as many different ways as possible. The Netta of London was the same, but the campaign was fought on a much wider front. One got an idea of how extensive it was when one stayed with her at Porchester Terrace. When she was elected President of the National Council of Women, its first professing Jewish president, her presidential address at the annual conference was outstanding and her chairmanship at subsequent business meetings was a model of how to play that difficult role. As well as being their president, Netta was, and continued for many years to be, Arts reporter to the Arts and Letters section of the N.C.W. This entailed visiting contemporary exhibitions and reporting on them later to her fellow members.

But, important as her many public functions were, it was the individual contact and the individual case which perhaps mattered most to her. There, she could feel that she might be rendering unique service to friend or protégé or stranger. No trouble was too great. The inquiry, or the letter that might make all the difference, went off by the very next post: if she was going to act, she acted immediately.

Hospitality at No. 50 was only one aspect of this ideal of service. It was pleasant to stay there. The atmosphere was quieter than the Glenalla atmosphere, and one felt that organization had been so perfected that the house ran itself, smoothly and silently. Poets and writers, though untidy, generally helpless, and disinclined to take the trouble to organize comfort for themselves, nevertheless have a very keen and distinctly valetudinarian appreciation of comfort, if someone else has taken the trouble to furnish it. "The Henrietta Arms" was a home from home. One arrived, dismissed one's taxi, rang the bell and waited, since it would be a little while before Elsie could mount from the distant 'servants' hall' alongside the kitchen in the basement. The first voice to greet one was a Donegal voice. "Mrs. Franklin is in the morning-room." "All right, Elsie, I think I'll just go up to my room first." Sometimes it was Geoffrey's room, if he was away; sometimes it was the official visitor's room; sometimes it was Michael's. Geoffrey's room had this advantage, that one had the benefit of all Geoffrey's fine array of books. He was a collector of Nonesuch Press limited editions, and it contributed to one's general sense of luxury to get into bed at night—different people have different ideas of luxury—and find oneself fingering a vellum-bound large paper Apocrypha with decorations by Stephen Gooden.

Everywhere in the house were beautiful and interesting pictures and cartoons, china and ceramics. The wall of the wide staircase was a little picture gallery in itself, where one passed drawings by Phil May and Max Beerbohm and Arthur Rackham on one's way to a Wilson Steer and—in later days—to an admirable painting of Glenalla under snow, by Archie Utin. The wide, two-flight staircase was well lit by a huge landing window, on whose ledge cats or a mischievous poltergeist had a way of setting off the burglar alarm when one tip-toed up the stairs late at night. The staircase was heated by a great radiator on the landing, alongside the bathroom door; and carpeted with a wide, lovely, pale green carpeting of the thickest pile. On this green stair-carpet, which was a Golden Wedding present from her children, I would spread long rows of 'stills' for selection when I came presently to write about films and the ballet. It was an ideal exhibition site, and Maggie, coming upstairs with a can of hot water, and unwilling to tread on the face of either Massine or Moira Shearer, would find herself turned back, as soon as she reached the landing.

In the centre of the house, sheltered from draughts, for Ernest's sake, by large screens, was the hall where, in later years, one breakfasted, lunched and often dined. From it mounted, as one descended the stairs in the morning, an agreeable aroma of hot coffee. Netta would be at the table already with a trolley beside her, occupied with the morning post, and in all likelihood another fellow-guest would be helping himself or herself to corn flakes, as one rounded the leather screen. Netta did not really want to talk at breakfast; she preferred to deal with her letters first. Her secretary would probably arrive just as we were finishing the meal, and would pass straight on into the morning-room beyond. Netta, after bequeathing you *The Times*, or perhaps the *Manchester Guardian*, would presently follow her. At the door she would pause.

"Sexton will be taking me to the P.N.E.U. office in Victoria Street at 12 o'clock, if a lift there would be of any use to you."

"No, I don't think so, thanks. I am going to stay here if I may, and read and be lazy."

"Will you be here to dinner tomorrow night? It's Friday, and my sisters and the Samuels will be coming."

"Yes, I'd like to very much, if I may."

It was the occasion of the Sabbath Eve service, and one sat down at table with a small Liberal Jewish prayer-book in each person's place. Lily read the prayers, and Netta, after the blessing of bread, would light the two candles and be the first to utter the ritual greeting, "Good Sabbath!" After that the bell would be rung, and the maids would appear with dinner, an excellent dinner, served with the best wines from Ernest's cellar.

Wine was appreciated in that household, but in strict moderation. Ernest liked his wines, and approached them with the same reverence as a Rhinelander connoisseur. But he and every member of his family drank in strict moderation. One could sense that they would all instinctively have shrunk from the libations of a Belloc or a Chesterton. The Jew tends to be abstemious. But he finds it harder to resist Nerea's curls.

Sometimes—generally in later days—prayers were read before dinner, seated round the drawing-room and overlooked by the Sargent, the Glyn Philpot, and the huge Elizabethan *petit-point*, now in the Victoria and Albert Museum. The car had been sent to fetch Lily and Marian and Miss Lewis, and it would take them back to The Red Lodge punctually at half-past nine. It was a family evening with an occasional privileged outsider present. Michael provided humor and repartee, Lord Samuel gravity and wit. I was flattered when, after one of these dinners, Michael said to me, "You know, you are the first person that I have ever known my Uncle Herbert discuss a serious philosophic question with at table."

No. 50 was at the disposal of all the causes which Netta had at heart. One of the biggest meetings held there was when Helen Keller, the blind, deaf and dumb writer, came to speak to the members of the National Council of Women. The audience overflowed through the doorways of the great drawing-room into the hall. Helen Keller spoke somewhat indistinctly, but one could follow her, and her secretary-companion interpreted for her when it was necessary. Coming into the house she passed her hands over Netta's face in order to get an idea of her hostess. Later she reached out to a branch of flowers on the table and touched them lightly "with her knowledgeable fingers."

But, despite all such comings and goings, No. 50 was primarily and emphatically a home. Even those members of the family who had left the home were continually coming and going. Sydney was in the banking firm, but he slept and spent all his spare time in the East End. Since 1918 he had been helping his friend Basil Henriques run the Bernhard Baron Boys' Club and Settlement. Henriques was a young relative of Claude Montefiore, and has been called his chief disciple. His family had been in England for generations, had contributed sons to the Army and to the Bar, but Basil, coming under Montefiore's influence in 1910, gave up all personal ambitions, went to live in the East End, and started a club for twenty-five Jewish boys (now increased to thousands), sons of foreign Jews, or of very poor people. His great desire, Lucy Cohen says, "was to infect them with a love for England and a desire to serve her, and to imbue them at the same time with the religious faith of Judaism." He married a social worker as ardent as himself, who carried on his work while he was away at the war.[29] This was the man whom Sydney would support with all his energies in the forty years that followed. Even today, in his seventies, although he is a wealthy man, he sleeps each night at the Settlement on a narrow iron bedstead.

He keeps card-index boxes containing addressed postcards to each member of the Club, past and present, greeting them on their birthday, which are posted all over the world at the appropriate time, thus forging invisible chains of friendship. One can imagine what this meant to boys serving in distant lands during the war.

Marjorie had qualified as a doctor in 1916. Then she had done war work, and, after the war, had gone to the United States to do post-graduate work in psychiatry. She then worked for a few years in mental hospitals in England, going presently to Budapest to train under Dr. Ferenczi and then qualifying as a member of the British Psycho-Analytical Society. Later she would specialize in juvenile delinquency and be a co-founder of the "Q" Camps, and the Alresford School.

Olive had married a Gentile, with Left-Wing sympathies, an action calculated to incur double disapproval. Not that I ever heard Netta or Ernest get angry about politics; their inherited liberalism forbade them doing so. In any case, Olive's marriage to Douglas Parsons was to turn out

---

29   Now Sir Basil Henriques, C.B.E., J.P.

a very happy one, and with the arrival of grandchildren the basic virtue of family affection, so strong in both Netta and Ernest, would melt away these earlier differences of outlook and restore complete concord.

Geoffrey had become something of a solitary. He had one or two close friends, but he lived at home, where he felt that his mother had need of him, and did not figure greatly in the Glenalla house-parties, any more than the recluse, Sydney. He seemed to find it hard to discover an outlet for his own very definite idealism. Sydney had an able brain; Michael had a quick brain; but both Geoffrey and Cyril had found school and university a distinct problem. Cyril with his very marked mechanical ingenuity could have become a highly successful engineer but only began to put this talent to use fairly late in life, and then in an entirely private capacity. His recordings of vocal and instrumental music are some of the best ever made. Geoffrey had left Oxford because he did not seem to be getting anywhere. In both these natures, perhaps most into Cyril's, had entered a fundamental diffidence, which may or may not have had its roots in either family competitiveness, or in their inability to live up to that tornado of energy, their own mother.

It was while recovering slowly from his Frankfurt accident that the thought came to Geoffrey one day of founding a travel agency of a different sort. Cooks' and American Express were huge, highly successful but largely impersonal organizations. What was needed was an agency that would think of clients primarily as human beings. He chose as his partner, David Gourlay, who had been a fellow-worker with him in the Friends' War Victims Relief Committee, and whose wife, Dame Janet Vaughan, is the able head of Somerville College, Oxford. Together they worked out a Fourteen Point list of objectives, with great stress upon their third point, "To study the taste of each individual, with a view to offering disinterested advice as regards hotels, routes, places of interest." The entire Franklin family had been brought up with the P.N.E.U. slogan "Children are born persons" ringing in their ears. The Wayfarers Travel Agency might well have adopted as its motto, "Travellers are Persons." Wai—helpful as ever—furnished the Agency with its name; and, after some time in the old nursery at 50 Porchester Terrace, it was soon making a modest beginning in a small room in Lily Montagu's Settlement. From there it moved to 33 Gordon Square, where it functioned for many years. Today, it is very comfortably installed in a fine old house, 20 Russell Square. It has had a number of imitators, but in 1920 it was unique in its line of approach, and it still remains one of the most human of the agencies, though it has continually enlarged the sphere of its activities ever since it was founded.

For ten years Geoffrey gave much thought and energy to this child of his brain. Then in 1930 he died. His friend Francis Birrell said of him after his death, "He was one of the most positively and even violently kind men who have ever lived. Nothing is easier than to be kind in an easy-going friendly sort of way—it is much rarer to have a demon of kindness in one's breast which will never be exorcised until some opportunity for benevolence has been unearthed." This friend writes of him jestingly, tenderly and with deep understanding; and Birrell is only one of a number of people who sang his praises in a memorial volume which was printed after his death.

From Netta, Geoffrey had inherited his fundamental idealism, and they were very close to one another. As Olive put it, he was his mother's "real friend." Despite the occasional, disregarded ragging he received at school, he had always been a cheerful person, and it had seemed at one time as though he might turn out to be the happiest of her children. Netta was in Ireland when he was first taken ill at No. 50. But her sister Lily wrote that there was nothing to worry about. Presently they recalled her. It was plain that some obscure and deadly virus was at work. Nursing him in those last days at Porchester Terrace she put down verbatim some of the things that he said, and those notes are touching in their simplicity and in their thoughtfulness for others. When his mother broke it to him that he was dying his comment was "I am not frightened—but it is a pity, a pity, such a pity!"

After his death she was to receive hundreds of letters of sympathy. In one of them was a phrase which might have been made his epitaph '... Geoffrey was always the one to do everything nobody else wanted to do.'

22

BOTH HER YOUNGER SONS were now married. Cyril had entered the family banking firm, and in 1925 had married Miriam Israels. Introduced by Dr. Stephen Wise, she had come on a visit to the 'Henrietta Arms' and intended studying art, but instead married Cyril. Her great uncle was the Dutch-Jewish artist Israels. Michael married in 1930 Irène Claire Bloch, whose father Amadée was a French Jew.

As a mother-in-law, Netta started with the best intentions. She sang the praises of Cyril's bride to her friends, told how talented she was as an artist, how deft with her fingers, how clever in the arrangement of flowers. She liked Miriam and did everything in her power to make the marriage a success within *the magic family circle.* Her diary records numerous activities with this daughter-in-law, whom Ernest used to take to sales at Sotheby's and to art exhibitions to cultivate her taste in the different schools. A house had been purchased for the young couple in Dawson Place, near to the aunts, and quite near to No. 50 itself. There Miriam painted, there she made good friends, among them Agnes de Mille, the dancer, whom she was always begging me to meet, but it was in the days before ballet had become a major pre-occupation. Orovida she did take me to see, Pissarro's granddaughter, in whose studio I saw wonderful paintings and etchings in an Eastern style, men, horses, mules, and donkeys, and where I purchased a fine etching of three galloping ponies, which decorates my staircase today. In the nineteenth century and even in some European countries today, the absorption of a daughter-in-law by the clan is an assumed fact, and the girl knows when she marries what will be expected of her. In bourgeois circles, she generally succeeds because her upbringing has not made her a rebel. But the Empress Frederick of Germany and the Empress Elizabeth of Austria are striking examples of failure in this process of family absorption. Miriam gained her mother-in-law's respect by her talent and apparent pliability. Irène had a much harder task, for her own mother, who was of cosmopolitan outlook, was persona non grata with Netta from the start. And in the long run, though for different reasons, neither of these Franklin daughters-in-law would succeed in achieving that relatively harmonious relationship which Ernest and Netta had eventually established in their own lives.

But in the early 1930s all looked hopeful. Michael discovered and purchased a charming little house on the Lower Mall at Hammersmith, facing the river and a few hundred yards from Hammersmith Bridge. There he had as neighbours A. P. Herbert and Maxwell Fry. And there he saw frequently Nigel Playfair, the actor-manager, who was bringing the Lyric Theatre into the forefront of the contemporary theatrical picture, and who remembered Michael's acting well from his Oxford days. Michael was now a director of The Wayfarers.

Michael might not be a 'spoiled priest,' like the hero of T. C. Murray's moving play *Maurice Harte*, but he was indubitably an 'actor *manqué*'. Years after his Oxford career had ended, he had only to enter a certain famous actor's dressing-room for the latter to exclaim immediately, 'Here comes the man who could have beaten us all!' Perhaps he could if he had been penniless first. But he lacked the spur of financial stringency. One can see Michael playing the part of Lear with a biblical grandeur and with unparalleled fervour, or one can see him, a music-hall comedian, bringing the house down before he has even opened his lips. What one cannot see him doing is sacrificing everything in life to the interests of an exclusive objective, and that is what acting demands of its devotees. One must be driven by an ambition that amounts almost to an obsession or else by the sharp spur of unpaid bills.

Cyril and Michael were married, and soon there would be five grandchildren to come to Glenalla at Easter and in the summer. A son was born to Miriam in 1927, another in 1929, and a third in 1933. Michael's daughter Angela and his son Peter were born in 1931 and 1935. The lives of all these grandchildren would be very greatly influenced by Netta, especially so in the case of Cyril's three boys, Roger, Joe, and Owen. Though she was on her guard against interference, suffering Roger to be sent to a kindergarten 'new school,' far removed from all P.N.E.U.'s cultural aspiration—'they teach them nothing, and they don't even interest him in stories!'—and making any suggestions with what she hoped was maximum tact, nevertheless with her temperament and with the veneration in which her sons held her, it would have been difficult for her not to be the matriarch. That she was on

TWO GRANDCHILDREN

ANGELA

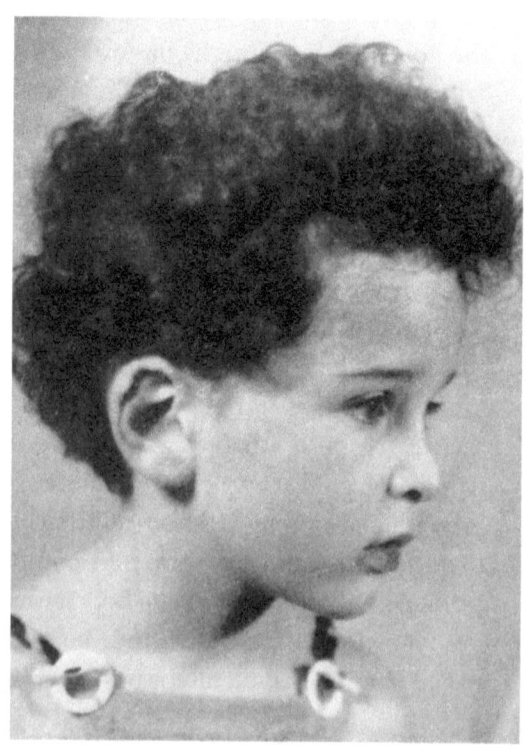

OWEN

her guard against it is unquestionable; that she was completely successful in the effort is another matter altogether.

The annals of Glenalla in the 1930s are bathed in a golden glow. Netta, Ernest, and Wai had sown, and now this new generation reaped. The huge household ran smoothly. Although they are volatile, impulsive, outspoken, and excitable, and quarrel amongst themselves in public, I have never heard a member of the Franklin family scold or be disagreeable to a servant. No one is regarded as a cipher in the household, and there is a spirit of real co-operation. Names of members of the staff are remembered long afterwards: Letty, Elsie, Annie Davis, the scullery maid; Peggy, the poultry maid; Mary Agnes; Ellen Brogan, in her beautifully starched apron, carrying baskets to the laundry; Mrs. Campbell, the Scottish cook, with a bunch of keys at her waist, who scorned the use of spoons and used to beat the butter and cream with her hands; Ethel, a niece of 'Tot,' for whom Ernest had a secret nickname, 'The Queen of the Slops,' partly derived from the fact that Glenalla, although it has four bathrooms, has no running water in any of its rooms.

>   And there's the redoubtable Ethel,
>   She's lawfully good with the slops;
>   She takes them away at the end of the day,
>   And never a particle drops.

For years the essential linchpin in the Glenalla economy was Frank, later to be succeeded by the tall, silent, utterly versatile, and ingenious George, who could turn his hand to anything from boat building to flower arrangement. Their epochs overlapped; George began as a boy in the garden at a time when Frank was still general factotum. A whole chapter might be written about Frank. His strong Northern burr suggested the Ulster Presbyterian, but he was a Catholic, and at one time intended to become a priest. He changed his mind and decided to train as a schoolteacher. Presently, however, he ran away from the training college and qualified as a master carpenter, that is to say, one who can take apprentice pupils. He came to Glenalla in 1914, after his marriage, and his daughter was born there. Soon afterwards his wife became ill and was in hospital for many years and was never able to join him again. During the First World War, Frank worked in an aircraft factory in Londonderry, which developed still further his range of accomplishment.

Frank could do anything except the thing on which he prided himself most—drive a car. On the occasion of my second Glenalla visit, he was sent with one of the cars to Letterkenny station to meet me. When I descended from a tiny, battered, unpleasantly-odoured, incredibly ancient, narrow carriage, which had started its life, proudly, as a 'First Class' in the year 1890, and which still had hanging about it—in its ornamented luggage rack and in the fringed end of its much-hacked leather window-strap—a faintly evocative flavour of the days of the Land League, and of fine gentlemen of the Protestant Ascendancy with curled moustaches, and ladies with trailing skirts and parasols, Frank was waiting for me, greeted me, and led me to the car. We drove back the seventeen miles along the twisting road to Ray, Frank talking the whole time in his broad Northern accent, swerving madly from side to side, missing farm-carts by inches, poising the car for a split second on the verge of ditches, and then swinging it back into the centre of the road, always at what might be called ironically a 'steady' fifty. Once in a while, as a concession to human cowardice, the brakes might be put on with a terrific screech, as though that in itself ought to act as a nerve-restorative to the apprehensive.

In later years, I would sit beside Michael when he touched seventy—'Relax, Monk, just relax!'—or watch Cyril put into practice his little trick, when asked to slow down by a nervous passenger, of replying, 'What? What?' while at the same time imperceptibly speeding up and then, dropping back again to his original pace, to their relief and reassurance. But at least Cyril and Michael were good drivers, and you knew that if you were killed it would be a case of a burst tyre or of somebody else's mistake. But with Frank, you knew that you were in the hands of the world's worst driver, a fact known to almost everybody except Frank himself.

Having written off two cars and become uninsurable, Frank had to be forbidden to drive at all. He loved the family, understood them, and he felt himself a very definite element in the Irish portion of their existence. Indeed, he overflowed into the English portion also; for he used to come to London for his annual holiday, and stay at No. 50, or in Michael's house at Hammersmith, generally doing a little house-decorating to help pass the time.

For Glenalla was really his whole life. He was its *deus ex machina*, capable of solving any problem, mechanical or otherwise. His favourite expression was, "Och, man dear, there's nae use in talkin'. And of course it was no use talking, since five or six Franklins were probably already doing so, all at the same time. 'Figaro here, Figaro there.' 'Frank, can you do anything about my wind-screen wiper?' 'Don't ask him now, you know he's promised to splice the top joint of that rod.' 'Frank, when you've a moment, Mrs. Franklin wants you to come to her on the terrace, she thinks something must be done about the waste pipe of the maids' bathroom.'

Then Glenalla and Glenbeg visitors' books are the measure of what these two houses have meant to their guests. The Glenbeg volume is vellum-bound and lettered by Phoebe Rennell, calligrapher, and has more room for ecstatic comment. In it the witty Ernest has permitted himself one brief and caustic gloss. Perhaps the Donegal weather had not been kind to the visiting family who had been loaned the little house; or the turf range of those days had given trouble. At any rate, a note of slight disillusion had crept into their entry. Ernest merely added, "Glenbeggars can't be Glenchoosers."

Inevitably, in the Donegal climate, weather figures preeminently in both books. Netta herself notes, "No rain for eight days. Glorious sunshine." "Chalet, except two nights." "No rain at all, not even at night." "Glorious weather." The very fact that these spells are noted as exceptional rather gives the show away, and Sir Frederick Keeble spills the beans completely:

> The miracle of Moses is surpassed,
> He smote the rock and made the water pour.
> By Netta's magic Moses is outclassed;
> She raised her staff and Ireland rained no more.

The kind of guest that Netta loved best of all was the child guest; like her niece, Judy Montagu. Judy, now a figure in society, and a friend of Princess Margaret, was a thin, rather spindly nine-year-old, with an agreeable, very intelligent face, and a great imagination. Her name appears from time to time in the visitors' book, at first in shaky block capitals, and accompanied by "Nannie" Hobbs. Sometimes our visits overlapped. She was a P.N.E.U. product, and quite early in our acquaintance she was indiscreet enough to announce to me that she was a prince. I refused to accept this claim. I vowed stoutly that her real name was Lambert Simnel, and that, like Perkin Warbeck, and other Pretenders, she would come to a bad end, unless, of course, she was lucky enough to find herself merely relegated to the kitchen with a job as scullion.

Netta's régime at Glenalla was one of benevolent autocracy. She knew what each guest liked best, but she knew also that they might not get it if the general clamour of tongues prevailed. So she was authoritarian, in so far as her very strong-willed offspring allowed her to be. At the same time, she showed considerable adjustability to the changing generations.

The different Glenalla epochs emerge quite distinctively. Nearly thirty years had passed since they drove up the avenue for the first time and a chink of the door had been opened to her by Colonel Symons' soldier servant. First, there had been the jaunting-car epoch and drives round the county with Davis. A girl from Lily's West Central Girls' Club, coming to Glenbeg, had got her travelling basket mixed with another of similar appearance on the ferry-boat. When it was eventually traced, Netta and the girl set off one afternoon to a small farmer's family up country to recover it. They reached the cottage only to discover that all of the treasured garments in the case had found new owners, the ends of the dresses had been hacked off with scissors, not even hemmed, and now the farmer's children were wearing them as they ran about on the midden. Even a much-prized dress brought for evening festivities had suffered the same barbarous treatment.

Later came the era of Wai and garden-making, which was concurrent with that of amateur theatricals and concerts at Rathmullen parochial hall. To the same epoch belongs the famous letter of protest from the older children to Ernest on the subject of his artistic taste, or rather his loyalty to an old friend.

> TO ERNEST LOUIS FRANKLIN, Justice of the Peace,
> WE, the undersigned, present a petition, that inasmuch as you pride yourself on the taste with which you have decorated your house, and in the name of Art, and for the sake of those younger members of the household who are not yet trained to choose between good and evil, and for our sakes, that you remove, on the immediate receipt of this petition, the loathsome mezzotint by Sir L. Alma-Tadema which for so long has turned our stomachs in the hall.
> We notice, with appreciation, that it has been placed conveniently, in case any person or persons perceiving same may feel overcome with nausea. But immediate withdrawal is requested by:
> Sydney Franklin (by proxy)
> Geoffrey Franklin (by proxy)
> Marjorie Franklin (by proxy)

Olive Franklin (in person)

The Glenalla of those days was still part of the Edwardian era, and that era was part of something far earlier. Netta can remember listening to an old woman keening in the churchyard just up the road on the way to Dixon's Lough. The last male owner of the house she and Ernest had bought had been a fascinating man, a great botanist and a Shakespearean scholar, and had travelled widely at one time. But in old age, a widower and lonely, he tended sometimes to drown his sorrows, and very late in life he married a second time, a quite young woman, thereby earning the frantic jealousy of his elderly housekeeper. Perhaps the housekeeper herself had loved him in her youth. At any rate, it is said that on one occasion the young wife, returning to her husband after a visit to Dublin, missed a train connection and reached Donegal so late that she stayed the night at Port Salon Hotel instead of going on to her home. The husband was in a state of frantic anxiety. This was the moment for the old housekeeper to whisper to him that his young wife had deserted him, that she would never come back, and to push the bottle across the table to console him. When the wife did return the next morning, she found him dead drunk, hardly the homecoming to soften marital asperities. And soon afterwards he died. How much of this is true, no one can say now. But what one can say is that Netta stood in the small churchyard at one side of Glenalla's trim little grey stone church and listened to the old housekeeper keening, while the young wife threw violets into the grave.

There had been the war epoch, and the post-war epoch. And now came what might be called the "Cyril-cum-Michael-cum-grandchildren" epoch. Netta had lost Geoffrey. Sydney had retired into the East End to his Settlement work with Basil Henriques, had become a J.P., and was greatly interested in his work in the Children's Court. Marjorie was busy practising, and was honorary physician to the London Clinic for Psycho-Analysis; Olive, with an Honours degree from Girton and a Social Science diploma from the London School of Economics, had been drawn into politics, loyally supporting her husband's views thereon. She had three children, Damien, Nicholas, and Diana, and was a director of Collet's bookshops. Both the sisters came to Glenalla from time to time and loved it; but it was just a brief respite from the breathlessness of other activities. Whereas to Cyril and Michael—as to Netta herself—Glenalla was an integral part of life and, from the point of view of happiness, perhaps its most important part. In the same way, it was becoming part of the lives of the two daughters-in-law, Miriam and Irène. Cyril and Michael could bring their young wives to this spot which they loved so well and introduce them to its multitudinous delights: bathing in deep, mauve-tinted seawater at Macarmish; tea on the wide beach at Kinnegar where one could find tiny, infinitesimal fan shells and still rarer necklace shells; picnics to that other, farther beach at Ballyhoorisky, long undiscovered, where numerous cowries lay, not on the surface but buried in the sand, so that Roger, when he was about twelve years old, would return with no less than a thousand, every one of them personally gathered.

In the summer, if the pressure of her own engagements made this necessary, Netta's daughters-in-law might precede her to Ireland. She would get happy letters from them. One summer Winifred, my wife, and John and Gilly joined them there, and there were picnics and fishing expeditions and bathing parties, while Miriam tried her hand at portrait-painting, including a large horizontal canvas—a nude study of a visitor who was there with her fiancé and who was asked to pose on a beach, with cowries slipping between her fingers. The picture—it is said—slightly shocked Netta when she arrived and saw it; or else it failed to establish artistic merit in her eyes. At any rate, it disappeared for several years, though it has now reappeared and is hung in one of the bathrooms, where those interested in cowries—or in comely female contours—are at liberty to study it.

Then, towards the end of July, Netta would arrive herself, and the house would fill up with guests as it had been doing at this season now for years. Michael, wearing the bright scarlet coat with green facings which his father had once sported regularly at Sandwich Golf Club, would be the life and soul of the party: capping stories with Ernest at the luncheon table, making puns, coming up late to meals from the tennis court, and helping to keep everyone entertained at the Saturday afternoon garden parties. Tradition still lingered in these; just as it lingered in the occasional Shakespeare reading in the evening; in the dispatch of visitors up Peat Hill to see the view, and in the almost daily picnic in one or other of the cars. Letty, Maggie, or George would see to it that all necessary gear was put in the boot, including the newfangled Volcano kettle, which, like all other gadgets, was the delight of Netta's heart, being supposed to need only a few broken twigs of heather or the flotsam of the last tide stuffed into its inner funnel in order to boil madly a few seconds later. It did undoubtedly boil, but it then required the courage of a Vulcan to pick it up and make the tea.

In 1930, Miriam was expecting her second baby. She stayed on at Glenalla after her husband had gone back to work in London, till the middle of September when the baby was nearly due. Netta realized that her daughter-in-law was nervous about traveling back to England alone and decided that she must go with her. The two-and-a-half-year-old Roger was to remain in Donegal with his nurse until the new baby was born, but his nurse was a martinet and seemed to lack sympathy for the child. Netta did not relish the idea of leaving Roger to her tender mercies for a moment longer than was necessary. It was a dilemma, and she solved it in her own heroic way. She traveled down with Miriam to Dublin, crossed that same night to Holyhead, and reached Euston at 5:50 the following afternoon. There Cyril met them, greeted his wife, greeted his mother, and they then made their way straight from the incoming platform across the station to the departure one, where Cyril put Netta back once more into a carriage on board the boat train, which was just about to start for Fleetwood. She crossed that night to Belfast and was in Glenalla again early the following afternoon, ready to keep a grandmotherly eye on the small boy whose mother had been forced to leave him. For someone aged sixty-five, this long double journey for the sake of a child showed considerable resolution.

The 1930s might be called the Daughter-in-law Epoch, or the Miriam Epoch, or even the Bathroom Epoch. Amateur theatricals were rather a thing of the past, but painting had come into its own and was now regarded as the most important of the arts.

An oval doorway with two sets of double doors, leaving a tiny closet-like breathing space between, connects the Glenalla drawing-room and dining-room. Over a century before, the eight panels on the drawing-room side had been decorated with a series of landscapes and seascapes, in brown tones, by the Reverend John Hunt, Dean of Derry—coastal, river, and estuary scenes in the contemporary mood of Rousseau's nature romanticism, and with the spire of Londonderry Cathedral showing in two of them. Miriam, who had considerable talent, now decided to decorate the farther pair of doors on the dining-room side which, hitherto, like all the rest of the room, had been plain white. She chose as themes various vegetarian contributions to the menu: a basket of potatoes in company with young onion thinnings; a spikily-leaved artichoke—Netta's favorite provender—a huge, flourishing green cabbage with a single stalk of red rhubarb laid beside it; and so on. She had already decorated the big yellow doors of the recessed linen cupboard on the landing upstairs with a series of typical Glenalla flowers: iris, fuchsia, japonica, and others.

But Miriam's *chefs-d'oeuvre* were her two bathrooms. To the Glenalla inhabitant, and to the Glenalla visitor, baths are almost as important as they were to the ancient Romans. Water pours into the bath in gushing torrents from the two great taps, having come not long before from the peaty hillside. Once in the white bath, it takes on a rich golden tone. To come down the passage in the morning, carrying one's towel, or to return late in the afternoon from a day's climbing or fishing and step into this warm, golden-hued liquid and lie there, still attuned to the mountainside by the mere fact that one is bathing in bog-water, is a most delightful sensation.

On the wall of one of the twin front bathrooms, Miriam depicted a long-haired ten-year-old girl in a bathing dress and with dripping tow-colored locks, riding on the back of an immense turtle. The turtle rises from behind the bath and swims upwards, and the turtle's eye is the wooden bell above the bath rim, with the white bell-push as its pupil. The other bathroom has been turned into a Gauguinesque South Sea Island scene. Michael, not to be outdone, decided to decorate one of the two remaining bathrooms and produced a rural scene, of charm and originality, with a glimpse of a great demesne through a wrought-iron gateway and with the wooden-framed shaving mirror on the wall playing the part of a window to a small thatched cottage.

23

SUMMER ENDED, Netta and Ernest would go back to London, leaving Cyril, perhaps, behind for ten days' further fishing. In London, there were friends waiting to descend upon the 'Henrietta Arms,' and all those multitudinous activities which had been continuing now for years without pause. They had not diminished. Rather, they had multiplied. A separate company, but under P.N.E.U. auspices and with capital subscribed by P.N.E.U. enthusiasts, had purchased the Philip Stott College, Overstone Park in Northamptonshire, rich in historical associations, so that, as well as well-known private schools like Burgess Hill, the Parents' Union could have a big public school for girls to which to recommend parents. It was called Overstone. Netta had been the first to have the idea and had been very much to the fore in its execution. She succeeded Dr. Costley-White as Chairman of the Governors, and in coming days, she would frequently go down to Northamptonshire to watch the classes or to speak to the girls. Its principal, Mrs. Esslemont, O.B.E., and its headmistress, Miss Wix, who had resigned a post as one of H.M. Inspectors of Schools in order to take up this position, were old friends and were often at No. 50. Overstone was quickly to justify the hopes which had been placed on it.

Other visits were to the primary schools in Gloucestershire, where H. W. Household's influence was still so strongly felt. One Whitsun, she found herself there and taken in charge by a small child on the way to school, who inquired, 'Would you like to see a wren's nest?' adding, 'We never noticed nests or birds till the new teacher came.' On Whit Monday, when the schools closed, a group of children gathered around her on a seat in the village and launched forth on their lesson preferences—the *Voyages of Ulysses*, the pictures of Fra Angelico. Herbert Samuel had said to her one day in London, 'I never hear nowadays the squabbling and screaming children that I used to in Hyde Park. I suppose that's due to P.N.E.U.?' Perhaps he *was* teasing her, but it was in large measure due to P.N.E.U. and to kindred sources of enlightenment. Some years later, she would, unconsciously, quote him at the Jubilee Celebrations of the Parents' Union

School: 'You never seem to hear children cry in the public places now. Why is that? Because people have learned to recognize the sweet reasonableness of children. They have learned that freedom is gained not by a *laissez-aller* treatment of children, which usually at the end results in such outbreaks of temper, but by a "masterly inactivity," an inactivity behind which there are principles of understanding and training. We remember the old Latin saying of Juvenal that we should show *respect* to the children—*maxima debetur puero reverentia.*' Yet, early in the 'thirties, she had already begun to throw out a warning against excessive libertarianism in relation to the child. In an article for a women's paper which she wrote then, she says: 'This very freedom on which we lay so much stress seems to be in danger of being misunderstood and of being itself responsible for much of the unhappiness of the day.

> Me this unfettered freedom tires,
> I feel the weight of chance desires.

We have ceased to make our children free inasmuch as they are enslaved to their own desires and have very often lost the self-compelling power of a well-trained will. Free to develop along their own lines, they are nominally free to choose their own lesson, though underlying this nominal freedom is very often a subtle form of influence and suggestion which is both soul-deadening and character-weakening. Punctuality, tidiness, good manners, consideration for others, which should all be the habits of a well-ordered life, are made into matters of choice and daily—yea, hourly—individual decisions. Action becomes a perpetual question of "Shall I?" or "Shall I not?" instead of a result of wise habits formed in early days, thus setting the will free to make wise decisions on important subjects. The children are made nervous and restless by this constant effort of decision, and the adolescent conforms to outward orders with either a will-less want of interest or with a senseless inner rebellion which naturally leads to constant change and discontent. One so longs to stem the restlessness of mind of so many of the delightful youth of the day. This inner restlessness shows itself by the inability to be alone, by constant talking and discussing when nothing really worthwhile is said.'

She had been in the forefront of a number of movements. But she did not believe in the divine right of novelty as such. Nor did she believe in labeling oneself with this 'ism' or that. When she spoke for the first time as

President at the Annual Council meeting of the National Council of Women, she was pressed by a journalist to define her position. She demurred to any such obligation. She was, she insisted, a human being first and foremost; whether of the 'old' or the 'new' feminism, she refused to divulge.

In the same way, on her South African tour, one of her hosts had asked her, as soon as she entered his house, 'Well, what is your particular fad?' She refused to tell him, replying, 'Everything interests me.' And it was true. Almost everything did interest her.

She returned to Burlington House six times to study the exhibition of Italian painting. She went to Paris to watch Duse act. She went to Swanwick for an Interdenominational Conference. She attended the annual dinner of the Royal Literary Fund to hear Baldwin make a speech in the course of which he asked anyone who had read Mary Webb's *Precious Bane* to hold up their hand. It was in the days before her fame, and only three persons in the room could do so; Netta was one of them. On the same occasion, Archbishop Lang announced that he had returned late the night before after witnessing a murder—the murder of a little prayer book. It had been assassinated in the House of Lords, and his distress was so great that when he got home, he had tried to steady his mind by reading Gertrude Bell's *Letters*. This disclosure delighted Gertrude Bell's stepmother, who was sitting next to Netta at the dinner. The brief entries in the diary show a wonderful balance between cultural activities, family activities, philanthropic activities, and educational activities. The last were not confined to speeches at meetings but included children's parties, treats to the theatre, and so on.

She was interested in 'everything,' but not in 'everyone.' There was that dreadful occasion at Glenalla when, after ten days, two guests happened to overhear her in an adjoining room saying something to Michael about the suitability of their departure. "Great storm and indignant letter, though I apologised," the diary records. And then, next day, "The S left. Terrible talk from I." Netta could be outspoken, even rude; but she was big enough to apologize, as on this occasion, if she felt that she was in the wrong. And for two unwelcome guests, thus insulted, there were hundreds on whom she had lavished infinite kindness and thoughtfulness. Forty or more would come to Glenalla in the course of a single summer.

One afternoon, she drove to Buckingham Palace and had tea there with Lady Elizabeth Motion, Lady-in-Waiting to Queen Mary. She had been summoned for consultation on the subject of a governess for the two little princesses, daughters of— as she was then—the Duchess of York. As it turned out, the governess eventually chosen was not Ambleside-trained, and the future Queen did not become a member of the P.U.S. But Netta had had an opportunity to preach the gospel to sympathetic ears, and some years later, when the centenary of Charlotte Mason's birth was being celebrated, the Queen would send a message to P.N.E.U. congratulating it upon its foundress and the great work which she had achieved[30].

As well as all this, there was the occasional trip abroad: to Cannes, to stay with Antoinette Campbell; to Lisbon, to establish a school for the English colony on the lines of Overstone; to Madeira, where disembarkation from the steamer down an exceedingly steep ladder into a small boat was a problem for someone with Netta's handicap; to Geneva, for a conference, where she met the explorer, Nansen. No. 50 saw the usual comings and goings. Edmond Fleg, the distinguished Jewish writer, came to stay. The Shakespeare Reading Society met there; Lillah McCarthy read, and Dunsany, its president. Marjorie's discovery, the talented Nina Milkina, gave a piano recital in the drawing-room at the age of twelve, and on another occasion, it was lent to Geoffrey's friend Dora Gordine for a reception before her first exhibition at the Leicester Galleries.

In October 1935, Netta and Ernest went to spend a weekend with Lillah and her husband in their home on Boar's Hill. They found that H.G. Wells was their fellow guest. Wells was in his seventieth year. He had given up his home, Easton Glebe, after his wife's death. "I should soon be an old man there, and I don't want to be old," he told a friend. He did not look old, any more than Netta, who was his contemporary; and he certainly did not seem old, apart from an occasional complaint about his health. In his loose, floppy, Basque beret and with his customary bow tie, he made an original and highly animated figure. He had been working hard on the film version of his "prophetic" *Things to Come* and was glad to relax in the Keebles' beautiful home. A photograph, taken by the local paper,

---

30
                                                Buckingham Palace,
                                                  November 1941

I am glad to have this opportunity of paying tribute to Charlotte Mason's work as an educationalist on the occasion of her Centenary.

Teachers owe much to her deep interest in child psychology and to the new principle in character building and mind training which she advocated. But parents owe her more. The gratitude of countless mothers in all parts of the world who have profited by her counsel will be her enduring memorial.

                                                                 Elizabeth R.

GROUP AT BOAR'S HILL
(Sir Frederick Keble, Lady Keble, Henrietta Franklin,
Baroness Budberg, H. G. Wells, Ernest Franklin)

NETTA AT HER DESK,
50 PORCHESTER TERRACE

ERNEST (AGED 90)

shows Netta wearing a short hand-woven cloak of Celtic style, and Wells leaning forward on a wooden bar midway across some stepping-stones, with Ernest, in distinctly good fettle, beside him. While at Boar's Hill, they called on Gilbert Murray, and there were poetry readings in the Keeble home in the evening.

One interesting occasion followed another, provided you knew how to simplify and fit them all in. You organized until you had things running smoothly; then, and then only, could you coast along. Netta ascribed much of her peace of mind to her domestic staff and to her secretaries. Frances Blogg had been General Secretary to the P.N.E.U., but after a time, abandoned that arduous task to take up the still more arduous one of being wife to G.K. Chesterton. But Netta's own personal secretaries were nearly always long-term enlistments. If they got married, it merely meant that Netta presently found herself dictating her letters, with a baby in a wicker basket, out on the balcony, or in a far corner of the room.

Evelyn Whyte, who was her personal secretary for fourteen years before taking over control of the P.N.E.U. head office in Victoria Street, dwells on Netta's love of service. "She is willing to lend everything she possesses—her houses, her drawing-room, garden, cars, often at great inconvenience, books, field-glasses. When she was asked if she went to King George VI's funeral, she replied with a smile, 'No, but my fur coat did!'"

Mrs. Bateman (Valerie Boon), who was with her for twenty-one years until her early death at the age of forty-six, has left on record another occasion when Netta was able to joke. She had had a morning visitor, who wished to see her alone, a lady to whom she had made a substantial loan, payment of which was long overdue. It was a considerable time before the visitor at last departed. When Mrs. Bateman returned to the room, Netta said to her, "Yes, that was." And then, with a smile, "No, of course she can't pay me, and she says that she is now so desperate that she 'will be forced to go to the Jews!'"

Her loyalty to her friends extended to their various activities. Humbert Wolfe suggested to Harold Monro's widow that she should ask me to read my own poems at one of the fortnightly winter readings over The Poetry Bookshop. Printed cards were sent out, but Mrs. Monro warned me that the audience would be "a very small one, but exceedingly select." In the event, it seemed that my own efforts and my wife's had collected about half of those present. But, well before I was due to begin, Netta, leaning on her stick, had hoisted herself slowly, step by step, up the steep and exceedingly narrow little staircase to that historic room above the bookshop where the readings were given.

Ernest had become an authority on silver, and his views on bimetallism, early in the 'thirties, had been given wide publicity in the *Financial Times*. Occasionally, he would write an article for his friend, Sidney Dark, in the *Contemporary Review*. Generally, it concerned pictures. His own taste had advanced with the years, and his walls were a tribute to the courage and soundness of his judgment. He liked much in modern art, but he refused to accept everything. In an article on "Fashions in Painting," he wrote: "The modern artist is not as insular as he was. He is influenced by the best foreign schools, but in many instances, not in too slavish a manner, so that there appears to be a better future for British painting than for a long time. I venture to think, however, that there is far too much striving after new styles. I may be wrong, but I think Cubism and many other 'isms' are only a passing phase and will die a natural death. Although I think very poorly of sentimental Victorian pictures, still they purport to represent something, generally very inadequately, but Cubism means to me nothing in 'the Heaven above, the Earth beneath, or the Waters under the Earth.'"

Fashion, it seemed to him, was both fickle and unsound; he instanced that Hogarth's delightful *Shrimp Girl* had been secured by the National Gallery for two hundred and fifty guineas at the very moment that Landseer's *Monarch of the Glen* was commanding seven thousand pounds. Greuze, once enormously popular, was now very largely forsaken.

In politics, he was temperamentally and, one suspects—despite the strong liberal tradition in his wife's family—in the polling booth, a consistent Conservative. It was never, however, a subject on which there was any need to get angry. "My father held strong views, but he always conceded that other people had the right to hold views equally strong," said Marjorie. Ernest's anger was reserved for Germany's treatment of the Jews, and occasionally he would give it violent expression in a way that Netta deprecated.

Times were worsening. One of Netta's very few diary comments upon public events occurs on 31 March 1933, when she notes, "Terrible news from Germany." Then in June, she writes, "Took German guests as far as Winchester"; in September, "Dr. Weiss arrived as refugee"; and on 3 October, "Took guests to great meeting at the Albert Hall to greet Professor Einstein, who had fled from Germany. Austen Chamberlain in the chair.

Dr. Einstein showed astonishment that all the hall rose to greet him and looked round for Royalty entering."

Always she speaks of the refugees as Germans. They were Germans just as she was English. They had come from Central Europe, and their brains, and the brains of their ancestors, had been a part of Germany's strength for centuries. The synagogue in Worms, which was burnt by the Nazis, had been built in A.D. 600.

From 1933 onwards, she was much occupied with refugee work for Hitler's victims, spending hours at Bloomsbury House, and Chairman for a time of the Special Domestic Employment Committee, since many of the refugees, who had been in professions, had, for a time, to be content to take household jobs. A doctor might find himself in the pantry, a musician blacking shoes. Schools had to be found for the children. Dr. Weiss had been Vice-President of the Berlin Police. He was forced to leave Germany, his property confiscated, his house raided by the Nazis—the German servants claiming various articles of clothing and jewelry as theirs in order to restore them secretly to Mrs. Weiss—and he was lucky to get safely to England with his wife and child. For five years, this trio were guests at Porchester Terrace. At the end of that time, Frau Weiss, after she had left the house, wrote a letter to Netta, intimate but so sincere, so moving, and revealing, that there seems justification for adding it to the record.

> Dearest Mrs. Franklin,
>
> Will you allow me to be serious for just a moment? Will you allow me to say in writing, because otherwise you would simply die, or get unpleasant by brushing it aside brusquely, that I would never have lived to see this day without you. You have—without any exception and without any fail—given me your utmost kindness, understanding, and help in all matters concerning us. Without your help—if only in this respect—I would not have recovered from this dreadful illness, at the time you rather accepted the inconvenience of having such a badly ill person in the house. And without your generous help in letting the three of us stay for five years in that beautiful house of yours—with the people you are—we would have had to live the sordid life of the average refugee.
>
> That you have been the models of tact and consideration, as how to make it easy for us to accept all you had to give, goes without saying for people like you all. And that we have, in response, been unpleasant and unresponsive to all the great kindness we received from everyone

in your family—Miss Lily, Lady Swaythling, Michael—and all your children and friends—goes also without saying, but was, which I am sure you did understand all along, only because of the hardship, unaccustomed for us, to have to accept it and to be frustrated and worried to our extent.

Keep well, dearest Mrs. Franklin, and forgive me for saying here what I felt and which, I fully realize, you will be very embarrassed to read. And all my love to you (the most wonderful person in the world) and to the family.

Lotte.

Weiss, like many another refugee, had to start life all over again in his fifties. He founded a successful printing business which, though he and Frau Weiss are both dead now, is still the property of, and managed by, his daughter, the shy, dark-eyed little girl whom I used to meet on the stairs at No. 50.

In addition to having the Weiss family living with her, Netta arranged a fortnightly evening reception at No. 50 for any of the London refugees who cared to come. At these, there were often as many as one hundred people present. Friends rediscovered one another at these gatherings, each of them with no idea that the other was in England, or, indeed, alive. And, as there were several well-known professional musicians amongst the refugees, there was no lack of entertainment. Only at one thing did Netta baulk. She could not bear to spend a whole evening hearing badly mangled English dutifully spoken all around her. And so large notices were hung up where they could be seen by everyone: HIER WIRD NUR DEUTSCH GESPROCHEN.

In a speech at Liverpool, Netta pleaded the cause of the Jew. She emphasized first his idealism and then his gift for initiative. Germany would be the loser by what she was doing. Jews had always been capable of serving the country of their adoption. Their record was good. They were neither parasitic nor anti-social. She reminded her audience of Zamenhof, who had founded the Esperanto movement, saying, "Wars and hatred are due to misunderstanding, and differences in language raise up walls of misunderstanding"; of Lubin, the modern Joseph, with his International Agricultural Institute in Rome; of Disraeli; of Rotheman, of her own brother Edwin Montagu. Jews, she said, had always realized the importance of education. They had been prominent in the foundation of Girton College and London University, and a Jew had been chairman of the Girls' Public Day Schools Trust, and of the Froebel Society.

The Froebel enthusiast was Montefiore. For years, he had been a munificent benefactor to that Society. He was now an old man. One Saturday morning when I was staying at No. 50, Netta invited me to accompany her to synagogue. After the service, she took me round to the vestry to introduce me to Montefiore, who had doffed his prayer shawl. He was old and frail, but he listened with patient attention as I told him how I had first encountered him in the pages of Von Hugel's wonderful letters. With his short beard, he looked a slightly older and more fragile version of the fine bronze bust which Benno Elkan executed of him about this time[31]. He had always been delicate; he had always had to conserve his energies, but he had kept his interest in life. In her book on him, Lucy Cohen says, of the year 1934, "On March 17th, to my surprise, he suddenly took it into his head to see the boat race. 'I had never seen the boat race before, and today I went for the first time. Michael Franklin has a house near Hammersmith Bridge, so I went there. Quite interesting for once. I would not care to see it again.'"

Montefiore was to die in 1938 before ruin overtook his world for the second time. Liberal Judaism in England was definitely his offspring, whatever he might say to the contrary. Liberal Jews are Protestants in a very real sense. In her youth, Netta had gone to hear most of the famous preachers of her day, of whatever sect, and had even attended the theosophic lectures of Annie Besant. Now, later in life, she supported the suggestion of Mrs. McArthur, a fellow member of her synagogue, that there should be a Society of Jews and Christians. The society was founded presently under the leadership of Dr. Mattuck, with wholehearted support from the Very Reverend W. R. Matthews, Dean of St. Paul's.

Netta accepts heartily her sister's definition of religion: "Religion is the binding of the soul to God, and it is expressed in the life of every man who seeks good and not evil all the days of his life. All through the ages

---

31   Benno Elkan had arrived in London as a refugee, and often visited at Netta's house, where for a long time she housed one of his seven-branched candelabra. Hitler had ordered the destruction of his tombs and monuments in Germany, erected mostly to the fallen in the First World War. In the new country of his adoption he became a most prolific sculptor, and among his achievements is a bronze candelabra with biblical figures at King's College Chapel, Cambridge, and the great bronze candelabra of the Old and New Testaments with about eighty figures erected in Westminster Abbey.

Judaism has been criticized as a legalistic religion. It is falsely believed that we consider obedience to the ceremonial law as the be-all and end-all of our religion. Liberal Jews hold that these ceremonies must be regarded as religious symbols, or as vehicles to hold ethical teaching. They are not ends in themselves but aids to right living. Judaism has morality as its basis, and only through the practice of righteousness can we fulfil the Jewish life."[32]

Lily had been the first woman to preach in a synagogue in Germany and had received the honorary degree of Doctor of Hebrew Law from the Hebrew Union College in Cincinnati. To her and to Marian, Netta had been a sort of guardian angel, modifying a little their own self-denying and strongly ascetic impulses, luring them occasionally to Glenalla, lending them her car in London, and arranging, whenever she was allowed the opportunity, "treats" for them. This cordial and devoted sisterhood was to continue into both Netta's and Marian's nineties, with Lily a year or two behind, leading to a typical incident the other day when Netta formed a plot to give Marian a special wireless and hearing-aid appliance as a ninetieth birthday present. Her intention was betrayed by mistake before ever the anniversary arrived, and Marian firmly insisted upon compounding for "a dressing-gown and some money for the completion of the building of the West Central Synagogue." At ninety, this younger sister, finding herself with a little more leisure on her hands, decided to join the Reverend John Rayner's correspondence class in theology, involving reading a number of stiff books and the periodic production of an essay.

---

[32] The Faith of a Jewish Woman by Lily H. Montagu, p. 68.

24

THE NAZI CLOUD on the horizon, once no larger than a brown shirt, was to spread across the whole European sky, and Hitler, generously publicized with ever-increasing effect by a press which, though loathing him, gave him just the notoriety that he needed, was to scream himself fanatically into power down that all-too-familiar psychological pathway of racial and political envy. National elation, as it has done on more than one occasion, took the place of extreme national chagrin. German liberalism has always been handed the baby in the moment of defeat and asked to take over responsibility until better times return. Then, when they do, it is pushed aside once more as anti-national, as soon as the fire-eaters, who vanish like mist when times are bad, think it safe to come out confidently into the open again.

War came in September and found Netta with her brood around her at Glenalla. The three or four years immediately before the war had not been particularly easy ones for her. Michael's marriage had threatened on several occasions to break down, and her anxiety on this count is reflected in her diaries. However much she might wish to see it a success, she perhaps should have realized more fully that the very closeness of the bond between her and her son, his admiration for her and at the same time his temperamental dependence upon her, were not really favourable to the success of the marriage. She could share various interests—picture exhibitions, concerts, and the like—with her other daughter-in-law, Miriam. But she had fewer points of contact with Michael's wife. Nor was the latter's role from any point of view a very easy one. "Mickirène"—a composite name invented by Michael—had always been a difficult partnership. With her conscious mind, certainly Netta wanted the marriage to succeed. That is plain from her diaries. But it would have been contrary to her nature if she had not, from time to time, given expression to momentary impatience, especially where there were so few intellectual or other links. All such expressions of impatience, in a family where remarks tend to carry and to be exhaustively debated, can do harm. Even more fatal was Michael's habit of sharing every trivial detail of his life with her.

When Mickirène went to Adelboden at Christmas, Netta sometimes went with them. There were late nights and fancy dress balls in the hotel, and the four-year-old Angela would sometimes sleep in her room on these occasions. Netta loved the privilege of putting her to bed, loved taking her for sleigh rides, or down to the rink to watch the skaters in the sun. Once the horse drawing the sleigh bolted, and Angela got a bad fright. Michael would have liked a second child, hoping for a son, but Irène was apprehensive of another confinement, not having had too easy a time with her first. When, however, another child did arrive, to everyone's delight it was the longed-for boy, and it looked as though with time and patience all might be well.

Meanwhile, Cyril's marriage, which had lasted for ten years, had foundered on a number of different rocks. He had married a talented girl of eighteen—which is too young to marry—and there had been genuine comradeship between them, and a number of happy and interesting years. But Cyril, despite his love and understanding of music, was not the ideal partner for an artist. Capable himself, in those days, of appreciating long hours alone fishing in a boat, he found it harder to concede that rather different solitude which a painter or writer needs. If he wanted the wireless on, the requirements of the contemplative artist tended to be forgotten.

Both brothers carried, perhaps as one of the results of survival in a large and highly individualistic family, a tendency to insist on their own way in trifles. But the desire to dominate—unless one has married a doormat—is fatal in marriage. Cyril, when his marriage broke up, was the wronged party, but he has always insisted that, because he was such a difficult husband in minor ways, the original blame must be his. For this, I admire him. Moreover, from the moment of his divorce, he took the line, "My children need a mother as well as a father," and by maintaining contact between them, he mitigated considerably the damage done by the divorce to his three boys. Later, Miriam married the now world-famous sculptor and painter, Nahum Gabo, finding happiness no longer in the practice of her own painting but in making a home in America for a man whose talent she revered enormously, and whom she has lived to see fully vindicated.

It was Miriam who used to call her Dutch grandmother "Ooma" (big mother), and Netta had adopted the name and become Ooma now to the younger generation. When the Jewish Fast, the Day of Atonement, came round, a time at which sins are reported, the eight-year-old Roger remarked, "I am sure you haven't much to be sorry for, good, kind Ooma." It was Roger too, who, at the age of four, had paid her the compliment which has probably given her most pleasure in her life. He was lying on the sofa in the drawing room at Glenalla for his midday rest. Netta was at her desk on the far side of the room reading to him when a small bird came and perched on the ledge of the window near her. "Shh!" she said. "Come and look at this little bird!" And then, a second later, "Oh, dear, it has flown away. It didn't like the look of me." To which Roger replied, "Yes. You have a face I love. But I don't think a bird would. It is too wrinkled."

Netta became a second mother to these three boys. She abandoned what she had looked forward to immensely, the conference of the International Council of Women in Dubrovnik, simply because she felt that they needed her. Once before, she had called off a trip to a similar conference in India. Then it was because of Ernest's vociferous protests. As time went on, she had come to mean more and more in the pattern of his life. Ernest liked people, but one felt that he really preferred them one at a time, and in a quiet armchair at his club. But Netta liked them *en masse*, or at any rate in a wide variety of species, and so the house had been filled with them for years, and Ernest had grown used to it and really survived it very well. Netta's protégés were legion. There must have been times when they seemed an infernal nuisance, but deep in his heart, I imagine, Ernest felt that Netta was right, and that, if fortune had favoured one, it was one's bounden duty to share the blessing with one's fellow creatures.

Netta's vitality and her wise planning meant much to him. Sexton, the chauffeur, was dispatched each afternoon to pick him up at the bank and take him to the Savile for his game of bridge. Later, he was collected again and brought back to Porchester Terrace for the family gatherings on Friday evenings and for all the comings and goings, from which he could retire if he wished into the privacy of his wood-panelled study, with its leather chairs and bookshelves and showcase of ceramic treasures. There, he could smoke a cigar and study the *Burlington Magazine*. But Netta was the centre of things. On one occasion, when she had been to the theatre with Michael, they went, contrary to all precedent, to have supper at a restaurant afterwards. When they returned to No. 50, they found Ernest in the porch in pyjamas and dressing gown, and in a ferment of anxiety. Netta teased him, asking if he thought that at her age she had been "picked up."

And now, after the outbreak of war, for fourteen months, these two grandparents were to enjoy a life of an almost patriarchal nature, surrounded by all their grandchildren in the house which they loved so well. It was a life shared for a good deal of the time by my wife and our two children. I had preferred to leave them at Fintragh in Donegal, where we were holidaying, rather than bring them back to England when war broke out in September. Netta, kept at Glenalla for the same reason, promptly decided on running a kind of home school for her grandchildren there and invited my wife to join her.

It was the year of "the phoney war," but happiness reigned still in that remote spot. Like the retreat from plague-stricken Florence of the characters in the *Decameron*, the household seemed to live a life apart, except that, instead of telling bawdy stories to one another, the inmates of Glenalla hastened hither and thither carrying P.N.E.U. notebooks and storybooks under their arms. There was the same feeling of retreat and safety from an inclement world; undeserved largesse in the midst of so much suffering elsewhere, but largesse which children at any rate could accept without any qualms of conscience.

Netta's reaction to being a school principal was characteristic. She was very far from dressing herself in a little brief authority. Her "school" was run on democratic and highly cooperative lines. It had for staff my wife, with an Oxford degree, Doreen Hickling and Kathleen Hipwell, both qualified Charlotte Mason College teachers. Then there was Dorothy Hurley, the ever-understanding companion of Cyril's three boys, and "Watty," nurse to Peter, Michael's small son. As well, one of the small houses on the estate held two German-Jewish refugees, a doctor and his wife, with their two children, Michael and Tania. The Franklin grandchildren, John and Gilly Gibbon, aged nine and seven, Veronica Hardy, a parson's daughter from the south of Ireland, Ian Scott, son of the Presbyterian minister at Ramelton, and Valerie Lyster-Smythe, daughter of Captain Lyster-Smythe, the land steward, who now lived at Glenbeg, made up the school roll.

There was nothing amateurish or easy-going about the timetable, which was practically the full P.U.S. programme. In the morning, the teachers could be seen scurrying about between the various rooms where lessons were given. The drawing room was used for painting classes and by Netta, both for her Latin class and for story reading and narration with the various ages. Doreen Hickling, in her bedroom over the kitchen, chosen because an explosion there would be less likely to reach the ears of Ernest, gave a "science" class to Roger and Joe. As Guy Fawkes Day approached, they made fireworks, to the great envy of John Gibbon, who considered he was old enough to risk his life. The veranda was in frequent use, and Netta's own bedroom was often a classroom too. Whenever it was possible, classes were given out of doors, and when the summer came, this was a regular occurrence. Peter's nanny, who had lived in Paris for some time, taught French, and Roger was coached in Latin by a retired clergyman in Rathmullen, whose daughter and daughter-in-law, both of whom had played tennis for Cambridge, were welcome visitors to the Glenalla hard court on Saturdays. Sometimes, all the classes would join forces for singing and would gather round the piano in the hall, that piano at which Enriqueta Crichton used to play her own accompaniments when she sang some of the great arias in the old days. Now childish trebles would offer "Green Grow the Rushes-O," and "Hoo-ray, Up She Rises," and when the singing was over, they would go in to dinner with Netta at one end and Ernest at the other of the huge, long dining room table.

Then there was the matter of exercise. Ropes and other gym apparatus had been put up in the barn. Once a week there was folk dancing, conducted by Doreen Hickling, an activity to which the maids, the schoolmistress of the local school, and some of her flock were invited. Even the three-year-old Peter joined in. There were nature walks and paper chases, with pieces of red wool tied to branches or dropped on the ground instead of desecrating newspaper—there were even occasional drives. Not long before the war, Glenalla had acquired its own tank and small petrol pump at one side of the courtyard. The pump was kept carefully locked by Frank, but the lock was filed off and the tank partially raided by ill-disposed persons later in the war. Still, for a time, and with the aid of petrol coupons from various members of the household who had cars, petrol could be found for a very special picnic or expedition.

On Saturdays, there was what might be called a non-denominational service in the drawing room. The children would sing previously chosen hymns, like "All Things Bright and Beautiful" by Mrs. Alexander, who, long years before she was the Primate of Ireland's wife, had presided in the small grey house a little up the road from the back avenue, which was then Glenalla Rectory. It had been written here in Donegal, and every word of it applied to the scenery around them:

> The purple-headed mountain,
>   The river running by,
> The sunset, and the morning
>   That brighten up the sky.
>
> The tall trees in the green wood,
>   The meadows where we play,
> The rushes by the water
>   We gather every day.
>
> *All things bright and beautiful,*
>   *All creatures great and small,*
> *All things wise and wonderful,*
>   *The Lord God made them all.*

Liberal Jewish children and Christian children alike could sing that. And on Sunday, there was another service in the little grey church up the road for Veronica, the Gibbons, Valerie Lyster-Smythe, and their adult relations, with George vigorously pump-handling the miniature organ.

Ernest became the official bard and versifier of the household. He had always loved making occasional verse. From his place at the end of the long table, he would read aloud his latest effort, scribbled on the back of an envelope or an odd scrap of paper. It was often a birthday ode. There was one even for Owen's teddy bear:—

> Dear Teddy, hip, hip, hooray,
> You are five years old today.
> But still you are hale and hearty,
> And Owen will give you a party.
> He's asking a lot of toys,
> I hope they won't make too much noise.
> Mrs. Campbell will make him a cake
> Of which all the guests will partake.
> If I may make a suggestion,
> See he don't get indigestion.

Or it might have nothing to do with a birthday at all but be just a rhyme of general appreciation:

> Roger brings me my coffee,
> Joey brings me my hat,
> Owen lights my lighter,
> And that, my friends, is that.
> Peter blows out my lighter
> And pushes the top bit down.
> If we play too much at breakfast,
> Watty begins to frown.
> John and Gilly Gibbon,
> And Angela the belle,
> Do nothing in particular
> And do it very well.[33]

Angela was indeed the belle, with her huge eyes and intelligent expression. She was a nervous child, liable to wake up in the middle of the night weeping bitterly and with perhaps a slight inferiority complex at being a mere girl among so many boys. In such a big household, unless you asserted yourself, people were inclined to regard you as a nonentity. But Angela was far from being a nonentity, and as she grew older, her character would show seriousness and genuine goodwill to those around her.

There was one theme even more in the octogenarian poet's thoughts than birthdays. This was the subject of doors and the closing of doors. It forms the footnote even to Teddy's birthday ode:

> I will just say one thing more,
> Please teach him to shut the door.

If Owen did succeed in teaching his five-year-old teddy bear to shut the door, that was about the only successful lesson on the subject ever given to anyone at Glenalla. Ernest was accustomed to wintering at No. 50, where there were warm radiators on every landing. He had always hated draughts, but now five doors, two corridors, and a staircase all abutted on the hall at Glenalla, with, at the top of the stairs, two more corridors and all their bedroom doors. In the hall by a great wood and turf fire, Ernest had his headquarters for most of the day, and as it was a thoroughfare for

---

33   A plagiarism from the peers in *Iolanthe*.

the whole household, there was abundant opening of doors and—according to him—practically no subsequent closing of them. Even nightfall did not bring him a respite. His nocturnal prowl around the upper regions of the house in pyjamas, in a state of righteous wrath, and his subsequent return in triumph to his room, exclaiming over his shoulder, "I knew there was a door open somewhere," were a feature of life at Glenalla.

It is pathetic to read the many excursions into ironic rhyme which this one theme wrung from his shivering Muse. It became an obsession with him. Since polite remonstrances and even roars had all failed, perhaps he could achieve his aim with the aid of golden numbers:

> Oh, leave the door open,
> A draught is so nice.
> Oh, do make the hall
> As frigid as ice.
>
> Ignore all the notices
> Stuck on the doors,
> Whenever it rains or
> Whenever it pours.
>
> Oh, don't close the door,
> Good folk, if you please,
> And then we can shiver,
> And then we can freeze.
>
> There are doors to the bedrooms
> And bathrooms galore,
> And these you will find
> Around the first floor.
>
> Of course, you'll catch cold,
> But that you must bear,
> So leave the doors open
> Is my most fervent prayer.

There was even a parody of "The Little Brown Jug," entitled "The Little Hall Door."

It's you who bring me all my woes,
It's you who give me my blue nose,
It's you I ever try to close,
I give it a bang, and shut it goes.

Hah, hah, hah! Hee, hee, hee!
You troublesome door,
How you bother me.

I pin up notices on the doors,
It's all in vain, I fear, because
Some of the children cannot read,
And others, who can, will give no heed.
Hah, hah, hah! Hee, hee, hee! etc.

It is not every eighty-year-old who can convert an acute annoyance into amiable light verse in the almost barren hope of alleviating it.

25

SOMEONE HAD GIVEN Ernest a present of a pedometer, and with this attached to his person, he would go for his morning or early afternoon walk and return to tell Netta exactly how much exercise he had taken. It was a pleasant life, even in winter, even with draughts. The grandchildren were charming, Owen particularly beautiful—a Raphaelesque six-year-old, with wonderful black curls and large, melting grey eyes. His skin was olive, and he might well have been from Italy or Greece; one moment he would look serious, and the next, a rather slow, mischievous smile would light up his face. Dorothy Hurley, who many years later would marry Cyril, was beloved by all three boys and made Owen her especial care. Netta had bought a large golden retriever, and 'Magnet' was already a part of the Glenalla household and a source of joy to all the children.

In the Christmas holidays, I rejoined my family, and there followed two gloriously happy weeks at Glenalla. It was a wonderful and unique Christmas, fine enough and warm enough even for tennis to be included in the day's activities. There were twenty-one of us in the house, and the eight maids—a fairly formidable household to cater for at such a time. But everything went off without the smallest hitch. Cyril and Michael—the latter soon to be wearing uniform—had come over, and Michael lent Cyril the treasured bright-red golf jacket which his father had assigned to him, so that, clad in it and with an immense white beard, Cyril could become not merely a creditable but a quite credible Father Christmas. His girth precluded the chimney. Eventually, it was settled that he should make a sudden appearance from behind a screen at the side of the drawing-room fireplace, which he did so convincingly that Peter wept in alarm. Then, having thus introduced himself, he departed through the double doors and reappeared almost immediately with a wheelbarrow full of presents. Two more wheelbarrow loads had to be brought in before everything had been safely delivered. Two days later, Glenalla gave a children's party with a play written and produced by Michael, and, the next day, Netta departed for London, taking my wife under her wing for the earlier part of her journey back to our home in Dorset, where she was to await the arrival of a third baby. Meanwhile, I took John and Gilly down to Dublin to spend the rest of their school holiday with my mother.

On the boat on his way back to England the previous October, the reticent Cyril had managed to put some of his thoughts and feelings upon paper. He had taken a party to the local village dance, a piece of democratic *camaraderie* disapproved by Captain Lyster-Smythe, and to which he was not certain his mother would take kindly. She had heard of this later and had been distressed that she was not taken into his confidence at the time. Cyril wrote frankly and with such obvious warmth of heart that his letter is worth giving as an indication of the relationship between mother and this particular son:

ON BOARD R.M.S.
SAILING FROM

ROYAL MAIL ROUTE OCT. 7TH '39.

My darling Mother,

It was a delightful week for me, and such a respite from the lonely and anxious time of waiting and doing nothing in London.

It is a great pity that I seem unable to 'purr' when we are together and that we can't have the long chats that we used to have. There seems to be a certain shyness in my make-up since Mirian left me that just shuts me up.

I do really appreciate immensely what you are doing for the children, whom we both love so much. They all seem so very happy and well-adjusted, with no atmosphere of strain of war. The arrangements and work programme are excellent, and I see your skill in organization in every item.

I was so sorry that we didn't have a nice long talk, and perhaps a walk round the garden, which is so beautiful. I wanted so much to do that this morning, but I seemed to just drift, and the time was gone. I did like being with the boys by the lake, however.

Winifred is really a good person and helps so well, and Doreen seems an excellent choice and much respected by my boys—a credit to P.N.E.U.

I am sorry about not telling you about the dancing, and I realize that you are broad-minded and understanding enough to sanction it, but I was afraid it might hurt you. Very silly of me. I hate scheming too. You are all a very happy family, and you the perfect and kindest of captains. I have seldom had such a mentally and physically helpful holiday.

I still hope the war will be very short and we will all have a happy, peaceful summer. Love and God bless you, and thank you with all my heart.

Love from Cyril

She was not far short of seventy-five, yet still the most vital person in the household. Everything started from her, and, for that matter, came back to her (like the village dance, for example!). Even in running the estate, all was planned in conjunction with her. There had been a number of stewards down the years, including Muriel Stubbs, who came as a qualified lady gardener and presently persuaded the Franklins to install a herd of small black Kerry cows—a venture which turned out most successfully and which added to the picturesqueness of the surrounding fields.

Muriel's successor as Glenalla steward was Captain Lyster-Smythe, who arrived in 1934 with his accomplished wife, Pat, and his small daughter, Valerie, and who remained until July 1940 when—although on a disablement pension from the previous war and with a silver plate in his head—the feeling that he ought to be back serving in some capacity took him away. Lyster-Smythe was an ideal man for the job. Heir to a large estate in Co. Meath, where his elderly and somewhat eccentric mother still resided, he had come partly with the idea of gaining experience in estate management. He and his wife and Valerie lived up at Glenbeg, where he installed a dynamo, which presently came to furnish electricity for Glenalla as well until the grid arrived in the district. He enlarged the garden, built a ha-ha and greenhouses, rebuilt the cow-byre, increased the size of the Kerry herd, planted twenty thousand trees, and improved and extended the amount of arable land on the estate. "Seven very busy and happy years," reads the entry in the Glenbeg Visitors' Book, when he left.

I was staying at Glenalla when Lyster-Smythe convinced Netta that the rhododendrons in front of the house ought to be drastically cut back and the ground turned into lawn, with ornamental flowering shrubs. I joined with Ernest—who was intensely conservative in outlook also—in declaring that this was desecration and sheer vandalism. Netta did not even bother to argue with us. She limped slowly around the area under discussion, agreed with Lyster-Smythe that the rhododendrons had gradually drawn much too near the house and must be driven back, and, the next morning, the assembled workers were there with axe and saw, and the shrubbery began to disappear.

They were right, and lawn and flowering shrubs, with the green forest rising behind them, now make a far more pleasing prospect from the house. But two other projects of Lyster-Smythe did not turn out quite so successfully. One was the Lyster-Smythe Avenue, unsuccessful only because, with the passage of time and a much-diminished staff of workers, it can no longer be properly looked after. It was an entirely new avenue that mounted through the woods from near the house and, after various twistings and windings, ascents and descents, returned to the real avenue at a point near the gate lodge. It would enable Netta in a wheelchair, or the children in a pony-trap, to explore the green depths of the wood, and it could be used by the estate men to bring peat down from the hill.

Meant to give Netta pleasure, in actual fact it gave her one extremely bad moment. The avenue was nearing completion when she started one afternoon on a tour of exploration in the rather elderly bath-chair, which had served her for such expeditions now for years. This was generally drawn by a donkey attached to its long, reversed, guiding handle, but on this occasion, the services of a pony had been secured. Owen was seated at her feet in the chair, and Joe walked beside her. Quite early in the expedition, a rusty screw defaulted, and the chair became detached from the pony. Netta had no means of guiding it, and it began to rush downhill uncontrolled. She ordered the five-year-old Owen to throw himself out, which he did, quickly and obediently. Shortly afterward, the chair hit a large rock, which stopped the descent, and Netta was thrown out onto her head. The pony had stood quietly by during all these catastrophic happenings. Joe, considerably alarmed at the sight of blood, went in search of help and returned with a workman. Netta then proceeded under her own steam down to the house. She had cut a gash two inches long in her scalp on a jagged point of rock and bruised the occipital bone. Dr. Boyle was summoned from Ramelton and put in three stitches, and the next day Netta was able to write in her diary, "A lovely day and sat out. Had guests to tea," and to continue with her preparations for departure to London.

The other Lyster-Smythe project, which turned out disastrously, had been planned as a great birthday surprise for Ernest. It was Lough Lyster. The Captain conceived the idea of building an earth and peat dam where the stream enters the wood, thus gathering its waters into a little lake, which could be stocked with trout, and where the younger generation could bathe in warm weather. I seem to remember hearing him explaining how the pressure of the mass of water against this great bank, constructed, as far as one could make out, simply from peat from the nearby hilltop, would, by some law of dynamics or hydraulics, or I know not what, merely press back harder than ever in the opposite direction. Anyhow, the scheme was approved, and with Ernest safely in London, the work went steadily forward. When he arrived in June, he and the new lake were introduced to one another, and the birthday present was acclaimed as a great success.

I cannot say how long exactly Lough Lyster lasted—some months certainly. Then a moment arrived in a rainy season—fortunately at 3 a.m. when everyone was in bed—when the great peat bank suddenly decided that it was time to refute all this dynamic and hydraulic nonsense. It suddenly burst asunder and liberated many hundred thousand cubic feet of water in one devastating rush. The roar, as the dam burst, woke people out of their sleep. The flood of water tore through the wood, uprooting a number of smaller trees on its way; it swept across the avenue—where if it had been daytime children might have been playing—it flooded madly across the bog garden, and then swept on down to the road, where it was still strong enough to do a certain amount of minor damage at the mill, more than a mile from where it started. And that was the end of Lough Lyster.

The Franklins get excited about trifles, but they take bigger things like this in their stride. The avenue was tidied up, and I never heard anyone reproach the Captain with this catastrophe or even refer to it in his presence. It had been a family scheme to increase general happiness, and all such schemes are sacred. Tolstoy's famous opening gambit to *Anna Karenina*, that all unhappy families are unhappy in their own peculiar fashion, whereas all happy families are happy in the same kind of way, has a large measure of truth in it. But though the Franklins share with other families this basic principle, which roots family happiness in a perpetual, surprised upsurge of mutual appreciation—so that even Michael would contend that no one makes such good tape recordings as his brother Cyril, and even Cyril would admit that Michael, when on his game, plays most formidable tennis—the Franklins have added to it a further corporate principle, which reaches out to and includes the whole circle of their friends, who are regarded as an essential element in family happiness and fully identified with it. This clearly stems from Netta in the first instance. As well as the inner family circle, bound to one another by the particularly firm bonds of Jewish cohesion, there is this other larger, outer circle, which includes friends and employees, who are made to feel that they are a definite part of the whole.

Occasions and anniversaries give family feeling its finest chances. Netta and Ernest had celebrated their Golden Wedding in 1935, and Ernest had celebrated his eightieth birthday on 16 August 1939, a little over a fortnight before war broke out. He could not be expected to versify about his own anniversary, and Michael had had to turn family bard for this occasion with a lengthy Gilbert and Sullivan imitation:

> I'm an Octogenarian Old Man
> An eighty-year young, old man,
> I *have* achieved four score,
> I *intend* to make more score,
> A very persistent old man.

There were numerous verses, covering all his different activities:

> I'm an Art benefactor old man,
> A plaster-the-wall-space old man,
> A Vyse in the Library, Nash in the Lavery,
> Keene on the stairs, old man.
> I'm a clock-golf invincible man,
> A seven-in-one old man,
> A scissors and secateurs, borrow from Netta her's
> Dead-leaf destroyer old man.

For the same occasion, getting into his poetic stride, Michael produced another song parody which covered not only the birthday celebrant, but all those in the house-party. There were verses for everyone at the table, including the Lyster-Smythes, Lord and Lady Samuel, Dorothy Hurley, and the various children.

> We take off our hats to Dorothy,
> Why do we do it? Because
> She's a habit of knowin' what's owin' to Owen,
> So give her your kind applause.

It was left to Lord Samuel to produce, on the spur of the moment, the only missing verse:

> We take off our hats to Michael,
> Why do we do it? Because
> He's the family poet, and all of us know it,
> So give him your kind applause.

The war continued. Netta noted, "A very beautiful and exceptionally cold winter, and the children had skating on the pond and tobogganing; the trees with frozen branches were exceptionally beautiful." The days slipped away, idyllic in many ways if it had not been for the thought of what was happening elsewhere. Dr. Rosenberg, playing chess in the hall, Mrs. Rosenberg taking walks in the grounds with her two little children, the fortunate exile, but with a slight look of the uprooted still in her face, these were a reminder of the far worse fate in store for one's own nearest and dearest, if Hitler came to Ireland, as many people said that he would. My wife returned from Dorset in April, bringing with her the six-week-old Penelope Anne, perhaps the youngest guest ever invited to Glenalla. Ernest made no protest against this latest affliction, welcomed the new arrival, and called to mind a song popular in his early manhood:—

> Penelope Anne, Penelope Anne,
> Must marry a highly respectable man.

Lessons were often out of doors, now that summer had come. One afternoon all the adults and children gathered in the garden to listen to the account of the Dunkirk evacuation being broadcast while—so my wife says—it actually went on. A week previously, there had been a big picnic to Ballymastoker Bay for Roger's thirteenth birthday, four car-loads of children and grown-ups, to the cove where we once found a baby seal amongst the great rounded stones at the far end of a cave, with its mother swimming anxiously up and down in the water outside.

Of that 1940 summer, Netta has written, "We did not allow the children to share our anxieties." But, after the fall of France, Cyril, like a number of other parents, began to wonder whether Canada was not indicated. The Hicksons were uprooting their school from Swanage on the now-threatened South Coast and were taking a party of children across the Atlantic to Stanstead College in the province of Quebec. Possibly it would be wise to dispatch Roger, Joe, and Owen with them. About this time, too, the bad raids on London started, and Ernest came to Netta saying that he would be quite unable to bear the anxiety if she went to England, as she was planning, for a meeting of the Ambleside Council in London. There was nothing to be done but to send off a wire canceling her plans. It was the first meeting of the Council since it had started many years before at which she had not been present; but it was some consolation to receive a cordial telegram from her fellow-members, accepting her apologies. Even in Ireland, there were P.N.E.U. duties and activities which she could undertake; for example, Speech Day at the Manor House School, where her charming and able friend, Mrs. Shelley, a frequent visitor at Glenalla, was the efficient if unconventional headmistress.

The Lyster-Smythes were leaving. They were going to do war work in England. I had been staying at Glenalla, was going down to Dublin for a visit to my mother, and was asked would I interview the various candidates who had replied to an advertisement in the *Irish Times* for a successor to the Captain. Netta would give them my mother's address, and they could call on me there. "All right, but." The "but" was a large and fairly obvious one; I did not relish the idea of choosing a candidate who might turn out to be unsuitable. In Dublin, a few days later, I gave my vote to a cheerful, alert, and quite evidently competent young lady who had been doing a job as companion-chauffeuse at Malahide. She was to come on a temporary basis for the rest of the summer.

I returned to Glenalla. The chosen candidate was to follow in a week's time. When she did so, I drove to Strabane to meet her, and, on the return journey, I did my best to outline for her the kind of household into which she was about to be plunged. "As a family, the Franklins are rather excitable. You must never mind if there are arguments at lunch. People sound rather heated, but it means nothing at all. It is all forgotten five minutes later. You are coming into a household where everyone speaks their mind. You might almost say that they think aloud. I know you will take to them greatly if you give yourself time to do so. But don't be put off by the general note of vehemence, because it means nothing. As for Mrs. Franklin, I can tell you in all honesty that she is one of the kindest people in the world. As soon as you get to know her you will realize that yourself."

All this was meant to be reassuring, and the new arrival, sitting beside me in the front of my very ancient Austin 12.8, listened to it and has, on various occasions since, laughed at the recollection, and assured me that it was most helpful. But actually, my nerve had gone. I remembered the precedent of Thomas Cromwell, who lost his head because Anne of Cleves had failed to live up to the glowing account which he had given of her to Henry VIII. And now, here I was, driving along with my Anne of Cleves, carefully selected in Dublin, seated beside me. Would my fate be the same?

It was not; for Kathleen Daly—to be known henceforth both to family and guests as Kay—came for six weeks and has remained for eighteen years. Like Cecil Lyster-Smythe, she has been one of Netta's most ardent admirers. She arrived at a difficult time, when the house was as full as it has ever been in its history; but a few weeks later it had emptied, and soon afterwards she was left in sole possession of it for nearly four years. Cyril had made up his mind; the boys had better go to Canada. Doreen Hickling would go with them. It was a blow to everyone concerned. The school, which had had one year of happy existence, dispersed. Years later, grown-up, and a textile designer in Galway, Veronica Harvey would tell Netta how she and the eight-year-old Gilly Gibbon had knelt down and prayed hard that the Canadian visas for the boys would not come, so that the school might continue.

But the visas did come, and the boys sailed on 20 September. On the 23rd, the wireless announced that the Benares had been torpedoed in the Atlantic, and eighty-three child evacuees had been drowned. It was bad news for any father with children of his own at sea, and the sensitive Cyril suffered tortures of remorse for having ever sent them. However, on the 28th, news came of their safe arrival in Canada.

Netta and Ernest remained at Glenalla until 21 October. Then they returned to England. For the first time since its inauguration in June 1914, the pale olive-green Visitors' Book went almost out of business. Between 21 October 1940 and 4 August 1945, only a single family entry is to be found in it. That entry is for Michael, who, as a Lieutenant—later Captain in the Royal Engineers—was able to get a travel permit, and was at Glenbeg from the 9th to the 18th of September in 1941. His entry reads, "Stayed at Glenbeg. Caught trout daily—a moment stolen from time—lovely and *peaceful*." As for the visitors' part of the book, there are no entries at all, except for a month's visit on the part of my family in the summer of 1941.

So ended Glenalla's brief history as a P.N.E.U. school. It had been a happy time for all concerned. Teaching her classes, reading aloud to a sick ten-year-old, touring the garden with Kay and Robert, the gardener, and holding subsequent consultations, entertaining her guests on Saturday afternoons—whenever the depleted petrol ration allowed them to visit her—the seventy-four-year-old Netta had been having just the sort of life she most enjoyed. To live amongst children is one way to remain young. A poem at the back of her Visitors' Book reminds her of that fact. It was written for her in wartime, and certainly, in her case, it is true:

> Lady, how wise in this, that, though life's day
>   Must lengthening shadows cast for all who live,
> And the best player tire of the play,
>   And even lovers lesser ardour give.
>
> Now, when regret most threatens many minds,
>   Your rooms are filled instead with present mirth,
> Laughter, and the slow speech that childhood finds
>   To voice its glad acceptance of this earth.
>
> So, though Time, overtaking, seems to gain
>   On each thing mortal in the unequal race,
> You, in light-hearted company, remain
>   With the undaunted, who press on apace,
>
> Holding your way, despite that tyrant grim,
>   With those whose eager feet would o'ertake him.

24

DESPITE THEIR AGE, and despite the fact that Ernest had no relish for air raids, neither he nor Netta ever contemplated for an instant safe retirement in neutral Donegal once the grandchildren had departed. Life for them was *family* life. Without the family, it would hardly be life at all. Besides, her sisters were continuing their social and communal work in London, and Netta wanted to be with them and help them in it.

And so, after a great struggle to obtain permits, they crossed back from Larne to Stranraer, spent a week or two at Grasmere, and thence moved down to Oxford until Beverley, a two-storey brick cottage beside Michael's home, Turkscroft, at Ifield, which he had bought a year or two before, when the war clouds were already gathering, should be ready. Thanks to Michael's foresight, Beverley Cottage had been purchased soon afterwards and was fitted out now with odd furniture from No. 50, whose real treasures had long before been moved to places of greater safety. Michael had spent the first year of the war teaching French and English at Ardingly College and producing *A Midsummer Night's Dream* in the open-air theatre where Ben Greet had produced it a generation before. He had now got a commission in the Royal Engineers and been posted as Railway Traffic Officer to Leicester. Irène was running the poultry farm which they had started just before the war, and Netta set herself to do two things: first, to learn to type, since she was going to be without a secretary, and then to learn how to pluck a fowl, so as to be of help on the farm. The diary contains frequent references: "Plucked chicken and walked." "Plucked two chickens and one duck." "Plucked. Madeleine Campbell came and went to a dance with Michael and Irène."

Netta's authoritative manner makes her awe-inspiring to most people, but at least one individual was not overawed by her. This was the temporary cook at Ifield, who, having listened to some cooking directions which she had been given one morning, remarked, "You know, you're a clever woman in some ways, but in this you're a perfect fool!" Netta was delighted. But her sister-in-law, Beatrice, when she heard the story, was a little shocked.

By using the Green Line bus as much as possible to save petrol, she was able, when the day came, to pay a surprise visit to her old friend, Ella Glover, in Holmbury St. Mary, for her Golden Wedding. Prompted by the same motive, she would walk to Ifield village and back—forty minutes each way—to leave petrol for an occasional game of bridge for Ernest in the evenings.

In April, a terrible air raid destroyed Lily's Girls' Club completely. Twenty-seven people were killed in the Club, including Miss Paynter, one of its secretaries. Two days later, Lily preached at Whitfield's Tabernacle to a congregation of five hundred. She and Marian were still living in Bayswater at the Red Lodge. It, too, was later damaged, so that before the war was over, she would have lost her synagogue, her Club, and her home.

Netta's educational activities continued. At the end of 1942, she could record that she had stayed at sixteen different places in the course of the year, speechifying and holding meetings for the P.N.E.U. From time to time, Ernest went with her, and even her young grandson, Peter. Once all three of them paid a visit to Westminster Abbey to see the great bronze candelabra recently placed there, the work of Benno Elkan, who had been so successful with his head of Montefiore. Another visit included Wilson Steer's pictures at the National Gallery, Pissarro's at the Leicester Galleries, followed by an air alert when she got back to Ifield. A few weeks later, the windows at No. 50 were all blown out in the course of a raid.

Olive's three children came to stay in Ifield from time to time. As well, Netta would have some of Dr. Barnardo's boys out to tea every week and would play games with them and read to them. But the 'doodle-bugs' had begun, their route to London took them over nearby Crawley, and Beverley became considerably less salubrious than when they first moved there. Oxford seemed preferable, and they departed thither. Cyril entertained them for a time at Headington; then followed a succession of boarding-houses. At one of these, kept by a Viennese couple, Ernest was able to get his game of bridge, but the quarrellings, disputes, and post-mortems were so violent that he soon desisted. Netta had volunteered to help in some form of munition-making under the guidance of the Hon. Eleanor Plumer, Principal of St. Hilda's, who had collected a number of wives of dons and other ladies for the purpose. Her work consisted of fitting minute objects into larger ones, and she found herself in receipt of a weekly pay packet of 12s 6d. After a few weeks, the secretary called her aside and asked her if she would mind very much not being paid, as the authorities had learned that her age was seventy-five and refused to believe that, under the circumstances, they could possibly be getting value for their money. They did not know Netta.

In August 1944, Roger arrived home from Canada, followed two months later by Joe and Owen. The war was drawing to its close. Peace came, with No. 50 badly damaged in a further air-raid, but not beyond repair, although the houses opposite had been wiped out. Netta and Ernest returned to London in April 1945 and stayed at the Cumberland Hotel while repairs and alterations were being made at Porchester Terrace. Only a limited sum could be expended, because of the regulations, so it seemed better to spend it almost exclusively downstairs. The dining-room must be sacrificed; then the space gained from it could be converted into two bedrooms and another bathroom. Upstairs, some of the visitors' rooms would have to become maids' bedrooms. Netta did not dare to let Ernest see anything until it was finished.

She and Ernest slept at No. 50 on 5 October for the first time since 1939. The following night, there was a family gathering for the Friday evening service—Sydney, Marjorie, Cyril, the three grandsons, the Red Lodge sisters. Next day, the Sabbath, was their Diamond Wedding. They went to synagogue in the morning, where Ernest was given the honour of opening the Ark. In the afternoon, they gave a big reception at No. 50 to friends and relatives. Netta began with the ancient Jewish blessings, in Hebrew, and afterwards translated:

> "Blessed art Thou, O Lord our God, Who hast kept us alive, preserved us in health, and brought us to this season:"

and followed it up with one of Wai's favourite quotations:

> "What need I more to ask of God, since He has brought me hereunto?"

Then, without a note, she went on to make a speech, ending it, to the amusement of everyone, with a few reflections on the subject of health:

"We rejoice, not at being just alive, but at being so well. You should have seen Ernest climbing up hill and down dale all day long in our Irish home and picking blackberries, a thousand at a time—he likes to count them—and I pottering about among my shrubs and flowers. I don't think I have ever missed an engagement through ill-health. I should like to impart the secret of long life to you, but it is very difficult since, as you will see in a moment, there are two secrets.

'I follow all the rules of hygiene—he none.

'I like open windows and fresh air. He likes stuffy rooms and hot baths.

'He eats meat. I don't.

'I don't take alcohol. He does.

'He smokes. I don't.

'We are both here—so you can take your choice. Perhaps it amounts to this: I don't like making an old crock of myself, and I don't let him do so either!'"

Michael, nevertheless, insists that, as the years passed, Netta had helped to keep her spouse in good trim by a modest display of what might almost be called fussing. He was reminded of his overcoat in cold weather, and of his head-gear in cold winds. Moreover, she was the rock of absolute certainty around which his whole life centred. She might still occasionally snap at him or disagree with him scornfully. But an existence in which she was not there to administer these rebukes would have been unthinkable.

To the guests who came to the house, Ernest was as much a part of No. 50 as Netta, though in less obvious ways. Her personality struck chords up the whole keyboard, but his provided a resonant bass echo, which was extremely effective. When I was a guest in the house, I used to love to come back in the late afternoon from some activity—perhaps merely a prowl round the Charing Cross Road bookshops—and to turn into the library about six o'clock. I would be met by the smell of Ernest's cigar, and would find him slumped in one of his huge leather armchairs, busily studying ancient Art Exhibition catalogues and auction lists. He had obviously discovered in this a way of making the far-distant past pay modest dividends to the present moment. Either he was reliving former thrills, experienced at Burlington House and elsewhere, or he may have been studying the vagaries of taste as reflected in sale prices. I never liked to ask. There was the heap of catalogues beside him, and from time to time he would get up and go to the cupboard below his bookshelves to search for another.

Ernest was a remarkable man. It was only because he happened to be married to a still more remarkable woman that one tended inevitably to think of him as merely part of her background. Both at Glenalla and No. 50, she was very definitely your hostess, since you knew that it was she who loved to keep open house. Ernest was your host, with his delightful and companionable manners, but he had not invited you there, and one always felt that it took Ernest about six hours to get used to any new arrival.

Anyone who wishes to meet Ernest can do so in Danny Kaye's *Me and the Colonel*. As the Jewish hero in that film, Danny, who is a Jew himself, shows all the gentle and lovable qualities that were so noticeable in Ernest. In intonation, manner, expression, whimsicality, general approach, and even appearance, he suggests Ernest to me, and this has been endorsed by my wife, who saw the film on a different occasion, and did not know what I felt about it. There is one slight difference, since Ernest, unlike the hero of the film, was quite without self-pity. He was a happy man, a lucky man; and he was still luckier in that he appreciated this fact. Nevertheless, buried deeply out of sight, he had, I suspect, not the Jew's sense of insecurity, but at least the Jew's sense of the pathos of circumstance. And it is this which Danny Kaye brings out so wonderfully and so touchingly in his magnificent playing of the part.

Ernest never talked business, but he was a force in his own business world. There is a letter from Franklin Roosevelt to his friend, Dr. Moskowitz, who had sent him on both a letter and a memorandum from Ernest on the subject of the silver market, at a time when America looked like doing some strange things with it. "China," Ernest pointed out, "thinks in terms of silver the same as most of the other countries of the world think of gold. It is my convinced opinion, and this is shared by all the great Anglo-Chinese merchants and bankers, that to raise materially the price of silver, and to fix its relation with gold, will have an effect on China that will lead to disaster. In fact, the only advantage that I could possibly see in a rise in the price of silver largely beyond that of commodities imported and exported by China, would only benefit the speculators in silver and retired Chinese merchants who wished to take a favourable opportunity of withdrawing their money from China." President Roosevelt wrote back to Dr. Moskowitz from the White House, "I am delighted to read the words of Mr. Ernest Franklin. I have heard of his great ability and knowledge—and he seems to understand our situation more clearly than most Englishmen."

Ernest belonged to the tradition of the nineteenth rather than the twentieth century. His business life was separate from his home and family life, and when at home he preferred to think of other things. Because he was a banker, that did not mean that he must sacrifice everything to banking. Thanks to transatlantic insistence on perpetual expansion and continual "pepping-up," lives have changed. The modern businessman is asked to slash himself with knives on the altar of his god, like the priests of Baal. Ernest looked at the thing from a more leisurely angle. Intelligence, integrity, and faith in God were to him all valuable business endowments. Chronic anxiety he would have regarded as a disease, and not a form of insurance. Three months before his Diamond Wedding, he had celebrated his sixtieth anniversary as a partner in Samuel Montagu & Co., and in a letter from some members of the staff—many of whom were still away on war service—he read, "Few of us have not personally experienced, at some time or other, the human kindness which has made you so dear to us all, and we wish to combine with this expression of our congratulations our grateful thanks and very best wishes for your happiness."

Proust, whose mother was Jewish, has said, "In the depth of almost every Jew there is an anti-Semite," and Cyril, smiling mischievously, once remarked to me in joke, "You know, I don't think I like Jews." But Ernest had no such latent, self-contained anti-Semitism. He loathed, Michael says, the idea of being in the least conspicuous. But, for the rest, he looked back on his forebears with pride, saw them practising a number of virtues which Christianity claimed specifically as its own, and was happy to be carrying on a tradition in which he would find so much that was good. It is surely not a crime to be intelligent, quick-witted, concerned about one's relatives and dependants, interested in the arts, and rigidly loyal to one's fellow-Jew in necessity. The Romans butchered the Jews because they found their monotheism made them utterly intractable upon one single issue—the Jew could not render even lip-service to the insignia of a deified emperor. Later, the Christians would persecute them for having crucified a fellow-Jew. Their cardinal crime, thenceforward, was merely that they were themselves, and if, coming into the world with this load of racial guilt, upon individually innocent shoulders, they developed traits that made them still more unpopular, it was their persecutors, even more than themselves, who were to blame. No Jew has ever stated the Jewish case more powerfully than Shakespeare did, or than Browning did. Where a nation—the French, for example—is quick-witted itself, it can absorb Jewish intelligence and compete with it. "The English know how to get on with the Jews," an Englishman once said to me, "because they know exactly when to tell them to stop." But, actually, a cultured Jew is not filled with any theoretical lust for power; his unpopularity far more often springs from the fact that his mind works more quickly, and that he is ready to work harder. He is never likely to be the school bully; but he is in danger of being the school buffoon, because, as Danny Kaye brings out so well, his down-to-earth realism makes him hate wasteful sacrifice or sterile gestures; and he is inclined to hide his inherited apprehensiveness under the cloak of humour.

Ernest would have said that his nationality was English, like Disraeli's, and his religion Jewish. But just as an Italian-American is Italian, and a German-American is German—and they are, in my opinion, until two or three generations of intermarriage have diluted the original mixture—so an English Jew is interesting to most of us because of his Jewishness. And yet this is largely an imaginary build-up on our part, for, very often, we only begin to notice this Jewishness after a person has, to our surprise, told us that he is a Jew. Our children, unless they are told, notice nothing.

Michael becomes a little indignant with me always when I hold forth on this question. "You have the wrong end of the stick altogether, Monk. Though your outlook is pro-Semitic, you are really heading in the same direction as the infamous Dr. Rosenberg. He liked to see us as a race apart, and so do you. But actually, Jewish blood is just as mixed as British or any other blood; if Ashkenazi, then there is an admixture of Silesian and even German; if Sephardi, of Spanish, Portuguese and Moorish. The average Jew is only about as Jewish, in a racial sense, as the average Britisher is pure Anglo-Saxon. That is why, when British, we object to being still given a special label. Our real Jewishness is a question of religion. Anti-Semitism exploits the racial idea, perhaps because, in these days, it isn't respectable to attack a man for his religion. But you can still voice prejudice against him on the score of his race. But Montefiore was proud to be English, and so are we. We are proud that our ancestors gave the Bible—or half of it—but don't care one jot or tittle for the fact that some scientist or author is Jewish unless he is a Jew by religion."

27

BACK IN LONDON after the war, Netta found her engagement calendar just as full as ever. There were daily visits to the P.N.E.U. office in Victoria Street. She had been made a member of the Advisory Council of Gordonstoun School, and Kurt Hahn, the school's founder, would often lunch at No. 50 before going on to the meeting of the Board with her. Other "educational" friends were Sir Richard Livingstone, the great Hellenist, and Vincent Massey, who later became Governor-General of Canada, and his wife. The P.N.E.U. had its own boys' preparatory school now, Desmoor, founded by Netta, and the diary records frequent meetings upon its account.

She still gave huge children's parties at No. 50. She still took her childhood friend, Rosie Elkin, now well into her eighties, for drives. She still served on countless committees. When she retired from the Council of the Liberal Jewish Synagogue in favour of her son, Michael, her colleagues presented her with five volumes of Anthony Trollope, all of them first editions. Ernest, about the same time, joined with his partners in giving a party for the staff of Samuel Montagu & Co. at the Café Royal. There were one hundred and twenty people there, and a conjuror, the discovery of Cyril, was the making of the occasion. Ernest was almost ninety, but he was still capable of enjoying life; and still in possession of all his teeth. Shortly before Christmas, 1947, he and Netta and the Samuels all migrated to Cheltenham, to the Queen's Hotel. On Christmas Eve, Ernest and Netta motored over to Gloucester to call on an old friend, Dr. Costley-White, the Dean of Gloucester and Chairman of the Executive of the P.N.E.U. for many years. He showed them round the Cathedral, and on Boxing Day he and his wife came over for lunch. On the 28th, Joe and Owen joined their grandparents, and while they attended dancing lessons, Netta invoked the aid of the philosopher Samuel to help her with The Times quiz at the hotel.

Her former pupil had, in the terminology of school reports, "gone steadily forward." As well as his distinguished political career, in the course of which he had put London's telephones underground, introduced the

Borstal system of reformatory schools, and been the first British High Commissioner in Palestine, he had won for himself recognition and regard as a thinker, writer, and philosopher, culminating, in 1959, in the reception of the Order of Merit. If Jowitt had been alive in 1937, when *Belief and Action* was published, he certainly would have approved that masterpiece of clear thinking. It was to him, as Master of Balliol, that Samuel had, years before, taken his essay on John Bunyan. Almost alone in modern times, Samuel has upheld the art of lucid philosophic statement. As a philosopher, he refuses to go one inch farther than his reasoning takes him. There he is content to stop, and to indicate the nature of the problem which remains. Einstein, when Samuel's *Essay in Physics* appeared, praised the independence of mind of its writer but maintained that all that we know is subjective, in that it is based on certain data of consciousness. Samuel argued that a certain unanimity of separate opinions was sufficient to indicate the objective existence of externals. Most of us will feel that he was right.

When he had given his lecture on "Creative Man" at the Sheldonian a few months before, Netta had driven him and Lady Samuel down to Oxford for it. Netta had lunched at the Randolph Hotel with two old friends, Daisy Turner, the widow of the Astronomer Royal, and Mary Hardcastle, now Principal of the Charlotte Mason College, and had then gone off to the Sheldonian to hear the lecture delivered to a highly distinguished audience. The pupil whom she had coached so long ago for a school holiday prize was now an honoured politician, of whom Gilbert Murray could say that his record had been governed "by an undaunted and infectious reasonableness," and a philosopher, of whom Einstein could write, "This man speaks as a doctor of the soul, as one who has a deep insight into the problems, possibilities, and goals of development of the human race."

Probably she praised him when he won the holiday prize. But I suspect that the occasion was unique. Her horror of effusiveness is so great that it may well have been the last word of praise he has ever had from her. Nevertheless, it is clear enough that she takes great pride in his achievements. In the Franklin circle, at Friday evening dinners, or, as a guest at Glenalla, where he admires the simplicity of life, describing it as "comfort without luxury," Lord Samuel is a well-disposed, slightly amused, largely passive spectator of the whirl of conversational or other activity around him. His manner at family gatherings is almost self-effacing, and he accepts their volatile excitability as philosophically as he accepts all human phenomena; reasoned acceptance being the keynote of his character.

Visits to Oxford, visits to Cheltenham, an afternoon visit to Wimbledon to watch the tennis, with her nephew, Kenneth Myer, editor of *The Writer*, to whom she had lately lent a room at No. 50 as a basement flat; a picnic in Regent's Park with Rosie Elkin; a Press Conference to publicize the P.U.S. jubilee; there was no lack of activity to fill Netta's days. But a serious blow now threatened. The London County Council had taken possession of all the lower, bombed portion of Porchester Terrace, and were going to build giant flats. And, although No. 50 was intact, they wanted possession of this site also, in order to make it part of a huge school playground. Netta had to appear before the Appeal Tribunal in Paddington Town Hall. I was present on that occasion. She had an excellent Scottish barrister, who conducted her examination with great effect, and she gave her own testimony clearly and forcibly, telling that she would like to save the house, and that she had always hoped to end her days there, and then to present it to Paddington as a Civic Centre. Her sister Ethel, who had married Henry D'Arcy Hart in 1893, was dying at this moment, and Netta had to divide her time between the hospital where her sister lay, and the public inquiry. Next morning, she had to return to the Town Hall; and, that afternoon, Ethel died. The L.C.C. Commission announced that they would give sympathetic consideration to the plea for No. 50.

The Parents' Union School needed a new Director. Elsie Kitching, the devoted 'Kit-Kit' of Charlotte Mason's letters, was retiring. She had served the Movement faithfully for many years. Netta travelled to Windermere for the appointment of her successor, Elizabeth Molyneux, an appointment which rejoiced her heart, and for which she had pleaded eloquently. An ex-pupil, she had had her own school in Golders Green, and had left it to do national service as a commissioned officer in the A.T.S. Now she returned to Ambleside and was to do admirable work there, and to produce the impressive P.U.S. Diamond Jubilee magazine when the jubilee of the school arrived in 1951. Everyone liked her, 'not only so able and active, but in every aspect of her personality so nobly good,' as Dr. Costley-White put it; but her work would be cut short a few years later by early death at the age of fifty-one.

Overstone Girls' Public School, which Netta founded as a memorial to Charlotte Mason, was well established by now, and Desmoor, the Boys'

Preparatory School, was forging ahead. There are frequent references to it in the diary, meetings of the Board of Governors, or visits to the school itself. Cyril's two boys had gone to Bryanston School. They attended the services in the school chapel, but were kept in touch with their own faith by Rabbi Mattuck's Correspondence Course. Owen had recently had his Jewish Confirmation, and had written a prayer for the occasion and sent it 'To Ooma with much love.' In it he refers to the Jew's mission in the world. 'We realise that it is our duty as confirmees to strive to carry out this mission. Because of the selfishness and greed of men, the world is at the moment in a state of chaos, and we ask Thee, O God, to help us to overcome these vices, and to become just and good. It would be easier to steer away from all hardship and to lead a protected and shallow life, doing no harm, but no particular good. We beseech Thee, O Lord, to help us to resist this temptation and to lead active and good lives in Thy service.'

Already at the age of six, in the days of the Glenalla school, he had decided what his own form of service would be—doctoring. The diary is full of references to him and to his brothers. 'Heard that Owen had passed his School Certificate with six credits, Angela also.' 'Roger had pneumonia at Cambridge.' 'The family climbed Errigal. Magnet fell over the cliff at Horn Head. Roger pulled him up.' 'Owen sprained his ankle at Ganemore.' 'The boys went to Horn Head and saw a snow-bunting.'

28

FOR GLENALLA AND DONEGAL and all the delights of Donegal were back once more in the picture. For five years, Glenalla had been left to the care of Miss Daly, with Frank, Robert, the head gardener, and the other loyal members of the staff to help her. Kay gives an amusing account of her suzerainty in those days, taking the roll-call on Saturday for wages, checking up on the activities of the half-dozen on an estate where legend said in the previous century forty had worked. 'What were you doing, Bigley?' 'Clanin' the shuck, miss.' 'I beg your pardon?' 'Clanin' the shuck.' Robert explains that this means clearing out the ditch at the side of the road. 'McNutt?' 'Here, miss.' 'Where were you?' 'Away with a cow.' 'One of your own?' 'One of Mrs. Franklin's, miss.' 'What made you take the cow away?' Deathly pause. 'Did you go to the fair?' No answer. Kay suddenly realizes, from the embarrassed faces around her, that modesty forbids any of them explaining to her that McNutt has been 'away with a cow' in order to take it to the bull. For a long time, the herd had had its own bull, but it had attacked Joe, the cowman, damaged him rather badly, and Netta had refused to run further risk with children about.

For five years, Kay, the versatile Frank, the faithful Robert, Joe, Danny, George, and the other employees had run the estate. Robert had been still a boy when the Franklin family first came, nearly thirty-two years before. Helen Webb had been his first instructress, supervising all he did, and he had proved an apt pupil. The new shrubbery, made in 1939, and planted mostly with rhododendrons sent over by Rose, Lord Swaythling's gardener, is called 'The Robert Shrubbery' in memory of him. At the end of each summer, Netta always left detailed gardening instructions, or she might write from London, as fully as if she carried a complete plan or panorama of the garden in her brain. 'Put rhododendrons now in pot in peach-house into new ground near Dirty Lane hedge.' 'Plant Montbretia in bed back of old greenhouse and divide and spread.' 'Replace Lily-of-the-Valley in Glenbeg steps shrubbery and near Buddleia already planted.' 'Remove Buddleia from dahlia bed near pergola.' 'In winter cover with bracken all rhododendron roots.' 'Take out Spanish Bluebells from rockery and herbaceous border, and put all over new shrubbery.' 'Take up Flea-bane erigeron. Increase Tangerine Poppy.' And so on for pages.

He had been head gardener for some time before the war, and two letters, written by him during the war, from the Mill House where he lived, give some idea of his devotion to his work and to the place.

> Dear Madam,
>
> I am so sorry I have been so long in writing to you. I meant to write long ago and tell you all about the garden. Well, everything looks very promising, the crops in the kitchen are very good, all the fruit very good, only strawberries ripe so far. It's a great pity we cannot send some to you. I am afraid it takes too long in the journey and would be useless. The herbaceous borders are just a blaze of colour at present, with poppies, lupins, and peonies. Also, the roses have started to bloom and look very healthy. The roses on the arch have been in bloom for some time. The red rose on Petrol Wall very good this year; also Lady Waterlow on Kitchen Wall, also Drawing-room Wall. The rose in box on terrace very good; also on porch at front door. The rhododendrons have been very good. Five that came from Lord Swaythling down in Road Garden have been in bloom. The blue poppies have done better this year. The roses are doing well in the bed where the poppies were. I re-made the whole bed and put in new soil.

There follows detailed information about the Rock Garden and the shrubbery. Then:—

> I cleared all the old ferns from around the fir tree behind the fuchsias in the shrubbery and planted some hydrangea. One of the Abutilon cuttings that I brought back from Glen Veigh has been in flower. The bog garden looks very charming just now with all the yellow primula, and Iris and Spiraea and white Lupins. The polyanthus were a mass of bloom everywhere, also wallflowers. I have planted dahlia along Petrol Wall, box on terrace, along Rose pergola, and herbaceous border. Mixed flowers in old Californian bed, the same as last year. The Ceanothus inside old greenhouse was a whole mass of bloom. The red Tropaeolum looks charming now. The Solanum on Petrol House and apple loft wall are very full of bloom now. All the Clematis have done very well this year, the Montania and Rhodo, very full of bloom, Nellie Moser, Lasurstern on the wall very good. The clematis

I moved from the old greenhouse to terrace steps has done well. The clematis on Petrol Wall, also rose pergola, Kitchen wall near terrace, very good. The wild hyacinths from herbaceous borders have done very well in Road shrubbery although there are still a few left in the border. I must lift this autumn.

This continues for another two pages, every sentence reflecting his intense interest in each detail of the garden that 'Wai' and Netta had taught him to tend with such care. The second letter is dated 14 March 1945:

Dear Madam,
   Some time ago I meant to write, but now I am sorry to say my letter won't be too cheerful.
   I cut the high hedge around the kitchen garden; it will help to let more air and sunshine in. The wire was all broken down, and the posts were all rotten. So I had oak posts sawn at the mill; they will last much longer. I creosoted the posts and repaired the wire that was all broken down.
   I made a complete new strawberry bed in the autumn; the strawberries did very badly last year. I hope we will have a better crop this year. I overhauled the maize[34] or Puzzle Garden; it looks very well now. From the entrance of the maze to the gate at roadside shrubbery, I planted a row of laburnum on each side of the path, so that in a few years they would arch over and make a Laburnum Walk.
   I am sorry to say the frost has done a terrible lot of damage. I am afraid the palm tree growing at the corner of the drive, also the other one near the old greenhouse, may have been killed. They may recover, I hope so. About twelve Eucalyptus trees have been killed; they had grown to a height of about 12 or 15 feet. (All the Veronicas also, but they will start from the base of the stem.)
   All the rambler and climbing roses suffered very badly, especially those grown on the wire at bog garden, tennis court, and pergola at Lane. Benthemea, fragfera, lithospernum, Euphorbia marginata, red-hot poker, cystus Datterandu, Indigofera, Paulownia, Scabious in bog garden: these plants have all suffered and may recover when growth starts now in the spring. I hope this war will soon be over and you will be over.
   The tennis court would need some top dressing to put it in proper order for the summer. About two years ago I could have got some

---

34   The original letter used the word 'maize', which was likely intended to be 'maze'.

at 3/- per ton; I must find out if I can still get some, about 10 tons or perhaps less would do.

I hope all are well, Mr. Franklin, Master Roger, Joe and Owen, Mr. Michael and family, also Mr. Cyril. We are all looking forward to seeing you all during the summer or perhaps at Easter.

I remain your obedient servant,
Robert.

Sometimes an individual's whole future would appear to have hung on quite a slender thread of circumstance. When the Franklins took over Glenbeg, it had no drainage and was served only by an outside earth closet. Girton College, when it opened, was the same. Victor Hugo and many others had waxed eloquent on the subject of the value of human waste as manure, and Netta put one of the farm men in charge of the Glenbeg bucket and instructed him to bury its contents on the land. When he died, however, all the other men on the estate refused to take on the job. It looked as if a critical labour situation had arisen in what was normally an abode of peace and harmony. Michael, who was about fourteen at the time, resolved it. He took Frank for a row on the lake and said to him, "You are very fond of my mother, and here is an opportunity to help her. Will you empty the earth-closet for a little while? If you, who are the head man, do it, nobody else will refuse?" Frank never lacked for courage, and he agreed immediately.

Soon afterwards, Netta needed a gardener's boy and selected Robert Alcorn out of a number of applicants. She already knew him by sight, for she had a library for the village children who used to come and borrow books after Mass and Church on Sundays, and she had noticed his quickness and intelligence. She engaged him now and told him that one of his duties would be to empty the earth closet. "Next day his mother came to see me and told me that he could not come, as, if he did, he would be laughed at by all the others and told he was only engaged for this purpose." Netta told her that she must act as she saw fit, but that if Frank did not mind doing the earth closet, nobody else ought to mind. She then added, "It would be a pity if your boy did not come; one day he might become head gardener." Mrs. Alcorn thought it over and consented, and years later the prediction was fulfilled. Robert was about nineteen when Netta sent him for a year to be trained as a gardener at Lord Swaythling's house under Mr. Rose. He was very much liked and thought very intelligent.

Frank was still alive to welcome them when they returned in 1945. He was still there when they came back in '46, but he had only another year to live. He had been poorly for some weeks with heart trouble, and Netta had offered to pay his expenses in any nursing home, but he implored Kay Daly, "Give me a bed down in the cellar, but let me die at Glenalla." Actually, he was given a room on the first floor, and his daughter, who had trained as a hospital nurse at the South London Hospital and was now working outside Derry, was invited to Glenalla to nurse him. Netta tells the story of his death thus: "On August Bank Holiday in 1946, when we were all at Glenalla, Frank persuaded his daughter to join the rest of the house staff and go to see the regatta at Rathmullen. Owen played patience with him that evening while they were away, and Dorothy (Hurley) went down to fetch his little supper and found him dead in his chair on her return. It was a great shock to Dorothy, and a terrible shock to his daughter when she came back at ten to find that his death had occurred in her absence. It was difficult to impress upon her that she could not have helped her father even if she had been there."

Robert had not lived to see his mistress's return in July of the previous year. The circumstances of his death were tragic. As early as 1943, he had developed skin trouble, which the doctors feared was of cancerous nature, and he was sent down to Dublin to the Skin Hospital in Hume Street. I was in Dublin at the time, and Netta wrote to me asking me to visit him. I did so, and we conversed shyly about Glenalla, and the happy days which each of us had known there. Robert seemed very cheerful, and soon afterwards the hospital discharged him. But about this very time his wife, Maggie, was writing to Netta in London:

MILL HOUSE,
GLENALLA.
28th December, 1943.

Dear Madam,
    I cannot find words to express my deep and heartfelt gratitude to you for what you are doing for my dear husband.
    So far, I have been able to hide from him the seriousness of his trouble. He left me in the best of form and was so cheerful about his return, that it is most trying for me to keep up the deception.
    I shall not discuss him with anyone outside my own family.

It must be a great source of comfort to my husband to know that he is so highly appreciated by his employers, and both he and I will always feel that our debt of gratitude will never be repaid.

I don't know if Robert has written to you, but he is well pleased with the hospital and the treatment he is getting. The doctors started the treatment on Monday, the 20th.

Thanking you again for your sympathetic letter.

I remain, Yours respectfully,

Maggie Alcorn.

Robert was given only a few weeks to live, but actually, he lived and worked for another whole year. A local healer or herbalist took over his cure, and we heard that he had worked wonders. But presently, the disease, which was sarcoma, gripped him again, and he died in July 1945, only four months after writing that second letter about the garden. He was only thirty-nine; nevertheless, he had been in Netta's employment for twenty-seven years. Maggie, whose services at the house had been part-time before, now became an indispensable adjunct of Netta's later years.

29

GLENALLA HAD BEEN PRIMITIVE in many ways when they took it over. The house was lit in those early days by oil lamps. Then, at much expense, Ernest had installed a petrol and air-gas plant, which necessitated hand-winding a cable with great weights on it up to roof level, at frequent intervals, to provide the pressure. Frank had been kept busy, and when the gas plant died of old age and disrepair, he was not sorry. Glenalla reverted to oil lamps; but this time, they were Aladdin mantle lamps or Tilly lamps, known familiarly as Roaring Willies. Then, a special electric light plant was instituted. Three Scottish youths arrived from Dublin and spent four months "sleeping all the morning, and fishing all the afternoon," ostensibly there to wire the house, cow-byres, laundry, out-offices, and so on, for electricity. Glenbeg was included, and the engine was put up there where Captain Lyster-Smythe could keep an eye on it. When the national grid arrived, the engine was brought down to the farm on sleds from Glenbeg and mounted in the open turf shed to turn the circular saw, which later was responsible for the death of Robert's brother, the devoted and heroic George.

Maintaining her Irish home had doubled all of Netta's problems of organization; but then, she liked organizations. And the whole of life would have been different if they had never discovered Glenalla.

Its history is a long, gradually unfolding saga of persons, plans, and projects achieved. The place has a special significance for each individual who comes there. Its significance, for example, to Gillian, Kenneth's pretty, thirteen-year-old daughter, is all summed up in those few words squeezed into the address column of the Visitors' Book: "Rode Bess, swam, played tennis. Adored Magnet, sweetest, kindest, nicest, best-trained dog I have ever met." And Gillian is only one of hundreds. One day, Netta took it into her head to reckon up the entries in this book, given to her by Sydney years before. There were nearly five hundred of them, apart from those made by Netta and Ernest themselves, and their nineteen direct descendants. And every entry, it could be fairly said, had meant some happiness, at some time, to someone.

Glenbeg is equally stocked with individual memories, most of them going back to Wai's day. Recent years have made the Gibbon family more Glenbeg-conscious, for it is there that they generally now make their eight-fold arrival. There is a happy coming and going all day, up and down the steep steps between the laurels. The octagonal tower, with its two rather clumsy one-storey wings, stands in the open gap amidst the trees. Behind it are the two grey cottages known as the Mill Houses, and the poultry runs. Geese chortle. White Aylesbury ducks quack loudly, or hang in silence at its back door. Glenalla itself is only one hundred and fifty yards away, although there are four different ways of getting to it.

Each of the two lower of Glenbeg's three storeys is a single octagonal sitting room. Over the brick fireplace are painted the Latin words: NUNC MEA MOX HUIUS SED POSTEA NESCIO CUIUS[35]. Over the fireplace in the room below are these two lines:

> "This tent is mine, said Yussouf, but no more mine
> Than it is God's; come in, and be at rest."

Wai had chosen them to go there, but the Franklin family had forgotten their origin until I introduced them recently to James Russell Lowell's fine poem from which they come: A stranger, fleeing from his enemies in the desert, takes refuge in Yussouf's tent. Yussouf entertains the outcast, rouses him before dawn, gives him gold, and has his swiftest horse saddled for him on which to continue his flight. This is too much for the conscience of the fugitive:

> That inward light the stranger's face made grand
>   Which shines from all self-conquest; kneeling low
> He bowed his forehead upon Yussouf's hand,
>   Sobbing, "O Sheik, I cannot leave thee so;
> I will repay thee: all this thou hast done
>   Unto that Ibrahim who slew thy son!"
>
> "Take thrice the gold," said Yussouf, "for with thee
>   Into the desert, never to return,

---

35   Mine today; yours tomorrow; the day after, who knows whose?

My one black thought shall ride away from me;
   First-born, for whom by day and night I yearn,
Balanced and just are all of God's decrees;
   Thou art avenged, my first-born, sleep in peace!"

It is part of the atmosphere, both of the big house itself and of this smaller tower, that in them one feels oneself in a setting where poetry, moral earnestness, and the idealism of an earlier generation are still exercising a strong, unseen influence. Netta is still on the scene, and Wai's ghost is not far off. And, together, they sustain the old values; just as the words above the blazing wood-fire suggest other days. It is consoling to stay in a house where poetry is still of prime importance; and where it is still read aloud. Admittedly, the initiative today always comes from Netta herself. It was her generation and Wai's that regarded it as the very breath and substance of life, and it is she who suggests—tentatively—that we might care to gather together in the drawing-room after lunch or dinner, to read a poem of our own choosing aloud. When the moment comes, she may read Christina's Goblin Market, or another poem, which seems to be her own special preserve, and which is not nearly widely enough known—George Eliot's Stradivarius—as telling as anything in Browning, and of similar substance. Her voice rings out clearly, and every dramatic inflection is effective. And the long white book-shelf in the drawing-room, reserved exclusively for poets, is another indication of the esteem in which the Muse has always been held, as are various additions to the bookshelves up at Glenbeg.

Glenbeg used to be concealed in the wood, but Michael has done some cutting, given it air, and opened up a magnificent vista out towards the gleaming silver ribbon of Lough Swilly, and the low, misty hills behind. At Glenbeg, one lives amongst trees and shrubs: beech, ash, sycamore, oak, eucalyptus, rhododendron, laurel, flowering currant, rowanberry, mountain-ash, creeping juniper, the slim-stemmed, feathery, Corot-loved birch, and innumerable firs and pines. Of all these, the umbrella, or Asiatic pine, clean-smelling, and with its sometimes grotesquely interwoven, salmon-pink branches standing out, glowing against an evening sky, is perhaps my own favourite; it is, for one visitor at least, the most welcome sight of all. Not even the trunks of the grey-stemmed and graceful beeches, black against a harvest moon, can oust it from favour. But everywhere there is greenery of some kind, graceful in its own peculiar way. Around the single pine, on the patch of grass where one turns to come up to Glenbeg, a mauve clematis has twined itself; it has enwreathed the lower portion of the trunk, and reached the first branches. Below the tree and between it, a great clump of giant bamboos is springing, and small purple autumn crocuses are growing. In the woods, the rocks are quilted with cushions of vivid green moss, the older elms have light jackets of olive-green lichen, the foot sinks in deep brown leaf-mould, there are ferns, and the long winding tendrils of young rhododendrons are woven into a complicated barrier.

From the big house, one looks across the cornfield to a sea of trees, a great green amphitheatre, with an occasional giant fir thrusting its top for a few feet above this general greenery. Some years ago, a violent storm brought down two hundred trees in a single night, and Kay telephoned to London for Cyril to come over and help her to face this scene of desolation. The great beech on the lawn received its *coup de grâce* then. It had had a reprieve a quarter of a century before, for in 1925, when Freddie and Lillah Keeble came to stay, Freddie insisted that this huge tree, which stood at the side of the house, just below Wai's rock-garden, ought to be cut down. He said that it robbed the bedrooms of light—it was twenty yards away or more, but a very big tree—and that it not only cut off the view down to the water-garden and the herbaceous border, but made it impossible to get the distant glimpse of Lough Swilly. As a horticultural expert at Oxford, he had spent his life deciding that certain trees should be planted, and certain others cut down. 'I know what I am saying.'

To Michael, this had seemed nothing less than assassination. After the Keebles were gone, Dr. Webb arrived, and Michael's first words to her had been, 'You are not going to let them cut down the beech tree, are you, Wai?' Her answer was, 'One never cuts trees down by the trunk: one starts by removing the big, sweeping, lower branches, to see what that will do.' And Wai had been right. Certain branches were cut, and this gave all the desired improvements; the view was opened up, and the big beech had been saved for another twenty-five years of life.

There had been another strange alteration of attitude towards the giant Araucaria. It stood on the front avenue just by the turn up to Glenbeg, and Netta greatly disliked it, only holding her hand because it was said to be the tallest tree in Donegal. Once she and a guest, Miss White, Principal of Alexandra College, Dublin, were walking up from the bog-garden together, both of them voicing their dislike of this poor Araucaria[36], when Miss

---

36   Monkey-puzzle.

White suddenly remarked, 'Don't distress yourself. Look at all the brown at the top. It is evidently dying. You won't be worried by it much longer.'

They drew nearer, and then they suddenly discovered that what they had been looking at was a wealth of huge brown cones. Miss White immediately became greatly excited. It is most rare for the tree to fruit in this climate. The despised Araucaria suddenly became an object of deep and widespread respect. It was photographed, and pictures of it appeared in the Irish gardening papers. Later it died, having first ensured an offspring to take its place.

Glenalla is full of memories like this. Tolstoy was right: happy families *are* happy in the same way: they find their happiness in little things, in quite little jokes. Coming down early, Michael discovers one of Netta's guests already pacing the lawn: 'How nice to see you down and out before breakfast'—followed by a roar of cheerful laughter. Later in the day, listening to the radio in the drawing-room, Netta says to him, 'You know, I'm really beginning to enjoy the Radio Doctor[37] more than I do Mrs. Dale's Diary.' 'Oh, I see, a case of up Hill and down Dale?' Ernest found a similar happiness in joking, watching his grandchildren, chaffing them, and versifying for and about them. Their private laureate produced what was almost a daily Peacock Pie, based upon actual happenings —

> Look at this huge potato!
> Isn't it immense?
> To grow to this enormous size
> Don't seem like common sense.
> I weighed it in the kitchen
> And as sure as I'm alive
> It turned the snow-white scales
> At over one pound five.
> There may be bigger taters,
> One hears such funny stuff,
> But, sure as eggs is eggs,
> This one is big enough.

Ernest's verses were a sort of barometrical indication of inner exuberance.

---

[37] Dr. Charles Hill.

He could get relish, even out of the occasional vicissitude. What he particularly liked to do was to record any incident that seemed likely to strike a child's imagination:

> When the enterprising corncrake starts a-craking,
> It makes our dear old Magnet start to bark.
> Then all the sleepers find themselves awaking.
> That's a nuisance, I would venture to remark.
>
> When the sanguine Michael Franklin goes a-fishing,
> He remains on Fern till very, very late.
> That he'll catch a lot, we all of us start wishing,
> But he doesn't, I regret to have to state.
>
> It's not his fault, for this I think's the reason,
> The weather now is very much too fine,
> The water's also far too low this season,
> And the canny fish can see his fly and line.
>
> One day when fish were honestly not rising,
> To the island Michael venturesomely paddled,
> And forthwith collected sixty-something gulls' eggs,
> Alas! he found out, later, they were addled.

The days seemed immeasurably remote since he had stormed and shouted at Netta that they should never have got married, and she had burst into tears. Equally remote, almost, were those other days when, to an onlooker, her own manner to him, in her late fifties, had sometimes seemed so crushing. The best way of finding happiness was to try to create it for others, and both she and Ernest had tried hard; for their children, for their grandchildren, and for their many friends. Now they were reaping the reward of their loyalty and steadfastness.

30

ERNEST WAS DUE TO CELEBRATE his ninetieth birthday at Glenalla on 16 August 1949. Netta and he were in Donegal in April with Cyril's boys, and again in June. On 4 July, Netta flew back to England, leaving Ernest in Kay's charge. Ten days later, he was writing to her in his rather frail, fine handwriting, made frailer by the use of a ball pen.

Glenalla,
Ray, Co. Donegal.
13th and 14th July, 1949.

Dearest Netta,

It is 6.30 and I shall continue this letter tomorrow. General Bush and Mrs. B. came to tea, and we had very nice talks with them. We are to go there soon. Mrs. Perry sends her love to you.

After some comment on the weather, and having recorded his disappointment at the non-arrival of his Times, which, however, had safely arrived before he posted his letter, he concluded with a list of his engagements:

15th. Tea at Bunlin
16th. Bridge, Gen. Cadell, Ramelton
17th. Bridge here with Dr. Boyle
18th. Bridge, Fullerton
21st. Chatelaine returns.

It is pretty cold today.
    Much love,
               Ernest.

Stuart is selling at Christie's the rest of your father's collection.

General Bush was another young fellow of ninety, living in a fine old house under the shelter of the hill at Kinnegar beach, owner of a good classical library, and still driving an incredibly antiquated Baby Austin. "Ought one to drive at that age?" people used to ask nervously, but the question never seemed to occur to General Bush himself. And his wife—a charming, gentle creature, who had once seen fairies, three feet high and wearing old-fashioned tailcoats, dancing a quadrille on Kinnegar beach—would never have dreamed of putting the question to her fine, upstanding, and still military-looking husband.

A few days later, a verse epistle followed. In a long poem on the various occupations of the different members of the household at Glenalla during the first year of the war, when the school was first in being, Ernest had written:

> What is everyone doing
>   This beautiful summer day?
> Robert is weeding the footpaths,
>   Four men are tossing the hay.
>
> Doreen is mowing the lawns,
>   And at intervals teaching the brats,
> Magnet is following Roger,
>   When he isn't chasing the cats.
>
> *I* am rooting up groundsel,
>   A quite unlimited task,
> "Where do they all of them spring from?"
>   I not infrequently ask.

But a curb had evidently now been put on that activity, and the groundsel was taking advantage of the fact:

> I don't know when you'll get this letter,
> The Sunday posts are queer, dear Netta.
> There's nothing much to write about,
> The weather's fine so I go out.
> I cut dead roses and faded lupin,
> These don't necessitate much stoopin'.
> One thing I very much bewail,
> I cannot find a slug or snail.
> I must not stoop—the doctor's orders,
> So groundsel thrives on all the borders!!

Ernest had noted hopefully 21 July as the date of Netta's return. She did manage to return on that day, but it was something in the nature of a miracle. On 11 July, she had had dinner out on the wooden terrace at the back of No. 50. A mosquito or some other insect bit her leg and infected it badly. She felt ill in the night and was worse next morning. Her friend, Dr. Gillie, came four times in the course of the day. There was a conference of the World Union for Progressive Judaism coming on in London, and Rabbi Kokoteck, who was to have been a visitor at No. 50, had to be put off and sent to a hotel instead. Dr. Gillie called in the specialist, Mr. Martin. The leg was badly swollen, and when I met Michael in London, he said to me, "My mother's temperature has got to come down within the next twenty-four hours, otherwise we may expect the worst." I remember my immediate reaction was, "How dreadful for Ernest, if he lives to have a ninetieth birthday and it should be without Netta." A day- and a night-nurse were in attendance. Two more rabbis, Rabbi Zaoui and Rabbi Elk, arrived, and No. 50 had not the heart to turn them away. In her ground-floor bedroom, Netta was worrying because she was missing, not only the conference, but a meeting of the P.N.E.U. Executive. A dinner party, planned for the conference for the 15th, was held without her, Lady Samuel acting as hostess.

By a merciful dispensation of providence, the apprehensive Ernest was far away from all this in Donegal, and had been told very little. By the 16th, Netta was better and was able to see several guests. On the 19th, she was able to go into the morning-room. That evening, there was a party for the World Union. Michael floodlit the garden for it, but Netta was not present, having been banished, very properly, back to bed.

Her air passage had been booked for the 21st, and she pleaded strongly to be allowed to go. Dr. Gillie agreed, if the journey could be done without any worry or fatigue. Cyril drove her to the airport. She was travelling with her dear Mrs. Freddie, and the latter's daughter. But when they got to Northolt, it was discovered that her seat in the 'plane had by some mistake been cancelled earlier in the week. "One passenger has not turned up. There is just a chance that there may be a vacant place." Netta, under strict doctor's orders not to worry, sat there, watching the face of the airport clock. The hand moved onward, slowly, all too slowly. At last, it reached the scheduled time-limit, and the waiting official—who by that time had been getting quite excited about the issue himself—shouted to an attendant to bring the chair, and Netta was hustled out quickly to where the 'plane was waiting, as though she were royalty escaping from a revolution. She was in Glenalla by 5.30 that afternoon, and—in obedience to her solemn undertakings to Dr. Gillie—in bed by 6.30. "Slept well," the diary records. There were further penicillin injections from Dr. Boyle about four days later. But she was soon herself again, completely.

Ernest's ninetieth birthday party was favoured by perfect weather. His sister Beatrice had come over to stay a fortnight previously, and his brother-in-law, WWW. Sydney, whose birthday it was too, and whose last visit had been in 1915, arrived as a surprise on the day itself, just in time for the birthday lunch. In the afternoon, there was a reception for one hundred and twenty guests from all over the county.

It was Ernest's last summer at Glenalla. The previous year, when he left in mid-September, he had written in the book, "Rather cold weather but enjoyed stay. Caught no slugs and only very small snails." Theoretically, a theme for rejoicing; but one catches a note of slight regret, the note of a nonagenarian Othello, a little sad at finding his "occupation gone."

In January, Netta received official intimation that the King had awarded her the C.B.E. There was a sudden bombardment of letters, telegrams, and congratulatory visits. The official citation was for work in the field of education, and Netta liked to think that this was an honour paid to the Union for which she had worked for so many years. She went to equip herself with a new dress, hat, handbag, and gloves for Buckingham Palace, and when she remarked to one of the girls behind the glove counter, "They're rather expensive, but I suppose I must have them to visit the King," to her amusement, the girl replied, "Yes, I sold a pair last week to another lady for the same reason," mentioning Dr. Janet Aitken, the only other woman C.B.E. to figure in that particular Honours list. The investiture took place on 14 March. Netta had written to the Lord Chamberlain explaining that she had an artificial limb and would not be able to curtsy. On the day she went off to the Palace, escorted by Cyril and Michael. When her turn came and she went up to receive her honour, an official tried to whisper something in the King's ear. The latter nodded and murmured, "Don't tell me, I know." Her family were delighted at the honour that had been paid her, but Ernest was not to be denied his little joke. "I can't think why they've given it to you, they never gave it to me!"

He had been poorly earlier in the year, but was well again. The diary for January records, "Ernest had a slight stroke and could not get out of his chair. Winnie Dowsett was in the house and helped. Had a nurse. I

MICHAEL AND NETTA

NETTA AND LORD SAMUEL

could not go to Datchet to see Valerie who was ill." Her beloved secretary, Valerie Bateman, who had written when she saw the Honours List, "Well, that is the nicest thing which has happened since I can't remember when! Almost the dearest wish of my heart come true. I am so happy," was seriously ill at her home at Datchet. Netta went to see her frequently. Ernest made a quick recovery and the nurse only remained one day. A week later, the diary reads, "Ernest went to the Club and I went to a Gallery." Ernest continued to play bridge almost daily at the Savile. He was a good player, and had always been, and still remained, a good-tempered player.

On 19 March, Ernest found that he could not get out of his bath unaided, and Sexton, the chauffeur, had to be summoned to help him. But next day he was back at the Club for his rubber of bridge. Ten days later, he felt unwell, and the doctor came. "March 29th. Sydney called. Ernest was less well." "March 31st. Ernest rallied. Bea and Herbert saw him and the boys before going to Glenalla, very happy." "April 2nd. Sydney slept at the house. I heard that Valerie was very ill."

The next few days were to hold much sorrow for her. But it is all recorded with the customary stoical brevity. "April 3rd. Not much change in Valerie's condition." "April 6th. Dr. Gillie broke the news of Valerie's death." "April 7th. Good Friday. Heard that Valerie Bateman's husband was dead. He was exhausted with nursing and watching his wife, and took an overdose of tablets. There was much telephoning re the two children." "April 8th. Ernest breathed quietly his last. Sydney and Marjorie were there."

Ernest had been gathered to his forefathers, old and full of years, and highly honoured by all who knew him. But Valerie Bateman was still quite a young woman and she left two children, a boy and a girl. The boy, James, aged ten, was with his aunt, and Henrietta, aged six, was with her paternal grandmother, because of their mother's illness. Netta's first thoughts were for the children. Cyril, who had delayed his departure for Glenalla when Ernest became ill, very kindly undertook to take the children with him. As though to add one more item to the sorrows and anxieties of the past few days, Olive, on 12 April, went into hospital for an operation. It was the day after her father's funeral, and as soon as the funeral was over, Cyril flew to Ireland with the Bateman children, to get them away to happier surroundings. Then Dorothy broke the sad news to the little girl; the boy had already heard it.

Nearly a quarter of a century before, Ernest had written on a slip of paper for his executors, a few wishes in connection with his funeral. He wished to be buried in whatever Jewish cemetery his wife, or, if she predeceased him, his children, should decide on. "I wish her to decide who shall perform the ceremony and where and under whose management any religious service shall be held. I only desire that it shall be according to the Jewish faith. I do not want any flowers. I am quite indifferent as to mourning. I certainly would prefer it not to be for more than a week. I would, if my wife has predeceased me, naturally expect that I should be buried near her."

At the Memorial Service, Rabbi Dr. Mattuck referred to Ernest's many philanthropies, but still more to the personal affection which he inspired. "We were fond of him. He had qualities of character and attainments that won admiration, an extensive knowledge and deep appreciation of art, a kindness ready to help those who needed help, expert authority in the field of his vocation. We were attracted by his sense of humour, by his combination of wisdom and simplicity, and by his warm friendliness. These qualities and attainments do not, however, fully describe his personality. It cannot be distilled into words; we just felt it, so that it was a pleasure to be in his company. The joy that his friends found in his friendship can help us to appreciate the rich meaning of his life to those, his wife and children, who shared fully in it, and in whose lives he shared fully."

31

AT 10:55 ON 25 OCTOBER 1953, the following curious telegram was delivered to Franklin, New Henrietta Arms, 88 Carlton Hill, N.W.8. The taped lines were pasted on a Greetings telegraph form, flanked by a most bellicose lion and equally excited unicorn. It may gradually have dawned on the post office attendant that what he was typing was verse. The telegram read:

> Fifty faithful unto death sends you with her final breath greetings and wishes you may find eighty-eight as dear and kind carlton eager bright and new delights and cheers to welcome you wishing you many years of life from parsons children man and wife.

Possibly it was the journalistic skill of Parsons *père* which produced this telling effort, or Olive herself. But one suspects that it was Parsons *fils*, the grandson bard, Damien, who was at the back of it. What the post office official almost certainly did not realize was that it was a message, not from one person, but from one house to another. Fifty Porchester Terrace, about to be pulled down, was sending a farewell and goodwill message to its successor at 88 Carlton Hill. Netta's pleas to the L.C.C. had prevailed for a time. She had asked to end her days in the house she loved so much. The only thing was, she showed so little inclination to end them. The L.C.C. had hardened its heart. No. 50 must come down. Netta was eighty-eight, but she was still going strong, and her plea must be disregarded. A long search for a suitable successor to the Porchester Terrace house led at last to the discovery of a very fine, modern, brick house with a walled garden at the foot of Carlton Hill, on a comparatively quiet road, yet only a few hundred yards from Kilburn.

Ernest had been spared the uprooting; but Netta, at the age of nearly eighty-eight, was being asked to pack up her possessions and start life all over again. She accepted it as calmly as she has always, throughout her whole life, accepted the inevitable. One may get excited about trifles, because trifles are avoidable with a little intelligence; but one does not get excited about the big things. Besides, this was a new experience. Retrospective sentiment being completely outside her line, it is more likely that she felt, like the aged Ulysses:

> Yet all experience is an arch wherethro'
> Gleams that untravell'd world.

The three years between Ernest's death and the departure from Porchester Terrace had been as active as ever. She had had one grief which touched her closely. The diary entry for 31 December 1950 reads, "Heard Robert Donat on seeing the New Year in. Very miserable over family matters." It was not a reference to her bereavement earlier in the year, but to the dissolution of her son Michael's marriage. It had lasted twenty years, though with ever-increasing stresses. But since the war, the prospects of its survival had become dimmer and dimmer. Yet Netta had continued to hope that it would survive and presently enter calmer waters. The divorce came at a time that was particularly distressing to the two children. Angela, just grown up and doing a three-year *hotelière* course at the wonderful Hotel School on the outskirts of Lausanne, had been deeply distressed by the ever-widening breach between her parents. Essentially a peace-maker, earnest in her outlook on life, and with a religious sense of her own, she needed all the help religion could give her at this moment in her life.

Netta may have contributed in one way or another to the break-up of the marriage. But certainly, as in Cyril and Miriam's case, she had not consciously wished to do so. Possibly, a son as attached to his mother as Michael was makes a mistake in marrying. He had run to her as a small boy in every difficulty; he had written to her daily from the moment he went to school; she was his confidante, he needed her opinion, her verdict, her sympathy, her praise, whatever the occasion.

Although she might oppose him, in the end, generally, he got his way. As in all human relationships, they quarrel over little things, and are unfair to each other. But this is only the sign-token of how essential they are to one another. He can occasionally be inconsiderate; and certain of Michael's traits seem infantile to Netta, his bickering with Cyril, for example. The gravest fault in her own character, I suspect, is that she would tend to condone his offence, even if he were in the wrong. At least it has the excuse of being *une faute maternelle*. And Michael's *petites soins* are a continual solace to her. He seldom arrives without some little gift: flowers, fruit, or some new gadget to give her pleasure.

Witty, gay, still with some of the elasticity of the child to whom everything is new, Michael has less melancholy, less sensitivity than his uncle Edwin, whom he resembles so much in appearance. But at heart he is not so very different. He has his moments of petulance, and perhaps of desolation. However, there is always one's little joke to cheer one up. Lunching with the novelist Charles Morgan and his talented wife, Hilda Vaughan, the former said to him across the table, "Oh, Michael, I've some good news that will interest you, my *Breeze at Morning* has been translated into German." "Splendid. I suppose they'll call it Morgen Windt?" The novelist did not smile. Perhaps there were too many subtle overtones to that polyglot pun. But Hilda Vaughan cried, "Oh! Michael, you are clever!"

Clever. Yes, and able to keep going with the aid of occasional nonsense. Michael is not the man with the one talent. He is the man with the five, who throws them all happily in the air. He rejoices in his virtuosity, but he is fundamentally humble about anything that he knows that he does really well. This is because he does not need the reassurance here which boasting momentarily gives. His career in the army was creditable, but all he has to say about it is, "I used my talents as an actor to become a quite successful officer." In other words, he was only playing one more part. He is perfectly aware of his own faults. "I am inclined, much to my chagrin and regret, to use people rather than to serve them." Overtaken by one of his bouts of self-pity, he can be heard groaning—quite unnecessarily— upon the procrustean bed of his own temperament. He is selfish, yet kind; maddeningly argumentative, but at times touchingly considerate. And the kindness and warmth of heart are perfectly genuine, even if they are one more aspect of his virtuosity.

When I think of him, a four-line poem by Yeats springs to mind:

> Hands do what you're bid:
> Bring the balloon of the mind
> That bellies and drags in the wind
> Into its narrow shed.

Michael would scorn to bring down the balloon of his mind. It is there to float gaily in the empyrean, and, from time to time, to jettison some observation—perhaps shrewd, perhaps absurd—like a sandbag thrown overboard. It would bore him to discipline any one of his gifts. It must be spontaneous. And because he has never tasted the appreciable rewards of patient persistence, he is all the greedier for ephemeral praise, which makes him often seem self-assertive and a conversational monopolist. He has never been able to channel his talent. But perhaps one day he will.

Michael's marriage came to an end in 1950. Thenceforward he used to sleep at Porchester Terrace during the middle of the week, and return to Turkscroft at the weekends. No. 50 had always been a second home to him, but it was nice to have him back now under the roof, coming and going, but considerably more restlessly than Geoffrey used to do. Nevertheless, Netta, because of the future, when she would no longer be there, wanted to see him married again. Sometimes it must have occurred, even to her, that it would need an exceptional individual, one who was neither a doormat nor a dominating type, to furnish the kind of companionship which Michael needed, without being overwhelmed by his volatile and capricious, and at the same time insistent nature.

Netta's life was just as active as ever. When I lectured to the Royal Society of Literature on Eddie Marsh's translation of *Dominique*, I could count on her punctual arrival at No. 1 Hyde Park Gardens to hear me. Her diary continues to show a multiplicity of activities of all sorts: a party for Old Girls from Overstone who were married and brought their children; a children's party for little motherless Henrietta Bateman; a visit to Agnew's Gallery to see the Turner exhibition. A big party for the older grandchildren, actually Angela's engagement party, took place on the night of the great smog. Half the guests were prevented from coming, and of those who did, a great number spent the night on improvised mattresses on the drawing-room floor. Netta herself succumbed to a sudden attack of bronchial asthma when she went to dress at seven o'clock, but was in with her guests at 9:30 p.m., when the dancing began. Then, in March 1953, only a few months before the house's demise, Angela was married to Gerald Loewi, a brilliantly clever, young, experimental pathologist of German-Jewish stock, who had been educated in England. After working both at Oxford and Cambridge, he was granted a Research Fellowship in biochemistry to Columbia University, New York, whither he departed, taking his good-looking young wife with him. When they returned, he would become a member of the Scientific Staff of the Medical Research Council. Angela, on her honeymoon, wrote to her grandmother: "I want you to know how terribly grateful I am to you for everything you have done and are doing for me—I really don't know what I should have done without your understanding and help. You have done far more for me than I deserved, and I want you to know how much I appreciate it—first for letting me come and stay at Porchester Terrace, then for everything you did for the wedding—the lunch was wonderful, and what could have been an awkward situation was made so easy—and happy. I enjoyed every minute of it—and then, we are both so grateful to you for letting us come and stay at Porchester Terrace, until we can move to Hammersmith. Once again, thank you more than I can say for everything. Very much love, Angela." This was from the heart, and the young bridegroom added, "I cannot say more to you than that you constantly remind me of the German poet's line: 'Wo Güte sich mit Geist Vereint.'[38] Much love to you."

Loewi, with his thoroughness and the deliberation of manner of a Heidelberg professor, makes one realize how strongly German the Central European German Jew could be. These were the people who, after several centuries of life in Germany, and service to Germany, were to be first outlawed, then labelled with a humiliating badge, and finally butchered by the million, an act of coldly-planned, modern, scientific barbarism that can only be compared in savagery to the mass vengeances of Assyrian tyrants. If, to some people, Jews seem unduly sensitive, and to have anti-Semitism on the brain, let it be remembered that in an age when religious intolerance was disappearing, they saw six million of their own people exterminated merely for the heinous offence of having omitted to be born pure Aryans. Such a race massacre, only yesterday, is not reassuring. The Glenalla Visitors' Book records a Monsieur and Madame Baur, a delightful young French couple, he President of the French Liberal Jewish Congregation, whom Michael had met and invited to Glenalla before the war. He was shot, and she and their three little children were all gassed later by the Nazis in France. Netta is constantly haunted by the vision of the pretty young French mother, whom she once watched playing tennis in Donegal.

Vetted and approved by the various members of the family, the new 'Henrietta Arms' was billed to open its doors late in October. Departure from No. 50 might have been made an occasion of lamentation and gnashing of teeth, but Netta refused to permit it. The house was packed with memories

---

38   Where goodness joins with wisdom.

of friends of former times. Famous people had come there: Baden-Powell, Thompson Seton, Helen Keller, Emile Cammaerts, the Belgian poet, Paul Robeson, Nina Milkina, Dunsany, Mrs. Naidu, Princess Alice, Countess of Athlone, Stephen Paget, Ramsay Macdonald; and it had been host also to a whole variety of associations, the 'Q' camps, the Liberal Jewish Movement, the National Vigilance Association, the Leper Colony Council. The British Friendship to Greece Society, which had occupied house room in its basement for a number of years, wrote now when they heard the news: "A terrible blow. It has indeed been the salvation of our Society, and has enabled us to carry on our work in a way that would otherwise have been impossible," together with their special thanks to the domestic staff "who have so often answered the door and taken in parcels and put up with all our packages in the passage, etc."

Amongst the many letters received by Netta on the subject of the passing of No. 50, was this one, received from a complete stranger:

June 18th, 1953.

Dear Madam,
 Will you please allow me to say how very sorry I am to read in the Press that you have to leave your house? I trust you will not think it presumptuous of me—but our family, too, have a very sentimental interest in it, as our (late) mother worked there over sixty years ago as a housemaid before she was married. It must be very hard to give it up when you have lived there SO long.
 I hope therefore you will excuse this letter, and understand why I felt I must write it, to say I am sorry, altho' a stranger to you.
 Yours very sincerely,
  R.E.G.

If a stranger could feel like this about the house, what were the feelings of those who had come there again and again? A month later, in July, her sister Lily wrote:

Dearest Netta,
 As you said there might be no reference to the sadness of leaving Porchester Terrace, Marian and I would like just to say "thank you" for all you have done to share your beautiful home with all who visited it. We do not forget what it has meant to our Club, what a comfort it

was to us when our old home broke up, and what your lovely 'home' Sabbaths have meant to us, and at all the other innumerable times. But you have interpreted the home feeling for us. Without you, the beautiful house would have had a very different and not a millionth part of its power to attract, to stimulate, and to comfort. Thank God we have got you still, and we shall be happy to be wherever you are. Your courage has left us very humble and very reverent. God bless you.

Your loving,

Lily.

There was too much to be grateful for to make it an occasion for sadness. Netta directed, and everyone helped in the ordeal of dismantling a house that had been occupied by the same family for a period of over fifty years. Books had to be given away to various members of the family and to friends; Carlton Hill was roomy, but not roomy enough to take all the contents of No. 50. Every piece of furniture was assigned its place before it left, and a number of the pictures were dispersed, loaned to public galleries, and to various members of the family. The great framed *petit point* in the drawing-room went now to the Victoria and Albert Museum, to which Ernest had bequeathed it after Netta's death. The Sargent portrait of Netta was sent on loan to the Walker Art Gallery, Liverpool; the Charles I cane-backed chairs to the National Trust. In fact, sixty different destinations were ultimately found. Cyril, who had bought a beautiful house with a large garden at Hampstead, was able to house the Glyn Philpot picture of the two boys, and much of the old Chinese collection, and Egyptian toys from the Tombs. On 25 September, the last Friday Sabbath evening service and dinner was held, with the Samuels present, the two sisters, Olive, Walter Hart, and Cyril's three boys. Roger, the eldest of the three, had married and brought with him his American colored wife, Beverley, who, thanks to this last-minute visit, when she hears No. 50 alluded to in years to come, will carry a picture of it in her mind.

A week or so later, a brief phrase in the diary indicates the beginning of the end: "Pam sold bits of old iron to rag-and-bone man. Took her and Maggie to 88."

Two poets celebrated the occasion of departure. Rosie Elkin, once Rosie Stiebel, who lately had celebrated her own ninetieth birthday, greeting her friends gathered at her home with a placard, "Genuine Antique," pinned to her back, sent a twenty-line poem Non omnis moriar in response to an invitation to pay a farewell visit to the house:

> How can I say with truth, 'I'll come with pleasure
> To bid adieu' to such a treasure
> As this old house, whose gracious door
> Has ever open been to old, young, rich or poor...

And Michael produced no less than a hundred and thirty-four lines of rhymed couplets in free meter, taking his reader on a complete tour of all the lower part of the house, and dwelling lovingly on each familiar detail, from the rug-covered pavement mosaic from Pompeii in the hall, to the huge petit point of Elizabeth and Leicester 'met at Kenilworth,' which some people say was the work of Mary Queen of Scots:

> Dear house of memories, house where I was born,
> Now derelict and desecrated, fractured and forlorn,
> Presenting a withered frontage to the eye,
> A house it seems that's just about to die.
>
> ....There's lots of time,
> Stay ere the marble steps you climb
> And let me paint the house in rhyme.

Nothing was forgotten: not even the sentimental terra-cotta bust which had been a wedding present to Ernest and which furnished striking proof, not of how far Rodin had gone as an artist by 1885, but rather of how far he was subsequently to go.

> At the foot of the stairs, we can't linger long,
> Except to admire the old Chinese gong,
> And, opposite it, a fine seascape of Boudin
> And opposite that a sugar-sweet Rodin.

The poem even managed to end on a cheerful note, with a *double entendre*, if not an actual pun:

> Now fifty's gone and with it part of us,
> But we need not really make too much a fuss
> For she who made it lovely's still in spate
> At eighty-seven, and will do the same at eighty-eight.

She did do the same. The new home was not only comfortable but provided an admirable setting for Netta's surviving treasures. A friend has told how, going there soon after Netta had taken up residence, she found herself passing from one room to another, and exclaiming, "I never saw that picture before! I don't remember this or that!" To all of which her hostess replied with patient amusement, "You saw them all the time at No. 50." After lunch, Netta offered the guest a lift home, since she was driving to see her sisters, Lily and Marian. They set off, and were in the car talking animatedly when Netta paused and said, "Look, Kitty." They were driving past some wasteland. It looked like a bombed site on which the bulldozers had just finished their work. This was the spot where No. 50 had once stood. The guest uttered a cry, "Oh, we needn't have come this way, surely. It must hurt you." "No, I just wanted you to see it." Netta accepted the *fait accompli* more philosophically than her friend.

In the new house, the Utrillo and many of the other paintings that came from No. 50 seemed to look better than ever, hung there by Michael, with the eye of a connoisseur. He has shown still greater ingenuity in exhibiting the best of his father's pottery collection without the appearance of overcrowding. The four Epstein bronzes came too; but the Rodin terra-cotta was sent to Christie's and sold for eighty guineas.

Carlton Hill is not quite the thoroughfare of a house that No. 50 was. Michael has his room there, and is there for the mid-week. Angela and her small daughter Diana stayed there for nine months after their return from America, joined by Dr. Loewi for the last three while a house was being built for them at Beaconsfield. There is a lovely visitor's room looking out on the garden, and with a small roof terrace if the visitor should wish to take the air. There are still Friday night family services and dinners, to which Netta's two sisters, Lily and Marian, come regularly, and Lord Samuel occasionally, to furnish an age total round the table which one imagines must be a record—three hundred and fifty-nine years, for its four senior members; yet comparing favorably in mental vigor with most dinner parties. To these "Friday nights" come great-nephews and great-nieces on the occasion of their engagement; various distant relatives in a family whose ramifications are extensive, as well as rabbis from all over the world.

To stay in London with Netta is what it has always been, a stimulating and at the same time a restful experience. She does not suggest age. A little before nine, every morning, Maggie carries up two breakfast trays to the morning-room, and places them on the table. When you appear ten minutes later, Netta is already dealing with her letters or immersed in the

Manchester Guardian. She pushes the marmalade an inch or two towards you and hands you *The Times;* but breakfast has never been her great conversational moment, and it is not now. Perhaps it is Sunday morning, and she says, "Where are you going to church?" "I haven't decided yet." "Well, Sir John Wolfenden is giving the second of a series of sermons by laymen at the church just down the road opposite us. It's on 'Religion and Education.' I thought you might be interested." Then, after a pause, she confesses to an ulterior motive. "I thought that, if you went, you could tell me whether I ought to ask him to let us print it in the *Parents' Review*," (which he subsequently did). She goes out almost as much as ever, even in winter. She still keeps up with art exhibitions and the like. Derek Hill, the painter, calls on her, and I listen to them chatting about Ernest's ceramic treasures. A lady arrives to tape-record an interview for a broadcast series in the Home Service. Netta reads as much as ever, with Milton and Chaucer as a "nightcap," and, when she goes off to bed at a quarter past nine, the wireless sounds immediately from her room, a medley of voices, for she loves listening to plays, and endeavoring to follow Russian radio lessons.

When Dr. Albert Schweitzer came to London in October 1955 to receive his Order of Merit, he asked might he visit Netta. He wanted to thank her for the gift of an indispensable assistant, his secretary, interpreter, and photographer, Erica Anderson, who, as Erica Kellner, an Austrian Jewish refugee, had stayed with her before the war. Netta "resisted the honour" from an old man who was so busy, and suggested that she should join the general gathering of his admirers which was to assemble in a restaurant in Petty France. But he insisted: he would like to pay her a special visit. So Peter fetched him in the car, a charming, courteous, and deeply impressive guest, humanly impressive in the same way that Nansen, Lord Robert Cecil, Smuts, and Gilbert Murray had seemed when she met them. Letty served tea, and they conversed together in French, as Schweitzer had done on his visit a few days before to the Queen. Netta and the Archbishop of Canterbury were the only two people he called on, apart from his Royal visit. Erica Anderson's book, with numerous photographs of his and of his work, was now duly inscribed for its new owner, as well as a photograph with a touching dedication. Netta was made to feel that some small part of herself, her love of organization and orderliness, had been trained and dispatched to Africa in the person of Erica, to aid this great man in old age in the work he was doing.

32

A RED-LETTER DAY was coming in her own life. Ernest had stolen a march on her by having a ninetieth birthday before she was in a position to do so. He had been born seven years earlier, which gave him an unfair advantage. However, in due course, she was to balance the account, a very necessary blow in the vindication of her sex. On 9 April 1956, Netta celebrated her ninetieth birthday. A huge birthday party was given for the occasion, in Cyril's house in Hampstead on Sunday, 15 April, the invitation card being sent out in the names of "Sydney, Marjorie, Cyril and Michael Franklin and Olive Parsons," with a thoughtful footnote: "We are looking forward to your *presence* but, at our mother's request, 'no *presents*, please.'" Hampstead Post Office was kept busy on the day itself, no less than eighty-one telegrams being delivered to 88 Carlton Hill. At the birthday party, Colonel Sir Louis Gluckstein, Q.C., T.D., Litt.D., who proposed her health, reminded the guests, as a matter of historical perspective, that the foundation-stone of the Royal Albert Hall had not yet been laid when Netta was born. The remarkable thing about her, he said, was "she never looks back, she is always looking forward, and that is, I think, the mark of real greatness." Netta, in her reply, noted that this was the first family function since her marriage seventy-one years before, in the organization of which she had been allowed to take absolutely no part. Her heart was full of gratitude: gratitude to God, gratitude to her friends, gratitude to the woman doctor who had kept her in health, gratitude to her children for this party, and especially to Sydney whose idea it was. "I think it is a lovely party. I have enjoyed it, and I hope you have and will, because you mustn't go yet. We want you to stop and enjoy the garden and enjoy talking to one another."

There had been a few presents, of course; and one particularly precious one. Michael, at the last minute, had had one of his inspirations. He had purchased a volume of blank pages, and hand-illuminated its vellum cover. Two slenderly-stemmed "trees," conveying the dual significance of Netta's life, public and private, wind upwards either side of the cover.

Their roots are in Religion; their leaves carry the initials of friends and children, and their fruits are the various causes which Netta has made her own. In the four corners of the cover are the symbols of her interests, cleverly epitomized: education by quill pen, ink, compass, etc.; her faith by a purple scroll embroidered with the Hebrew B for Shaddai, the holiest name of God; Nature by flowers; and needlework by symbols of the visual arts. Every tiny part of the design, painted with the minute care and delicacy shown of a medieval scribe, has its significance, and into this book, Netta has collected the signatures of her guests and friends and the various newspaper accounts of the occasion.

There was a further celebration to follow. Under the headline "Indomitable Woman," the *Evening Standard* announced that the National Council of Women were preparing to celebrate the birthday of their past President with a dinner at the Savoy. The dinner was to be shared with another nonagenarian ex-President, Mrs. F. A. Keynes, J.P., the mother of Lord Keynes and former Mayor of Cambridge, and it took place on May the 10th. Netta began her reply to the speeches of congratulation by thanking the kind friends who had said such wonderful things about her, but she confessed that she did not recognize the portrait. It was some other woman whom she would like to have known, and she must thank them, although she believed they had made a mistake. She went on to say:—

> I have indeed seen many changes in my long life. For example, we have just been drinking the loyal toast. I learnt to associate the word "Queen" not with a beautiful smiling young woman waving from an aeroplane as she flies off to visit the distant parts of her Commonwealth, but with a little old lady in a black bonnet and silk cape, Empress of India, to whom I was taught to bow when, after tea, I and a bevy of little sisters in white piqué frocks, blue sashes, Leghorn hats, and bronze button boots, were taken by our mother driving in a barouche round and round Hyde Park. It was an elegant, leisurely, but rather boring experience; furthermore, driving back to the horses usually made me feel sick.

She went on to indicate the extent of women's achievements within her own lifetime. Was there any walk of life, she asked, into which women had not penetrated?

> Today we hear of a woman being asked to become financial adviser to John Lewis & Son. I have even seen in the paper a woman has won the post of slinger in a hop-field, whatever that may be—and with it all, are they any worse mothers? When I was a young mother and very boldly pushed my own children's pram in Kensington Gardens—an almost unknown feat—it was quite usual to hear screams and tantrums and to witness battles of will. I remember my blood boiling at one of these scenes, following a nanny to her home and shyly stammering my say to the indignant mother—only to have the door slammed in my face—"Thank you, I can look after my own nurse and child."

She was convinced, she said, that all the many changes had resulted in greater general happiness. Then she went on:

> You know, it has been said, though not by Shakespeare, that there are three stages in a woman's life. She is young and beautiful, middle-aged and nondescript, old and wonderful. I am certainly not wonderful. I suppose I am old, but I don't feel it. You all tell me I am, and I have even seen it in print, so it must be true.

What she was aware of, however, was an overflowing sense of gratitude. And on that note, she concluded.

Both at the birthday party and at the subsequent public dinner, Netta did what she hardly ever does: made an allusion to health. Her practice through life has been to assume health, to plan for health, to exercise intelligence in the interests of health, but not talk too much of health. People who talk about health generally talk about ill-health. During sixty-five years of social service, Netta had not missed as many as half a dozen meetings. The amputation of her leg took place during the summer, the off-season for council meetings, and she was back in circulation again before autumn. Her general good health, she insists, is attributable to the hygiene taught her long ago by Dr. Helen Webb, and to the wise care, continued today by her friend, Dr. Annis Gillie. "My faith in, and help towards, the opening of the medical profession to women, is thus rewarded."

33

THIS BOOK BEGAN on the terrace at Glenalla, and it is going to end there too. Some activities are creative in a quite obvious manner, such as the founding of schools and the preaching of a particular educational gospel. Others are rather different, subterraneously creative, with results that lie in the invisible depths of a number of different souls and cannot be demonstrated to order. Netta's half century of association with Glenalla is of this order. I have written throughout of Glenalla as though I had a share in it, and I have a share in it, since every one of Netta's friends has a share in her possessions. Her mode of enjoying them is to give them to others. She has no solitary delights—except that of reading, letter-writing, and embroidery. All her other pleasures are communal pleasures.

Even the inanimate object in this house in the remote wilds of Donegal has a faintly personal effluvium. The warped tilt of the ping-pong table in the hall has its pleasing, familiar significance. Each room is, not weighted down with, but lightened by, past memories. The drawing-room, with its plain white mantelpiece and blue-and-white Dutch tiles, its rose-coloured curtains and pelmets, is redolent of its mistress. A single white-wood bookshelf runs from the fireplace to the left-hand one of the group of three front windows, with their gracious hangings. On this shelf are gathered all the poets dearest to Netta's heart, just as in the small bookshelves on the other side of the fireplace are books on Judaism and the works of Charlotte Mason; and, under a curtain in the front window, are the service books for the Jewish Sabbath. The colour scheme of the room is white and old rose. Netta's Chippendale desk stands between the triple windows that open onto the sweep of gravel, and the great bow-window which juts out at the side onto the terrace. There she sits towards six o'clock, waiting until it is time to turn on the news. One side of this bow-window is a two-part door, which is generally open, or at least its larger, upper glass portion. Near it, looking out towards the lemon-scented verbena shrub against the side of the house, from which a few green leaves are regularly plucked each afternoon to flavour her, or a guest's, tea, Netta sits, watching the bird-table on the terrace with its hanging tit-bits. A tiny, red-brown field-mouse comes out from the deep green carpeting of rock plant on the stone surround of the terrace and makes lightning-swift forays to and fro for crumbs that have fallen from the table. He is quite safe since, because she is a bird-lover, Netta has banned Glenalla to cats.

The drawing-room is full of light and air, not crowded, although the objects in it are heterogeneous, every one of them a symbol of past happiness and affection. The tiered cabinet of shallow shelves in the front window carries memories of three generations. Netta herself began its collection of shells at St. Andrews; her children carried it on; it was completed by Roger, her grandson. In a brass-handled oak chest-of-drawers under the poetry bookshelf are novelties and games for child visitors. A few things in the room—three Japanese prints, a circular gold mirror, two framed samplers over the Chippendale desk, one of them worked by a child, Sarah Ensworth, and finished in August 1795,[39] a small Arthur Rackham water-colour of an elf and some bees—may have no special association. But most of the things in this glowing, gracious room and elsewhere in the house are associative, like Michael's marvellous piece of coloured embroidery on blue silk done at the age of sixteen, which qualifies as a family heirloom.

It is Netta's room, but ours also. We count on finding her here. And even when she is not here, the room carries an indefinable essence of her. Here she sits in the morning at her desk, and we come to borrow stamps from her if the box in the hall is empty. Here she does housekeeping accounts with Kay. Here she reads to eight- and nine-year-olds after lunch. Here she gets Cyril to arrange the chairs for the Saturday morning family service.

---

39   One on 'Youth':
　　　　Fragrant the Rose is but it fades in Time,
　　　　The Violet sweet, but quickly past its prime,
　　　　White Lilies hang their heads but soon decay
　　　　And whiter Snow in minutes melts away
　　　　So, and so with'ring are our early Toys
　　　　Which Time or Sickness speedily Destroys.

and one on 'Thankfulness':
　　　　Next to God, dear Parents I address
　　　　Myself to you in humble thankfulness,
　　　　For all your Care and Charge on me Bestowed
　　　　And Means of Living unto me Allowed,
　　　　Go on I Pray and let me still Pursue
　　　　Such arts as Vulgar People never knew.
　　　　It's education forms the common Mind
　　　　Just as the Twig is bent the Tree inclines.

Here she waits for Michael to return from fishing, so that we can begin the Shakespeare reading. About half-past two, she may very occasionally indulge herself so far as to take the briefest forty-wink "shut-eye" when she sits on the sofa in the bow-window. But it is unofficial, and if one bursts in on her, no apology must be offered. And at three she is in her place in the car, waiting, very often, for some of those unpunctual Gibbons up at Glenbeg to come down and join her picnic party.

About five-thirty she returns, and there is her book on the arm of the sofa in the drawing-room to while away half an hour before turning on the news, or a chat with some lady visitor, or a letter from a grandchild in England or in America to be read aloud.

Sometimes, if she has not left the place all afternoon, she will sit for a few minutes on the bench outside the study window, looking across the courtyard to the serenity of a pale, eggshell-green evening sky, with the tumbled hills and a line of fantastically shaped black pines silhouetted against it.

The era of grandchildren is already past; the era of great-grandchildren has begun. Roger's children have not yet been here, but Joe's two little boys have flown from America and are completely at home. Or there is "Di-Di", for example—that is to say, Diana Clare Loewi, born at Oxford on 24 September 1955, Angela's daughter, Michael's granddaughter, Netta's great-granddaughter. She is a living testimonial to the truth of Charlotte Mason's dictum, that "Children are born Persons." Even at two years old, she revealed much of Netta's resolution and stoicism, accepting car-sickness almost without complaint, despite the fact that her head must be periodically thrust hastily out of the window, and held there, till the spasm had passed. Like Angela, she is a beauty. And in the extreme, intent gaze of her steadfast blue eyes, there is a remarkable suggestion of her great-grandmother. This is the gaze of someone who does not want her time wasted and is most unlikely to waste yours. She even gives me a lesson in good manners. I am seated at the end of the dining-room table late one afternoon, in a mood of some abstraction, when she comes to my elbow and says, "Good night, Monk." There is no answer. She repeats her good night; this time a little more loudly. Still no answer. Whereupon a "good night" like the roar of an angry bull greets my ears, which quickly brings me to my senses, and leads to that exchange of salutations which she, quite rightly, has considered is her due.

Netta's faith in the young receives striking confirmation in the shape of this young person. Diana speaks deliberately, acts deliberately, eats deliberately. Netta sits at the corner of the table in the dining-room watching her have her six o'clock supper. There is a considerable degree of accord between them. The young have no difficulty in getting on with the old, because they know that they themselves are old, with aeons of race-experience behind them. And the old—like Netta—can establish contact quite easily with the young, since they feel themselves to be young, and are still young in all that matters most. There is no gulf to be bridged; only nine decades of varied adventures. Diana is conscious of her limitations. She may return from the glass door of the dining-room and say to Netta very deliberately, "I cannot close the door for you because I cannot reach the handle." But Netta has her limitations too. And Diana remembers them. At the top of the steps down from the terrace to the rock-garden, this diminutive figure pauses one morning and remarks to her great-grandmother, "I want to go down. Can you manage, or shall I help you?" There is nearly a century between them, but what does it matter? It is life that matters, and kindness, and courage, and consideration. Looking at these two figures together, I realize that, in Di-Di, all Netta's hopes have been reborn.

Netta loves Glenalla. She has always loved it. But she has never been greedy about it. If the Day of Atonement happens to fall early in September, she will leave her beloved spot a fortnight earlier than usual in order to be with her sisters in London for it. Nowadays she avoids making plans too far ahead—"It will be better to wait and decide nearer the time"—but give her the present moment, and she knows better what to do with it than almost any person I know. Sometimes I add up what might be called my own psychological debt to her. Amongst the many items are a belief in ruthless candour, if backed by genuine and evident goodwill; a refusal to waste time on perfunctory polite-nesses, which are only the debased coinage of the real currency of courtesy; and a conviction that, by using one's intelligence and planning, one can conserve one's energies, greatly ameliorate one's annoyances, and, at the same time, serve the cause of corporate happiness.

A well-loved friend, a retired Indian Civil Servant, with a face like Punch, gave me years ago in Chateau d'Oex his considered advice as to how to get through life. It was this: "Trust God and keep the bowels open." Netta's advice, I believe, would be: "Trust God and never be anything but yourself." She would cordially endorse the poet Graves' counsel to his daughter on her wedding day, to remain

> ....with features
> Resolutely and unchangeably your own.

Thanks to her courage, to her faith, and to her ability to merge herself in the happiness of others, she has been able to rise above all vicissitudes. She is an incentive to others not to be afraid of life, but to love it. The best of it is a delicious experience. The worst of it can be borne. In almost ninety-four years of life, she must have had her disappointments, but she refuses to speak of them—there are better topics. In Masefield's phrase, she is:—

Proud to belong to the old proud pageant of man.

INDEX

Aberdeen, Marchioness of, 71, 77, 112ff.
Aberdeen, John, 1st Marquess of, 77
Adelboden, 181
AE., see Russell, George W, 76
Aigues-Mortes, 144
Aitken, Dr Janet, 225
Albert, Prince Consort, 19, 99
Alcorn, George, 161, 166, 185, 210, 216
Alcorn, Mrs Maggie, 153, 166, 214f., 235, 237
Alcorn, Robert, 129, 198, 210ff.
Alexander, Mrs Cecil Frances, 184
Alice, Princess, Countess of Athlone, 87, 234
Allen, Miss, 44
Allenby, Field-Marshal Edmund, 1st Viscount, 140
Ambleside, 37, 44, 51, 57, 96, 139ff., 196, 208
Anderson, (née Kellner), Erica, 238
Annie Bevand (maid), 104
Anne of Cleves, 197
Anson, Mrs, 47
Arezzo, 74
Arles, 144
Arnold, Matthew, 51, 102
Arnott, Sir John, 112
Asquith, H. H., see Oxford and Asquith, Earl of
Avignon, 144, 150
Ayliff, Robert, 145

Baden-Powell, Robert, 1st Baron, 140f., 234
Baeck, Rabbi, Leo, 150
Baldwin, Stanley, 1st Earl, 171
Balfour, Lady Frances, 54
Barnes, Earl, 68, 147
Barrow (coachman), 139
Bateman, Henrietta, 232f.
Bateman, James, 227f.
Bateman, Mrs Valerie (née Boon), 174f., 227
Baur, M. and Mme, 233f.

Bedales, 73, 97f., 115f., 123, 145
Beerbohm, (Sir) Max, 126, 153
Bell, Gertrude, 171
Belloc, Hilaire, 41, 154, 112f.
Berlin, 84, 150, 176, 112f.
Bernhard Baron Boys' Settlement, 155
Berks, Sister Adelaide, 124
Besant, Annie, 30, 99, 178
Beverley (House), 199
Billing, Pemberton, 118
Birchington, 35, 47
Birmingham, 92
Birrell, Francis, 116, 157
Blake, Dame Louise Aldrich, 91, 92
Bloch, Amédée, 158
Blogg, Frances, see Chesterton, Mrs G.K.
Bone, Stephen, 33
Boswell, Mrs Jean (née Farquharson), 137
Boudin, Eugène Louis, 33
Boyle, Dr, 192, 222, 225
Bradley, T. H., 59
Breslau, 19, 149
Bridges, Robert, 103, 145
Brighton, 5, 8, 11, 79
Brogan, Ellen, 161
Brooke, Stopford, 63
Brown, Dr William, 87
Brown, Ivor, 145
Brown, Miss, 93
Browning, Robert, 210
Bryant, Sir Arthur, 124
Buchanan, Mr, 104, 106
Buckle, George E., 49
Bulfinch, Thomas, 141
Burne-Jones, Sir Edward, 34
Burney, Venetia, 141f.
Burns, John, 98
Burton, Sir Richard, 48
Bush, General, 222f.
Bussé, Annie, 47

Cadbury, Dame Elizabeth, 54f.
Caine, Sir Hall, 35
Cammaerts, Emile, 234
Canada, 89ff.
Campbell, Antoinette, 172
Campbell, Lady, 43
Campbell, Madeleine, 199
Campbell, Mrs (cook), 161
Campbell, Sir Guy, 43
Campbell, Rev. R. J., 63
Cannes, 172
Carcassonne, 144
Carlton Hill (88), 133, 229, 235f., 239
Carlyle, Thomas, 13, 41
Caterham, 28f.
Cecil of Chelwood, Robert, Viscount (Lord Robert Cecil), 238
Chadburne, Miss, 93
Chamberlain, Sir Austen, 175
Chesterton, G. K., 41, 154, 174
Chesterton, Mrs G. K. (née Blogg), 174
China, 203f.
Christiana, 123
Claxton, Miss K. M., 141
Clifton College, 68, 97
Coal Commission, 58
Cohen, Harry, 28
Cohen, Lucy, 61, 155, 178
Cohen, Walter, 34
Conway, Moncure, 63
Coote, Sir Algernon, 77
Copenhagen, 103
Costley-White, Dr, 169, 206, 208
Crawford, Hughie, 80
Crewe, 94
Crichton, Enriqueta, 131f., 171, 184
Crichton, John, 137
Cromwell, Thomas, 197

Daly, Catherine (Kay), 2, 3, 18, 197, 210, 214
Danny (farmhand), 210
Danton, 69, 93
D'Arcy Hart, see Hart
Dark, Sidney, 175
D'Avigdor, Countess, 26
Davis, 63, 80f., 164
Davis, Annie, 161
Dean, Basil, 145
de Mille, Agnes, 158

Derby, 94
Desmoor, 206, 208
Devonshire, Mrs, 43, 114
Dickens, Charles, 83
Disraeli, Benjamin, Earl of Beaconsfield, 177, 205
Donat, Robert, 230
Doreck College, 9
Dove, Miss, 85
Dowden, Edward and Mrs, 103
Dowsett, Winnie, 225
Dublin, 121
Dubrovnik, 182
Dulcie, see Sassoon, Dulcie
Dunsany, Edward, Baron, 172, 234
Duse, Eleanora, 74, 113, 171

Elizabeth, Empress of Austria, 158
Elizabeth, the Queen Mother, 171
Elk, Rabbi, 224
Elkan, Benno, 178, 200
Elkin, Charlie, 47
Elkin, Rosie (Mrs William), née Stiebel, 28f., 32, 89, 206, 208, 235
Elkin, 'Willy', 30, 34
Elsie (maid), 152, 161
Emerson, R. W., 13
Emma (maid), 8, 24
Ensworth, Sarah, 243
Epstein, Jacob, 33, 237
Essex Education Committee, 42
Esslemont, Mrs, 169
Esterre, Mme d', 43
Ethel (maid), 161
Eumorfopoulos, George, 33

Fagan, J. B., 145
Faithful, Miss, 12
'Fairless, Michael', 116
Faunce, Miss, 44, 125
Fawcett, Mrs Millicent Garrett, 121
Ferenczi, Sandor, Dr, 155
Figgis, Robert, 146
Fisher, Herbert A. L., 60
Fitzgerald, Lord Frederick, 121
Fleg, Edmond, 135, 172
Flockhart, Mr, 54f.
Folkestone, 8
Foote, Rev. Mr, 82, 90

Forbes-Robertson, Sir Johnston, 146
Forster, Megan, 118
France, Liberal Synagogue, 66
Franckel, Benjamin Wolf, 19
Franckel, Menachem Mendel, 149
Frank, (MacConighey), 113, 161-4, 184, 210, 213, 216
Frankfurt-am-Main, 123
Franklin, A. Joseph (Joe), 161, 194, 203, 210
Franklin, Abraham, 18f.
Franklin, Adelaide, 19
Franklin, Angela, see Loewi, Angela
Franklin, Beverley, 238
Franklin, Cyril, 52, 53, 71, 72, 89, 94, 96-9, 103, 104, 105, 116f., 123, 131, 156, 158, 159, 162, 165, 166, 169, 181, 183, 189, 190, 191, 195, 197, 201, 204, 206, 209, 213, 219, 222, 224-7, 230, 235, 239, 243
Franklin, Dorothy-(Mrs Cyril Franklin), see Hurley, Dorothy
Franklin, Ellis Abraham, 19, 54
Franklin, Ernest Louis, passim, esp. 1, 8, 16ff., 23ff., 31ff, 47ff., 175f., 182ff., 204ff., 229
Franklin, Geoffrey, 35, 69, 71, 82, 89f., 97, 99f., 103, 115f., 123f., 147, 153, 156ff., 164, 172, 232
Franklin, Henrietta ('Netta'); birth, 5; childhood, 5ff.; marriage, 16, 20; family, 18ff.; health, 31, 48, 241; births of children, 34, 35; and P.N.E.U., 37ff.; as public speaker, 84f.; amputation of leg, 90ff.; awarded C.B.E., 225; 90th birthday, 239
Franklin, Irène Claire (née Bloch), 158, 166, 181f., 199
Franklin, Jaques, 29
Franklin, Laura, 35
Franklin, Marjorie, 34, 35, 44, 47, 53, 71, 79, 90-2, 99, 103, 104, 114, 115, 117, 143, 155, 164, 165, 172, 175, 201, 227, 239, 244
Franklin, Michael, 49, 50, 52, 70-75f., 78, 89, 90, 92, 96-100, 103, 104, 115, 117f., 122f., 128, 129, 133f., 136, 139, 144ff., 149ff., 158f., 162, 165-8, 171, 178, 180f., 189, 193-5, 199, 202, 204, 205, 206, 213, 218, 219, 219-1, 224, 230f., 236, 237, 239, 243, 244

Franklin, Miriam (née Israels), 158f., 166-8, 180ff.
Franklin, Olive, see Parsons, Olive
Franklin, Owen, 159, 189, 192, 194, 201, 206, 209, 213, 214
Franklin, Peter, 159, 183, 184, 189, 200, 238
Franklin, Roger, 159f., 166, 167, 182, 184, 186, 195, 196, 201, 209, 213, 235, 243, 244
Franklin, Sydney, 21, 34, 35, 44, 47, 48, 53, 71, 72, 76, 77, 90, 93, 97, 103, 115f., 124, 155, 156, 164f., 201, 216, 225, 227, 239
Frederick, Empress, 158
Fry, Maxwell, 159

Gabo, Nahum, 181
Gandhi, M. K., 125
Geneva, 172
George VI, King, 225
Gernsheim, 80
Gibran, Kahlil, 51
Gillie, Dr Annis, 224, 225, 227, 241
Gladstone, W. E., 21, 25
Glenalla, 1-3, 18, 63, 66, 77ff., 103ff., 128ff., 242ff., et passim
Glover, Ella, 43, 47, 90, 95, 99, 200
Gluckstein, Col. Sir Louis, 239
Gogarty, Oliver St. John, 33
Goldsmid, Sir Isaac, 58
Gollancz, Mrs Ruth (née Lowy), 131
Gooden, Stephen, 153
Gordine, Dora, 172
Gould, Daphne, 147
Gourlay, Dame Janet, see Vaughan
Gourlay, David, 156
Graves, Alfred Percival, 99
Graves, Robert, 246
Gray, Miss, 91
Gray, Mrs Edwin, 89
Greek Refugee Society, 58, 234
Greet, (Sir) Ben, 199
Gregory, Lady (Augusta), 112, 120
Grenoble, 123
Greuze, Jean Baptiste, 175
Grey, Edward, 1st Viscount Grey of Fallodon, 58
Grindelwald, 35
Gullant, Mr, 104

Gwynn, Stephen, 76
Gwynne-Jones, Allan, 137

Hahn, Kurt, 206
Hardcastle, Mary, 207
Hardy, Veronica, 183
Harris (servant), 96
Harris, Bernard, 101
Harris, Sir Augustus, 45
Hart, Ethel d'Arcy (née Montagu), the Hon. Mrs d'Arcy Hart, 8, 208
Hart, Henry Chichester, 105
Hart, Henry d'Arcy, 208
Hart, Maria Henrietta, 105
Hart, Rev. G. V., 80
Hart, Rosamund, 104, 105
Hart-Davis, Mrs, 47
Harvey, Rev. Arnold, 82
Harvey, Veronica, 197
Haslam, Mr and Mrs, 99
Henriques, Sir Basil Q., J.P., 66, 155, 165
Herbert, Auberon ('Bron'), 58
Herbert, (Sir) Alan P., 159
Hickling, Doreen, 183, 184, 190, 197
Hickson, Mr and Mrs, 98, 195
Hill, Derek, 238
Hill, Dr (Sir) Charles, 220
Hipwell, Kathleen, 183
Hobbs, 'Nannie,' 163
Hogarth, William, 175
Hone, Joseph, 120
Horsley, Sir Victor, 92
Houghton, Rev. Mr, 63
Household, H. W., 40, 44, 120, 147, 169
Hubback, Eva, Mrs, 121
Hugo, Victor, 213
Hume, John, 79
Hunt, Rev. John, 167
Hurley, Dorothy (Mrs Cyril Franklin), 183, 189, 194, 214, 227
Hyam, I., 31
Hyde, Douglas, 76
Hyson, 81, 96, 103

Ifield, 199f.
Ireland, 76ff., 103
Isham, Sir Gyles, 145
Italy, 25, 74f.

James II, 104
Jammes, Francis, 141
Jarinzoff, Mrs, 69, 70
Jewish Religious Union (U.L.P.S.), 64
Joe (cowman), 210
Johnson, Dr, 40
Jones, Mrs (cook), 24
Jowitt, Benjamin, 59, 64, 70n., 207

Kaye, Danny, 203, 205
Keeble, Lillah (Lady McCarthy), see McCarthy, Lillah
Keeble, Sir Frederick, 145, 163, 219
Keighley, 94
Keller, Helen, 154, 234
Kemp-Welch, Lucy, 113
Kemper, 19
Keynes, Mrs F. A., 240
Kingsley, Charles, 13
Kingsley, Mary, 61n.
Kipling, Rudyard, 102
Kitching, Elsie, 114, 140, 208
Knittel, Dr, 45
Kokoteck, Rabbi, 224

Lambert, Miss, 44, 125
Landseer, Sir Edwin, 175
Lane, Sir Hugh, 33
Lang, Rt. Rev. Cosmo Gordon, 171
Law, Hugh, 76, 104, 107
Law, Lola, 76, 107
Leatherhead, 47
Le Lauteret, 123
Lemare, Iris, 137
Leney, Rose, 20, 28
Lennox-Boyd, M.P., Alan, 146
Leonardo da Vinci, 68
Letts, Winifred, 129
Letty (maid), 161, 166, 238
Lewis, Miss Connie, 133
Lewis, Rabbi, 151
Liberal Judaism, 58ff., 178
Lisbon, 172
Liverpool, 177
Livingstone, Richard, 206
Loewi, Angela (née Franklin), 159, 181, 186, 209, 230, 232, 233, 237, 244
Loewi, Diana Clare, 165, 237, 244f.
Loewi, Gerald, 230, 237

Lombardi, Signor, 5
London, Bishop of, 45
Lowell, James Russell, 217
Lubin, 177
Lunn, Sir Arnold, 35
Lyster-Smythe, Capt. Cecil, 183, 190, 191-4, 197, 216
Lyster-Smythe, Valerie, 183, 185, 191
Lyttleton, Edward, 41, 125f.

MacArthur, Mrs, 178
MacCarthy, Lillah (Lady Keeble), 125, 145, 172, 172, 219
Macdermott, Mrs, 132
MacDonald, J. Ramsay, 234
MacNeil, Lord, 39
MacNutt, Hesther, 109
Madan, Falconer, 141f.
Madeira, 172
Maggie (maid), see Alcorn, Maggie
Magnus, Lady, 9, 10, 69, 70
Magnus, Sir Laurie, 34, 66, 102
Malory, Sir Thomas, Morte d'Arthur, 53
Manners, Lady Diana, 127
Margaret, Princess, 163
Margesson, Lady Isabel, 39
Margherita, Queen of Italy, 113
Marjoribanks, Dudley Coutts, 112
Marks, 19
Marsden-Smedley, Basil, 88
Martin, E. K., 224
Mary Agnes (maid), 161
Mary Queen of Scots, 236
Masefield, John, 146, 246
Mason, A. E. W., 128
Mason, Charlotte, 39ff., 43ff., 57, 69, 84, 85, 95, 96, 113, 114, 120, 132, 139f., 142, 144, 172, 208, 244
Massey, Sir Vincent, 206
Matoppo, 148
Matthews, Very Rev. W. R., 146, 150, 178
Mattuck, Dr Israel I., 66, 147, 178, 209, 228
Matzke, Miss, 48
Maud, Queen of Norway, 47, 125
May, Phil, 153
Mendelssohn, Mr, 66
Milkina, Nina, 172, 234
Milner, Alfred, Viscount, 58
Molyneux, Elizabeth, 208f.

Monro, Mrs Harold, 174
Montagu, The Rt. Hon. Edwin S., 5, 7, 58, 61, 69, 70, 98, 104, 117, 127, 177, 231
Montagu, Ellen (née Cohen), 20
Montagu, Judy, 117f., 163f.
Montagu, The Hon. Lily, C.B.E., 10, 11, 13, 26, 60f., 89, 100, 125, 130, 133, 137, 150, 154, 156, 164, 179, 200, 234, 237
Montagu, The Hon. Lionel, 13
Montagu, The Hon. Marian, 133, 154, 179f., 200, 234
Montagu, Sir Samuel, see Swaythling, Lord
Montefiore, Claude G., 42, 57ff., 67, 147, 150, 156, 179f., 208
Montefiore, Mrs Claude, 67
Montefiore, Leonard, 58
Montgomery, Field-Marshal Bernard, Viscount, 49
Montreal, 89
Moore, T. Sturge, 113
Morgan, Charles, 231
Morison, Fynes, 80
'Moser, Nelly', 2
Moskowitz, Mrs Henry, 149
Moskowitz, Dr Henry, 203f.
Motion, Lady Elizabeth, 171
Mulvaney, Dr, 85
Murdoch, Dr Mary, 94
Murray, (Sir) Gilbert, O.M., 174, 207, 238
Murray, T. C., 159
Myer, Gillian, 216
Myer, Kenneth, 208, 216

Naidu, Sarojini, 53, 125, 234
Nansen, Fridtjof, 172, 238
Nathan, Sir Matthew, 34
Nathan, Maud (Lady), 34
Neville, Mme, 126
Newman, John Henry, 83
Nightingale, Florence, 88
Nîmes, 144
Noblett, Hamish, 142
Norton, James, 124
Norway, 123
Nuremberg, 23

Oakes, Miss, 117
O'Neil, Joseph, 120
O'Neill, Moira, 129

Osborne, Mr and Mrs, 104
O'Shea, Capt. William, 21
Osler, Sir William, 68
Ottawa, 90
Overstone, 169, 208
Oxford, 141, 205
Oxford and Asquith, Herbert, 1st Earl of, 98

Pam, 66
Paine, Tom, 13
Paget, Stephen, 234
Pankhurst, Emmeline, 121
Paravicini, Baron, 58
Parents' National Education Union (P.N.E.U.), 37ff., 85, 120, et passim
Parish, Miss, 45
Parsons, Mrs Clement, 43
Parsons, Damien, 74, 165, 229
Parsons, Henry Douglas, 155
Parsons, Nicholas, 165
Parsons, Olive (née Franklin), 18, 35
Paynter, Miss, 200
Pearse, Padraic, 112, 129, 137
Peggy (poultry maid), 161
Pembridge Gardens (9), 21, 54
Pennethorne, Amy, 85, 132, 139
Perrin, Mrs Henry, 47
Perry, Mrs, 107, 222
Philpot, Glyn, 33, 96, 97, 235
Pioneer Club, 43
Pisa, 74
Playfair, (Sir) Nigel, 159
Plumer, Hon. Eleanor, 200
Plumptre, Miss E., 149
Pluto (planet), 14f.
Pont du Gard, 144
Porchester Terrace (50), 55, 58, 201, 238
Portsmouth, 95
Proust, Marcel, 73, 204
Puccini, Madame Butterfly, 29, 131f.
Purnode, Marthe, 114f.

Rackham, Arthur, 153, 243
Raphael, Willy, 34
Rayner, Rev. John, 179
refugees, German, 176f.
Rennell, Phoebe, 163
Rhodes, Cecil, 148
Rhodesia, 147

Rimbaud, Arthur, 93
Robert (gardener), see Alcorn, Robert
Robeson, Paul, 124, 125, 234
Rodin, Auguste, 236, 237
Rolland, Romain, 99
Rome, 113
Roosevelt, Franklin D., 203f.
Rose (gardener), 213
Rosenberg, Dr and Mrs, 195
Rosenberg, Dr Alfred, 205
Rosie (nurse), 5, 9, 61, 73, 82
Rossetti, Christina, 218
Rotheman, 177
Rowbotham, Mr, 47
Royden, Maude, 125
Ruskin, John, 41, 45
Russell, G. W., 'AE', 76, 78, 104, 112

Sadler, Sir Michael, 39
Salaman), 137
Samuel, Asher, 19
Samuel, Beatrice (Lady), 224-7, 235
Samuel, Gilbert, 35, 137
Samuel, Hannah (née Israel), 19
Samuel, Harriet (née Israel), 19
Samuel, Henrietta (née Israel), 19
Samuel, Herbert, 1st Viscount, O.M., 10, 34, 58, 137, 154, 170, 194, 207f., 225, 227, 235, 236
Samuel, Louis, 19
Samuel, Menachem, 19
Samuel, Moses, 19, 254
Samuel, Nancy (The Hon. Mrs), 137
Samuel Montagu and Co., 16, 156, 166, 227, 235, 239
Samuel, Sir Stuart M., 55
Sargent, J. S., 33, 55, 235
Sassoon, Dulcie (née Franklin), 10
Schaumann, Dr., 68-9
Schiller, Friedrich, 14
Schlösser, Maud, 47
Scott, Ian, 183
Sebag-Montefiore, Adelaide, 34
Sebag-Montefiore, Sir Joseph, 34
Seligmann, Dr., 66
Seton, Ernest Thompson, 234
Sexton (chauffeur), 182, 227
Shaftesbury, Lord, 83
Shanklin, 8

Shedlock, Marie, 84
Shelley, Mrs., 196
Sickert, Walter, 33
Silver, Hillel, 150
Simon, John, 1st Viscount, 137
Singer, Mrs., 31
Singer, Rabbi, 10
Sitwell, Edith, 125
Slater, Mr., 104
Smuts, Field-Marshal Jan, 238
Society of Jews and Christians, 178
Solomon, Solomon J., 34
Solomons, Bethel, 11
South Africa, 147f.
South Stoneham, 35, 99f.
Speaight, Robert, 145
Spencer, Herbert, 113
Spielmann, Sir Isidor, 66
Stanley, Sir Herbert, 148
Stead, W. T., 30
Steer, Wilson, 153
Steinthal, Mrs. Francis, 37
Stephens, James, 112
Stiebel, Rose, see Elkin, Rose
Stocks, Mary, 121
Stuart, Rev. W., 76, 106
Stubbs, Muriel, 191
Sutherland, Duchess of, 126
Swanage, 98
Swanwick, 171
Swaythling, Samuel Montagu, 1st Baron, 10, 11-12, 18, 20, 30, 62, 99f.
Switzerland, 74
Symons, Col., 77, 90, 103
Synge, J. M., 112, 129

Tadema, Sir L. Alma, 164
Tarascon, 144
Thompson, Mrs. Whitaker, 38
Thorndike, Dame Sybil, 145
Tolstoy, Leo, 193, 220
Tomlins, Miss, 94
Toynbee, Arnold, 58
Turberville, Edith Picton, 121
Turner, Daisy, 207
Turner, H. H., 141

U.L.P.S., see Jewish Religious Union
Underhill, Mr., 48

Ussons-les-Bains, 144
Utin, Archie, 131, 137, 153
Utrillo, Maurice, 33, 237

van Gogh, Vincent, 33
Varengeville, 76
Vaughan, Dame Janet (Dame Janet Gourlay), 156
Vaughan, Hilda (Mrs. Charles Morgan), 231
Venice, 103
Vigniols, Mr., 12, 35
Vlaminck, Maurice, 33
von Arnheim, Count, 98
von Hugel, Baron, 60, 178

Waley, Sir David, 28
Waley, The Hon. Mrs. (Florence), 44, 137
Wallace, Kathleen, 72f., 89, 126, 130ff., 142
Walton-on-the-Hill, 34
Wayfarers Travel Agency, The, 156, 159
Webb, Dr. Helen ('Wai'), 49, 51ff., 57, 68, 74, 81, 90-93, 94, 104, 105f., 115, 122, 126, 129, 136, 156, 210, 216, 219, 241
Webb, Mary, 171
Weiss, Dr. and Frau, 175f.
Wells, H. G., 172
Wemyss, Admiral, 115
West London Reform Synagogue, 64
Wharncliffe Rooms, 64
Whichcote, Benjamin, 37
White, Miss, 219, 220
Whyte, Evelyn, 70, 82, 139, 147, 174
Wilcox, Miss, 103
Wilhelm II, Emperor of Germany, 8
Williams, Emlyn, 145
Wilson, Woodrow, 57
Wise, Rabbi Stephen, 66, 147, 149, 150, 158
Wix, Helen, 169
Wolfe, Humbert, 174
Wolfenden, Sir John, 101, 238
Wordsworth, William, 102
Worms, 80, 176

Yates, Fred, 57f.
Yeats, W. B., 112, 113, 120-1, 231
Yorke, Mrs. Dallas, 44

Zamenhof, Dr., 177
Zaoui, Rabbi, 224

www.ingramcontent.com/pod-product-compliance
Lightning Source LLC
Chambersburg PA
CBHW021952160426

43209CB00001B/14